The Battle of
New Orleans

Also by Robert V. Remini

Andrew Jackson: Vol. 1
The Course of American Empire 1767–1821

Andrew Jackson: Vol. 2
The Course of American Freedom 1822–32

Andrew Jackson: Vol. 3
The Course of American Democracy 1833–45

Daniel Webster: The Man and His Time

Henry Clay: Statesman for the Union

The Election of Andrew Jackson

Andrew Jackson and the Bank War

Martin Van Buren and the Making of
the Democratic Party

The Battle of
New Orleans

Robert V. Remini

Viking

VIKING
Published by the Penguin Group
Penguin Putnam Inc., 375 Hudson Street,
New York, New York 10014, U.S.A.
Penguin Books Ltd, 27 Wrights Lane, London W8 5TZ, England
Penguin Books Australia Ltd, Ringwood, Victoria, Australia
Penguin Books Canada Ltd, 10 Alcorn Avenue,
Toronto, Ontario, Canada M4V 3B2
Penguin Books (N.Z.) Ltd, 182–190 Wairau Road,
Auckland 10, New Zealand

Penguin Books Ltd, Registered Offices:
Harmondsworth, Middlesex, England

First published in 1999 by Viking Penguin,
a member of Penguin Putnam Inc.

1   3   5   7   9   10   8   6   4   2

LIBRARY OF CONGRESS CATALOGING-IN-PUBLICATION DATA
Remini, Robert Vincent, 1921–
The Battle of New Orleans / Robert V. Remini.
p.   cm.
Includes bibliographical references and index.
ISBN 0-670-88551-7
1. New Orleans (La.), Battle of, 1815.   I. Title.
E356.N5R46   1999
973.2'239—dc21   99-19837

This book is printed on acid-free paper.
∞

Printed in the United States of America
Set in Times Roman
Designed by Betty Lew

Illustration credits

Frontis: *Battle of New Orleans*. Engraving by Thomas Phillibrown after a
painting by D. M. Carter, published by Martin, Johnson & Co., New York.
Print courtesy of a Private Collection and the Hermitage: Home of
President Andrew Jackson, Nashville, Tenn.

Insert
Pages 1,8 (top): The Hermitage: Home of President Andrew Jackson,
Nashville, Tenn.
Pages 2,4: The Historic New Orleans Collection, Accession Numbers
1991.34.32i, 1991.34.32ii, 1991.34.33, 1994.34.2, 1959.2.347, 1983.123.8
Page 3 (top): Chrysler Museum of Art, Norfolk, Va.: Museum Purchase 65.34.6
Pages 5 (top), 7 (bottom), 8 (bottom): The Collection of the Louisiana
State Museum
Pages 6 (bottom), 7 (top): Library of Congress
The author and publisher would like to thank the staffs of the Eisenhower
Center for American Studies at the University of New Orleans and the
Hermitage for their help in assembling these illustrations.

For Joan Marie Costello,

Beloved Daughter

Contents

List of Maps

Preface

There was a time when the United States had heroes and reveled in them. There was a time when Andrew Jackson was one of those heroes, along with the men and women who stood with him at New Orleans and drove an invading British army back into the sea.

The purpose of this book is an attempt to recount one extraordinary event in the nation's past that produced not only a stupendous military victory that helped define the country but a towering hero who became a symbol of what was best in American society. It is an attempt to explain the reasons that produced this phenomenon, and why the victory was so important at the time.

In the past I have had occasion to write extensively about the Battle of New Orleans, but this effort was sharply focused on Andrew Jackson. Then Wendy Wolf, an editor at Viking, invited me to broaden my perspective and write a work that would go beyond the limitations of a single biography and include the vast numbers of men and women who in one way or another contributed to the outcome of that conflict. I am very grateful to her. The invitation allowed me to rethink the event and delve more deeply into certain aspects of it that had larger and more national significance. In the process I found an extraordinary degree of heroism demonstrated by all its participants, both the invaders and the defenders. For the first time I came to admire the sheer pluck, determination, and endurance of the British sailors and soldiers who were forced to endure incredible hardships. They were ordered into what can only be described as mass slaughter and yet they did not hesitate to face it bravely and resolutely.

The Americans, too, responded to the challenge of the invasion of their homeland in a manner that exceeded expectations. A population of many ethnic and racial backgrounds who frequently quarreled with one another put aside their differences and joined together to save their city and safeguard their liberty. Their heroic deed and accomplishment proved to many that a union of people had at last taken place in this country. The Battle convinced them that a republican society which rewarded individual effort, not class or heredity, could and would survive.

Robert V. Remini
Wilmette, Illinois

Chronology

1812

June   United States declares war against Great Britain.

1813

August 30   Massacre at Fort Mims and entrance of United States in Creek War.

October   Jackson leads troops against Creeks.

1814

March 27   Jackson defeats Creeks at Battle of Horseshoe Bend.

May   British attempt to recruit Indian and Spanish allies for an invasion of the United States from the Gulf.

August   British invade Chesapeake Bay, capture Washington, and burn the Capitol, the White House, and other public buildings.

August   U.S. and British peace envoys meet in Ghent, Belgium, and begin negotiations.

August   British attempt and fail to recruit Baratarian pirates.

August 22   Jackson occupies Mobile and garrisons Fort Bowyer.

September 6	British invade United States from Canada.
September 15	Jackson repulses British attack at Mobile.
October 4	British fleet sails from Chesapeake to Jamaica.
October 25	Jackson begins invasion of Florida.
November	British army and navy rendezvous in Jamaica.
November 7	Jackson captures Pensacola.
November 9	Jackson evacuates Pensacola and returns to Mobile.
November 22	Jackson departs Mobile for New Orleans.
November 26	British fleet and army sail for New Orleans.
December 1	Jackson arrives in New Orleans.
December 12	British sighted off Lake Borgne.
December 14	British defeat American gunboats.
December 16	British begin landing troops on Pea Island.
December 16	Jackson imposes martial law in New Orleans.
December 22	British land troops at Bayou Bienvenu.
December 23	British occupy Villeré plantation.
December 23	Jackson forms his line at Lacoste's plantation and halts British invasion with night attack.
December 24	Jackson withdraws his army to the Rodriguez Canal between the Macarty and Chalmette plantations, and British complete ferrying of troops from Pea Island to Villeré plantation.
December 24	American and British commissioners in Ghent, Belgium, sign Treaty of Peace.
December 25	General Pakenham assumes command of British forces.
December 27	British sink USS *Carolina*.
December 28	Jackson repulses British advance toward New Orleans.

1815

January 1	Artillery duel.
January 8	British defeated at New Orleans.
February 16	Senate ratifies Treaty of Peace.
March 13	Martial law lifted.

The Battle of
New Orleans

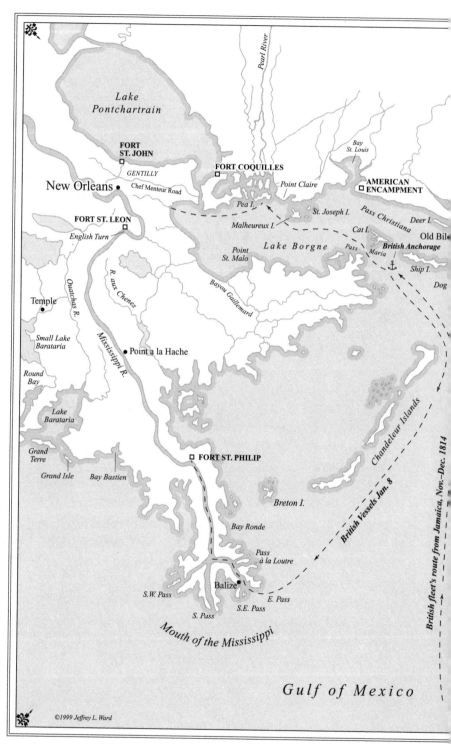

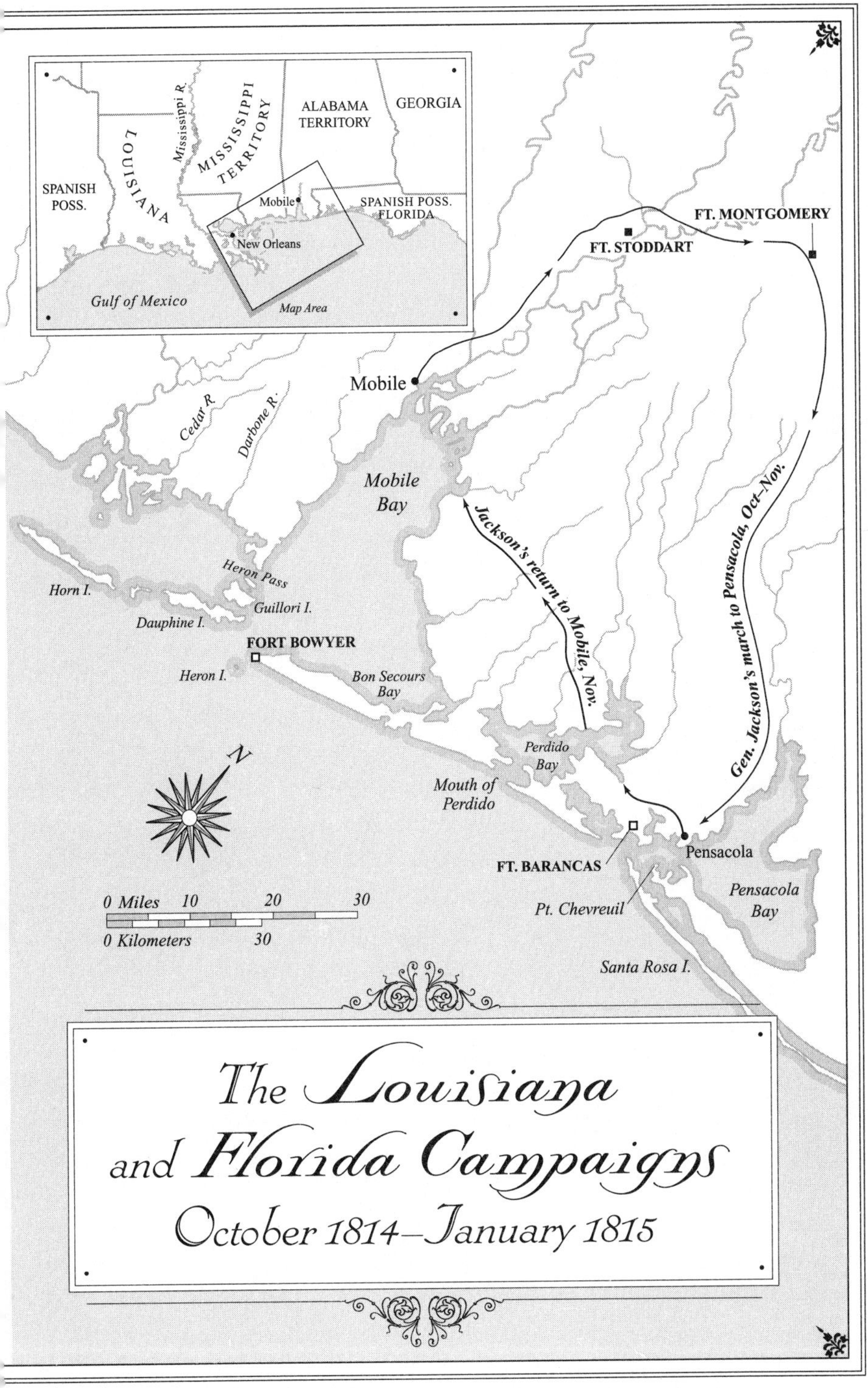

The Louisiana and Florida Campaigns

October 1814–January 1815

Inset map labels:
LOUISIANA
MISSISSIPPI TERRITORY
ALABAMA TERRITORY
GEORGIA
SPANISH POSS.
SPANISH POSS. FLORIDA
Mississippi R.
Mobile
New Orleans
Gulf of Mexico
Map Area

Main map labels:
FT. MONTGOMERY
FT. STODDART
Mobile
Cedar R.
Darbone R.
Mobile Bay
Heron Pass
Horn I.
Guillori I.
Dauphine I.
FORT BOWYER
Heron I.
Bon Secours Bay
Perdido Bay
Mouth of Perdido
Jackson's return to Mobile, Nov.
Gen. Jackson's march to Pensacola, Oct.–Nov.
FT. BARANCAS
Pt. Chevreuil
Pensacola
Pensacola Bay
Santa Rosa I.

N

0 Miles 10 20 30
0 Kilometers 30

Chapter 1

❦

The War in the South

It was a battle that changed the course of American history; a battle that convinced Americans they had earned the right to be independent and that their sovereignty would be respected once and for all around the globe; a battle that thundered a once-poor, wretchedly educated orphan boy into the White House.

The battle took place during the War of 1812 between Great Britain and the United States on the Plains of Chalmette, approximately ten miles south of New Orleans on the east bank of the Mississippi River. Two armies faced each other. The attacking force consisted of roughly eight thousand disciplined regulars of the British army, including the Royal Fusiliers, Highlanders, Light Infantry, and Light Dragoons, a West Indian regiment, and sailors from the fleet anchored in the Gulf of Mexico. They expected to punch their way straight north to New Orleans, collect the "Beauty and Booty" that awaited them, and then head up the Mississippi Valley to join with British troops coming from Canada, effectively slicing the United States in two. As Lord Castlereagh, the British foreign secretary, put it, once the large seaport towns of America were "laid in ashes" and New Orleans captured, and the British had command of "all the rivers of the Mississippi valley and the Lakes . . . the Americans [would be] little better than prisoners in their own country."[1]

The defending army consisted of about four thousand frontiersmen, militiamen, regular soldiers, free men of color, Indians, pirates, and townspeople who were strung along a line from the Mississippi River to a cypress swamp and crouched behind a millrace ditch that had bales of cotton placed atop its northern edge.

It was January 8, 1815, and as the light of a new day dawned, a Congreve rocket, followed immediately by another, soared from behind the British line and hung for moments in midair before exploding over the field below. Red-coated officers ordered an advance; the disciplined veterans of the army of the Duke of Wellington rushed forward; the battle between these two armies began. When it was over, nothing for the young country would be the same.

The War of 1812—the "forgotten war"—began when the Speaker of the House of Representatives, Henry Clay of Kentucky, his principal assistant, John C. Calhoun of South Carolina, and other southern and western representatives, collectively known as the Warhawks, pressured President James Madison into asking Congress to declare war against Great Britain. Madison's message listed several provocations. The British were impressing American seamen to help fight the war against Napoleon and seizing American ships. They were inciting Indians to attack the frontier, and had not evacuated forts held on American soil along the northern frontier as had been stipulated in the 1783 Treaty of Paris, which had ended the American Revolution. But perhaps a more important reason than those given by Madison was the need the country felt to prove to itself and the rest of the world that this new experiment in republican government was a permanent fixture in the family of nations and that the contempt shown by Britain in persistently violating American rights would not go unchallenged or unpunished.

But the English sneered at U.S. pretensions. They insisted that these former colonies had not legitimately won their independence, certainly not by the force of arms. After all, what major military triumph could the former colonists point to as proof that by their own efforts they had won their freedom? Certainly not Saratoga or Yorktown. They were simply surrenders, nothing more. The English chose to believe that American independence resulted because they had grown weary of the rebellion and the accompanying European wars and simply agreed to let the colonies go.

The years following the Revolution demonstrated continued British disdain for American independence. England by its arrogance and condescension acted as though the United States would never survive as an independent republic. And America's great ally during the Revolution hardly behaved any better. France had guillotined its king, formed the Directory, and then succumbed to the dictatorship of Napoleon Bonaparte. At one point in this remarkable period the United States was invited to bribe French officials as a way of obtaining recognition for its ministers. The "XYZ Affair" caused such a furor in America when it became known—"Millions for defense but not one penny for tribute," went the cry—that a formal declaration of war almost resulted. To make matters worse, the French imitated the British in seizing American ships when they docked in French ports.

But war with France made no sense. The real enemy was Great Britain, and it remained America's enemy for well into the nineteenth century. Only a great military victory over the English could convince the world that our independence had been fairly won and that it was permanent. Only such a military victory would give Americans the self-confidence they needed to face a hostile Europe with its kings and czars and dictators.

So the Warhawks demanded that President Madison take action to smite the nation that unceasingly humiliated and shamed the American people. When Madison finally capitulated, the House of Representatives responded with a declaration of war on June 4, 1812, by a vote of seventy-nine to forty, and the Senate followed on June 17 by a vote of nineteen to thirteen. The President signed the measure the following day. But the congressional vote revealed a dangerous split within the country. Western and southwestern states enthusiastically favored the war; but the commercial and maritime east almost solidly opposed it.

In the succeeding months and years following the outbreak of war, the hapless young nation experienced one military disaster and reversal after another. General William Hull failed in his invasion of Canada, retreated to Detroit, and foolishly surrendered the town to a decidedly inferior force of British soldiers and their Indian allies. Invasions of Canada from Niagara and Lake Champlain collapsed when American troops refused on constitutional grounds to cross the border. Then the frigate USS *Chesapeake* was captured, its captain, James Lawrence, killed along with a number of crewmen, and the ship taken to Halifax. The British also blockaded the entire American coastline except for New England, in the hope that that commercial section might be persuaded to secede from the Union and return as a British colony or dependency. The situation really worsened for the American cause when Napoleon retreated from Moscow and subsequently abdicated, leaving Britain free to throw its considerable military power entirely against its former colonies.

To bring the American nation to heel, the British cabinet worked out a grand plan of conquest. The goal was "to destroy and lay waste the principal towns and commercial cities assailable either by their land or naval forces." The strategy consisted of a three-pronged invasion from three widely separated areas of the continent: an amphibian thrust into the Chesapeake Bay area aimed at Washington, Baltimore, and other coastal cities; another from Montreal into New York State via Lake Champlain; and a third from the Gulf of Mexico into Louisiana with the purpose of seizing New Orleans and detaching the Mississippi Valley from the Union.[2]

The first part of this grand strategy enjoyed an initial success that further devastated the American people. An amphibian force under Admiral Sir George Cockburn sailed into Chesapeake Bay in August 1814. A crack army of four thousand British soldiers and marines under Major General Robert Ross landed at Benedict, Maryland, and marched on Washington, easily knocking aside a superior number of American militiamen gathered at Bladensburg to block the invasion.

President Madison fled to Virginia. His wife, Dolley, managed to make her escape in a wagon filled with "valuable portable articles," including a large portrait of General Washington that had to be unscrewed from the wall of the presidential mansion.

The British entered the unprotected city on August 24, 1814, and set fire to the Capitol, the White House, and all other public buildings with the exception of the Patent Office. They also burned any private dwelling from which shots were fired at the invaders. But the advance to Baltimore on September 13 was repulsed by thirteen thousand Americans, who had fortified the heights around the city. A British fleet tried to bombard Fort McHenry into submission, and when the attempt failed the invaders withdrew.

At approximately the same time that Ross and his men advanced on Baltimore, a red-coated army of ten thousand veterans, commanded by General Sir George Prevost, crossed the Canadian border and arrived at Plattsburg, New York, on September 6, 1814. Before continuing his advance, Prevost decided to wait until a British fleet could enter Plattsburg Bay and assist him in storming the American position. But Lieutenant Thomas Macdonough of the U.S. Navy and his squadron outfought the superior British fleet and prevented it from entering the bay, thereby retaining control of the strategic Lake Champlain. Without that naval assistance and unable to proceed further, General Prevost turned around and retreated back to Canada.

The only really encouraging military news for Americans during these dark days of humiliating invasion came from the southwest. The Creek Indians had been engaged in a deadly civil war going back several years. There were numerous causes for this conflict: factional enmities within the Creek Nation, the building of a federal road from the Georgia frontier to new settlements along the Alabama River, the encroachment of whites on Creek land, and violent differences of opinion over the intrusion of white culture on Creek life and society. One group, known as Red Sticks because of their custom of painting their war clubs a bright red color, and led by such prophets as Peter McQueen, Josiah Francis (Hilis Hadjo), Paddy Walsh, and others, attracted a large following, mostly through magic, prophecy, and spell-binding oratory. These men preached the necessity of maintaining Indian cultural purity.[3]

The Creeks friendly to the whites understood the likely consequences if they waged war against the United States, so they refused the appeals and demands of the prophets. The Red Sticks subsequently threatened a massive bloodletting, and as their numbers swelled, especially among young warriors, they began a systemic assault against their own people, attacking and burning several villages allied with white traders, killing livestock, and burning homes and fields. Big Warrior, a Creek chieftain who was pro-white, appealed to Benjamin Hawkins, the U.S. Indian agent, for help, and the agent responded with military assistance. Thus, when the United States intruded in the summer of 1813, the Creek civil war became a war within the larger war against Great Britain.

Shortly thereafter, in July 1813, at a crossing of Burnt Corn Creek on the Pensacola Road, a group of whites and mixed-blood Creeks attacked a number of Red Sticks, led by Peter McQueen and High Head Jim, who were transporting a packtrain of powder and shot obtained from the Spanish in Florida, who were allied with the British. The Red Sticks drove off their attackers but lost their gunpowder. The whites and their friends took refuge in Fort Mims, a makeshift structure built around the house of Samuel Mims, a Georgia trader. It was a mile from the Alabama River in the Mississippi Territory and about forty miles north of Mobile.

At noon on August 30, 1813, the Red Sticks, led by a new recruit, William Weatherford (Chief Red Eagle), counterattacked. They entered through an open gate, slaughtered the defenders, and burned the fort. It was one of the most appalling massacres in frontier history. "The fearful shrieks of women and children put to death in ways as horrible as Indian barbarity could invent" echoed around the fort. The victims were "butchered in the quickest manner, and blood and brains bespattered the whole earth. The children were seized by the legs, and killed by batting their heads against the stockading. The women were scalped, and those who were pregnant were opened, while they were alive and the embryo infants let out of the womb." Red Eagle tried to stop this savagery, but many red clubs were raised over his head and he was forced to withdraw to save his own life. Between 250 and 275 white settlers, friendly Indians, and mixed-bloods were killed; between twenty and forty escaped.[4]

The horror of the massacre at Fort Mims, the savagery and audaciousness of it, rolled over the western country of America like a shock wave. Anger and fear and a demand for revenge ricocheted up and down the frontier. The governor of Tennessee, Willie Blount, responded immediately to the outcry. Empowered by the legislature to raise five thousand men for a three-month tour of duty, he ordered Major General Andrew Jackson of the Tennessee militia to "call out organize rendezvous and march without delay" 2,500 volunteers and militia "to repel an approaching invasion . . . and to afford aid and relief to the suffering citizens of the Mississippi Territory."[5]

On October 7, 1813, although pale and weak from the loss of blood from a bullet wound in his shoulder suffered in a barroom gunfight with Jesse and Thomas Hart Benton, and with his left arm in a sling, the six-foot-tall, cadaverous Jackson took command of the West Tennessee army at Fayetteville. His complexion was sallow and rather unhealthy-looking; nonetheless, the rest of his overall appearance exuded strength, if not fierceness. He always carried himself very erect, and his manner radiated confidence and sureness of command. He was forty-six years old and his steely blue eyes invariably registered his thoughts and feelings. At one instant they could blaze with anger and fury, at another with gentleness and understanding. Because of his strength and toughness as well as his constant attention to the welfare of his army, his soldiers affectionately called him Old Hickory. Hickory was as tough a substance as they knew, and General Andrew Jackson was, in their minds, indomitable.

Born in the Lancaster district of South Carolina on March 15, 1767, Andrew Jackson participated in the American Revolution as a messenger boy for Colonel William R. Davie. Only thirteen at the time, he was captured by British soldiers, mutilated on the wrist and forehead, imprisoned at Camden, South Carolina, where he contracted smallpox, but later released in a prisoner exchange arranged by his mother.

His entire immediate family died during the Revolution: first his older brothers, then his mother. (His father had died shortly before his birth.) His hatred of the British lasted for the remainder of his life and no doubt accounts in large measure for his fierce determination to defeat them in battle.

After the war he moved to Salisbury, North Carolina, where he studied law, first in the office of Spruce McCay and later in the office of Colonel John Stokes. Lacking opportunities for a lucrative law practice in North Carolina, he migrated west and established himself in Nashville. He married into one of the first families of Tennessee, established himself as a successful politician in the state, both as a congressional representative and a senator and as a judge on the state's superior court. In 1802, at the age of thirty-five, he won election as major general of the Tennessee militia.

The call by Governor Blount to avenge the Fort Mims massacre set Andrew Jackson on the course to national fame. He led his army deep into Creek country, speeding along at the incredible rate of thirty-six miles a day, and halted momentarily at the southernmost tip of the Tennessee River to build Fort Deposit as a depot for supplies. He then pushed on to the Coosa River, cutting a road over the mountains as he went and establishing a base at Fort Strother near Ten Islands. He and his army were now within striking distance of the Red Sticks, who were encamped thirteen miles to the east in the hostile village of Tallushatchee. On November 3, 1813, a thousand soldiers surrounded Tallushatchee and then closed in for the kill. It did not take long. They systematically slaughtered most of the warriors. "We shot them like dogs," boasted Davy Crockett. The town was then burned to the ground.[6]

Jackson won another victory at Talladega and killed three hundred warriors, but many more escaped, and he was forced to wait for reinforcements before renewing the war.

Governor Blount finally responded to Jackson's repeated appeals for additional troops, and on March 14, 1814, Old Hickory and an army of about two thousand infantry, seven hundred cavalry and mounted riflemen, and six hundred friendly Indians, of whom five hundred were Cherokees and one hundred Creeks, wheeled out of Fort Strother and headed directly for the heavy entrenchment of the Red Sticks at Horseshoe Bend.

Horseshoe Bend was a heavily wooded peninsula almost completely enclosed by the looping course of the Tallapoosa River. The Indians had built a stout breastwork running across its narrow 350-yard neck. It was made of timber and trunks of trees "laid horizontally on each other, leaving but a single place of entrance." At a height of five to eight feet it had a double row of portholes "artfully arranged" to give the defenders "complete direction of their fire." Since the breastwork was a curved zigzag structure, attackers could not advance upon it without being exposed to a deadly crossfire, while the defenders themselves were well protected and could not be enfiladed. It was "a place well formed by Nature for defence & rendered more secure by Art," Jackson reported to Secretary of War John Armstrong. Within the fort the finest gathering of hostile strength from the towns of Oakfuskee, New Youka, Oakchays, Hillabee, the Fish Ponds, and Eufala had been assembled. The principal chief in the fort was the Prophet Monahee, but the warrior in command of the fighting was Menewa (Great Warrior), a mixed-blood.[7]

The punishing hand of Andrew Jackson arrived at Horseshoe Bend at approximately ten o'clock in the morning on March 27. Facing the barricade, which was the focus of the main attack, Jackson stationed his artillery, one six-pounder and one three-pounder (not a particularly powerful battery), on a small eminence about 80 yards from the nearest and 250 yards from the farthest points of the breastwork. At 10:30 A.M. he opened fire.

The Indians inside the fortification began beating their war drums and screaming their defiance. Then, without warning and apparently without specific orders from Old Hickory, the friendly Creeks, part of the Cherokee force and the company of spies who had been sent to the other side of the Tallapoosa to cut off a retreat by the Red Sticks, crossed the river in canoes and set fire to buildings near the shore, attacking the hostiles at the rear of their fortification. This diversion gave Jackson the opportunity he needed, and he quickly seized it.[8]

He stormed the breastwork. The troops raced forward under a withering hail of Indian bullets and arrows. The 39th Regiment reached the barrier first, and Major Lemuel P. Montgomery leaped onto the top of the breastwork and called to his men to follow, the screams of the Red Sticks almost drowning him out. No sooner had his words been spoken than a bullet struck him in the head and he fell lifeless to the ground. Ensign Sam Houston mounted the wall and repeated Montgomery's cry, whereupon an arrow pierced his thigh. Unmindful of his wound, he jumped into the compound, followed by a large contingent of regulars. Within moments the breastwork was breached, and the army scaled the rampart in force.[9] With the capture of the fortification, the infantry moved in force from the forward position while the friendly Indians and spies advanced from the rear. Caught in this pincer, the hostiles could not escape. They tried to hide in the thick brush that covered the ground but were flushed out and shot at close range.

Once the troops gained the upper hand they set the village on fire. For five hours, Horseshoe Bend became a killing field, "but the firing and the slaughter continued until it was suspended by the darkness of the night," reported Jackson. "It was dark before we finished killing them."[10]

As the sun went down it also set on the once great and proud Creek Nation. For the Americans the victory came at the most opportune time imaginable. The hostiles were crushed just when the British were about to land troops in the south to initiate the third prong of their grand strategy to conquer the American nation. Had the Creek civil war been delayed and synchronized with the landing of the British troops, the combined forces might well have overcome Jackson's army and gone on to capture New Orleans and the lower Mississippi Valley.

About three thousand Creeks, estimated at approximately 15 percent of the entire Creek Nation, lost their lives in this war.[11] Numerous Creek towns had been destroyed, along with an abundance of foodstuffs. Jackson moved his army to the juncture of the Coosa and Tallapoosa rivers, and there he raised the American flag on April 17 over the old French fort, which was rebuilt and renamed Fort Jackson. There at 2:00 P.M. on August 9, 1814, Old Hickory imposed on the defeated Creek Nation a treaty in which he obtained for the United States some 23 million acres of land, roughly half of all the land held by the Creeks. It was approximately three-fifths of the present state of Alabama and one-fifth of Georgia, and extended from Georgia to the Mississippi Territory. As a reward, Andrew Jackson was appointed major general in the United States Army and placed in command of the Seventh Military District, which consisted of Tennessee, Louisiana, and the Mississippi Territory.

Once elevated to this exalted rank, the proud conqueror of the Creek Nation immediately assumed all the trappings of his high office. He even informed his wife, Rachel, that "you are now a Major Generals lady—in the service of the U.S. and as such you must appear, elegant and plain, not extravagant—but in such stile as strangers expect to see you."[12]

He had brought, to use his own words, "retaliation and vengeance" to the Creeks. And Great Britain and Spain, those two despicable allies, deserved no less. "I owe to Britain a debt of retaliatory vengeance," he told Rachel, "should our forces meet I trust I shall pay the debt—she is in conjunction with Spain arming the hostile Indians to butcher our women & children."[13]

Although the United States was not technically at war with Spain, and therefore any attack on it or its possessions would constitute an act of unauthorized aggression, Jackson had no compunction against invading Spanish Florida, because Spain cooperated with the British and Indians and indeed supplied the Indians with arms and ammunition. In addition, many of the leaders of the Red Sticks had escaped into Florida, where they continued to plot against the United States. So Jackson wrote to the Spanish governor in Pensacola and instructed him on his duties. There are "refugee banditti from the creek nation swarming into Florida," he wrote Don Matteo González Manrique, and "drawing rations from your government and under the drill of a British officer." Such renegades as Peter McQueen, Josiah Francis (Hilis Hadjo), and other hostiles constituted a "matricidal band for

whom your christian bowls seem to sympathise and bleed so freely."
They should be arrested, confined, and tried for their crimes, he insisted. The United States would not tolerate any attempt to protect
them. Be aware of my creed, he warned. "An Eye for an Eye, Toothe
for Toothe and Scalp for Scalp."[14]

As Jackson turned his attention toward Florida, the third phase of
the British grand strategy finally came into play. Vice Admiral Sir
Alexander Forrester Inglis Cochrane, commander of the North American station, had recommended to his government an invasion of the
United States from the Gulf of Mexico, an expedition by which he felt
certain he could bring about the conquest of New Orleans and the entire Mississippi Valley. Cochrane was the youngest son of the eighth
Earl of Dundonald. A stern, proud, domineering Scot, he entered the
navy at an early age, served in the West Indies during the closing days
of the American Revolution, and, with the renewal of the war by Great
Britain against Napoleon, was named a rear admiral in 1804. He was
knighted for bravery in the naval victory off San Domingo and later
promoted to vice admiral. He was a very courtly man, quite proud of
his achievements. Once raised to flag rank, he expected and received
the deference due him. Early in 1814 he was placed in command of
the entire North American naval station.

In his argument to his superiors about this invasion from the Gulf,
Cochrane declared that few troops would be needed—perhaps three
thousand regulars, perhaps less—because they would be joined by Indians and Spanish. He also believed that slaves in great numbers could
be recruited to fight the United States. Their hatred for their masters
and their masters' fear of them combined to make them especially
valuable. With Indians, Spanish, and slaves it would take as little as a
few thousand regulars to capture Mobile, drive on to Baton Rouge,
and from there seize New Orleans.[15] Once the great city was taken, the
invading force could march up the Mississippi Valley to Canada and
reduce the United States to an island territorially surrounded by
Britain and Spain. He, like other commanding officers, was also certain that the people of Louisiana would not be loyal to the United
States and would welcome British "liberation." Since American peace

commissioners had already departed for Europe to meet in Ghent, Belgium, with their counterparts from England, a victory such as he anticipated would enable the British envoys to dictate peace terms, in particular the creation of a semi-independent Indian state in the southwest under British protection and the acquisition of territory around the Great Lakes to be added to Canada. In August 1814 the American and British peace envoys would meet in Ghent and begin their negotiations.

London approved Cochrane's plan, and on July 30, 1814, Lord Bathurst, the secretary of state for war and the colonies, directed General Ross to sail his army to Jamaica and rendezvous with additional troops that would be sent him from England. As part of the invasion Ross was also ordered to obtain command of the lower Mississippi so as to deprive Americans any access to the Gulf of Mexico and to occupy a large stretch of important and valuable territory in the area that could be demanded as the price of peace. Less than two weeks later, on August 10, John Wilson Croker, secretary to the Lords Commissioners of the Admiralty, wrote Cochrane and approved his plan; five thousand—later the figure was raised to fourteen thousand—men would be dispatched over a period of time to join him in the invasion. The bulk of them could be expected to arrive in Jamaica around mid-November.[16]

In executing his plan,[17] even before it had been officially approved by Croker, Cochrane first dispatched Captain Hugh Pigot in May 1814 to the mouth of the Apalachicola in Florida, just east of Pensacola, to begin rounding up Indian and Spanish allies. Pigot later reported that over three thousand Creeks and Seminoles had agreed to join in raids against the Americans. With Spanish consent, Cochrane initially planned to invade through Pensacola and Mobile—the latter recently seized by the United States from Spain. So he sent Lieutenant Colonel Edward Nicholls to Pensacola with two naval vessels, the *Hermes* and the *Carron*, plus a small force of one hundred troops and a supply of arms and ammunition, to begin training the Indians. Nicholls, "an impatient blustering Irishman" known to be brave but cruel, was directed to scout the area and determine all the possible routes to New Orleans.

He first landed at Apalachicola, where he issued several proclamations in which he said that all slaves who joined him would be freed and all Indians who took up arms against the United States would regain the lands taken from them, which would be guaranteed to them forever.[18]

Nicholls arrived outside the port of Pensacola on August 14, 1814, and immediately received permission to land from Governor González Manrique. This was a clear and indisputable violation of Spanish neutrality, but González Manrique felt justified, since he expected an American invasion at any time.

As early as June 1814, General Jackson learned of the British operations in Florida. He notified Secretary of War John Armstrong that "300 British had landed and are fortifying at the mouth of the Apalachicola, and are arming and exciting the Indians to acts of hostility against the United States." Under the circumstances he requested permission to initiate an assault against Pensacola. "Will the government say to me . . . proceed to ——— and reduce it—If so I promise the war in the south has a speedy termination and British influence forever cut off from the Indians in that quarter."[19] Such permission would of course constitute a declaration of war against Spain, which the Madison administration was reluctant to grant. "I am directed by the President to say," replied Secretary Armstrong, "that there is a disposition on the part of the Spanish Government not to break with the U.S." You must distinguish between "the effect of menace & compulsion" and "choice & policy. The result of this enquiry must govern." If the Spanish are arming and feeding the Indians and cooperating with the British, then "we must strike on the broad principle of preservation."[20]

It is unlikely that Jackson received this letter before he made plans to invade Florida. Not that it would have made a particle of difference. He received many reports about the intentions of the British invading force, particularly the proclamations of Nicholls. He knew that they included an attack on Mobile, followed by a general assault against New Orleans.[21] He therefore "finished the business with the creeks" by forcing them to sign the Treaty of Fort Jackson, and then hastily moved down the Coosa and Alabama rivers with his army to the American-occupied town of Mobile, arriving on August 22. He and his army had traversed four hundred miles through a wilderness in eleven days.[22]

Roughly 140 miles east of New Orleans, Mobile figured prominently in British invasion plans for three reasons: it provided the best route for an invasion of Louisiana; it would strengthen ties and lines of communication with the Indians; and it guaranteed the severing of Louisiana trade to the rest of the country and Europe. The chief American defense of the town consisted of Fort Bowyer, built at the extreme end of a long spit that extended many miles out across the entrance of Mobile Bay and "commanded the passes at the entrance of the bay." It provided almost exclusive control over the navigation of the coast of West Florida and allowed easy access to Pensacola. In the first of a whole series of costly mistakes, the British, in particular Admiral Cochrane, decided that the fort was weak and did not require a large force to subdue it.[23]

On arriving at Mobile, Jackson sent Major William Lawrence and a contingent of 160 regular soldiers to repair and defend the dilapidated fort. Working at top speed, they managed within two weeks to bring the fort to an acceptable level of defense. Then on September 12 a British force of 225 marines and Indians was put ashore nine miles east of the fort and a naval squadron consisting of the *Hermes*, *Carron*, *Sophie*, and *Childers* with a total of seventy-eight guns under Captain William H. Percy arrived at Mobile Bay to begin the land-sea invasion. The *Hermes* and *Sophie* got within range of the fort and opened up with their heavy guns at 4:20 P.M. But the shallowness of the channel and the dying wind made it impossible for these ships to maneuver. By 7:00 P.M. the *Hermes* had gone aground with her sails shredded and her rigging shot away by the returning fire from the American fort. After transferring his men to other ships, Percy abandoned the *Hermes* and set it ablaze. The resulting explosion of her magazine could be heard by Jackson thirty miles away in Mobile. The destruction of the *Hermes* marked the end of the engagement.

Realizing that he could not capture the fort, Percy withdrew and sailed back to Pensacola. The marines and Indians who had landed got within a thousand yards of the fort and attempted a feeble assault, but when they saw the fleet sailing off they turned around and retreated to Pensacola. In the engagement Nicholls was wounded in the leg and blinded in one eye. The British lost twenty-two dead aboard the *Hermes* and twenty wounded; the *Sophie* had nine killed and thirteen wounded, while the *Carron* sustained one killed and four wounded. Lawrence lost only four killed and five wounded.[24]

The loss of this battle was catastrophic for British plans—and it could have been prevented. The strategy of a land-sea operation to capture Mobile and thereby provide the location for a massive invasion by the army gathering in Jamaica had great merit and should have been better planned and organized. Defeat resulted because shallow-bottomed boats were needed to properly navigate the waters of Mobile Bay so as to get into position to bombard the fort. In addition, the land force was too small for the task of capturing the fort and faced a highly disciplined and well-entrenched contingent of American soldiers.

Now convinced that the British planned their invasion through Mobile with Pensacola as a base of operation, Jackson decided to pursue the retreating British marines and Indians and invade Florida. Such an action would disrupt British plans, punish the Spanish for violating their neutrality, and put an end to the Indian war in the south.[25] Although he admitted in a letter to the new secretary of war, James Monroe, that "I act without the orders of the government," still he said he felt "a confidence that I shall stand Justified to my government for having undertaken the expedition."[26]

But he needed additional troops for such an expedition. Fortunately, his friend General John Coffee started southward from West Tennessee with more than two thousand cavalry and even picked up several hundred more troops along the way. When he learned of Coffee's approach and the size of his force, Jackson wheeled out of Mobile on October 25 to rendezvous with him. By the time the combined force reached Pensacola the American army comprised over 4,000 men, including 1,000 regulars and several hundred Choctaw and Chickasaw allies.

Pensacola was a small village of a few streets connected to a square and defended by two forts, St. Rose and St. Michael, which were poorly garrisoned with approximately five hundred men. Real strength lay in Fort Barrancas, which guarded the entrance of the bay, and it was held by the British.

Under a flag of truce, Jackson demanded the surrender of the forts from Governor González Manrique and the immediate evacuation of the British from Pensacola. "I have come not as an enemy of Spain," he assured the governor, "but I come with a force sufficient to prevent the repetition of those acts so injurious to the U.S. and so inconsistent with the neutral character of Spain." If his demands were refused he would not be responsible, he said, for the conduct of "my enraged soldiers and the Indian warriors."[27]

The governor rejected the demands, and Jackson attacked the town on November 7, employing one column of five hundred men to make a noisy demonstration on the west side of the town while he led the main force through the woods before dawn on the east side. The Spanish had expected the attack to come from the west side because that was the site of Jackson's camp. Moreover their heaviest artillery was located in that section. So they were completely surprised when the Americans poured into Pensacola from the east. Jackson anticipated that the British ships anchored in the harbor would open fire on his army, "but they remained silent from a dread of our Artillery." Actually the British, like the Spanish, had expected the assault to come from the west, and the surprise attack on the east developed so swiftly that the ships could not make the necessary adjustments to bring Jackson's force within range of their guns. Indeed, the attack moved so quickly that resistance collapsed within minutes, and González Manrique soon surrendered the town and its fortifications. However, the commanders of the forts delayed their surrender for several hours in the hope of receiving British support—"Spanish treachery," Jackson fumed—which meant that the attack on Barrancas had to wait until the following morning.[28]

The next day the town was rocked with a tremendous explosion. The British had destroyed Fort Barrancas, and Nicholls, the British garrison, and hundreds of their Indian allies sailed out into the Gulf of

Mexico. At least, Jackson reported to Secretary Monroe, "I had the Satisfaction to see the whole British force leave the port and their friends to our Mercy."[29]

In the engagement the Americans lost seven dead and eleven wounded, while the Spanish suffered fourteen killed and six wounded. British and Indian casualties went unrecorded.[30]

Rather than remain in Pensacola, since it was now totally defenseless against invasion because of the loss of Barrancas and was therefore a waste of effort and manpower, Jackson decided to return to Mobile, still the focal point, in his mind, of invasion by the main British force. If nothing else, the continuing presence in Pensacola of his army was a violation of international law and an act of provocation that could trigger open warfare between the two countries. He was also convinced that he had "broken up the hot bed of the Indian war," since many starving Indians wandered about the area in desperate search for food. In addition, he believed the Spanish recognized that any further violation of their neutrality would bring swift retaliatory action by the United States. So he departed the town fairly certain that he had seriously disrupted the overall British strategy in the Gulf area.

And indeed he had. The defeat at Mobile and the expulsion from Pensacola forced the English to change their invasion plans and target New Orleans directly as the point of invasion—probably the worst site they could have chosen. An attacking force of professional soldiers coming from Mobile or somewhere in East Florida could easily sweep across the Mississippi Territory to Louisiana above New Orleans. Such an invasion would cut off the city from supplies, especially with the British fleet patrolling the Gulf of Mexico. Also, the terrain across Louisiana was far better than what an attacking force faced in a frontal assault up the Mississippi River with its bayous, creeks, and soggy ground, which could play havoc with the movement of heavy equipment and a large army. And the river itself could be treacherous, with its shifting tides and erratic movement.[31]

Even the British acknowledged the damage that Jackson had inflicted on their plans. "The attack made by the Americans upon Pensacola," wrote Admiral Cochrane, "has in a great measure retarded this service." Jackson also appreciated the extent of his success. "Our conduct," he told his wife, "has obtained from our enemy [a] tribute of Just respect. It is said that Colo. Nicholls, exclaimed from the shipping that he never beheld such o[r]der and determined bravery and the universal good conduct of our troops whilst in Pensacola, has inspired the Spaniards with the highest confidence in the americans, and the citizens exclaimed that the choctaws were more civilized than the British."[32]

Jackson's victories also deprived the British of any real help from the Spanish population living in East Florida. Not only had the invaders proved their inability to lend useful support, but their behavior in Pensacola shocked and outraged the inhabitants of the town. They kidnaped slaves, stole property, and acted with "typical British arrogance" toward occupied peoples. Any attempt on their part to invade from Florida in the future would have been met with hostility and possibly concerted opposition. As for the Indians, they were so demoralized and disorganized as to be of little use to the British.

On November 9, Jackson handed the town back to the governor, but not without a typical Jacksonian flourish. The "enemy having disappeared and the hostile creeks fled to the Forest," he wrote Governor González Manrique, "I retire from your Town, and leave you again at liberty to occupy your Fort." Or what was left of it. And Gonzalez Manrique responded in like manner, asking "God to preserve your life many years."[33]

And on that pleasant note, Jackson departed Pensacola and headed for Mobile, where he arrived on November 19. It is quite possible that before he left he received a letter written by Secretary of War Monroe almost three weeks earlier. In the letter, written at the direction of the President, the secretary directly forbade Jackson to take any "measure which would involve this Government in a contest with Spain." A minister to Spain had just been appointed, and since U.S. relations with that country were still officially amicable, it seemed more appropriate for this country to make a "representation" to the Spanish government about "the insolent and unjustifiable conduct of the Governor of Pensacola" through its minister than to have Jackson take military action.

Fortunately for the ultimate success of American arms, this letter arrived too late to forestall the invasion of Florida.

But the letter had added significance in that it relayed to Jackson the information the administration had heard about Britain's invasion plans. Monroe told Old Hickory that a large force under Lord Rowland Hill would be directed at Louisiana.[34] In fact he informed the American peace commissioners meeting in Ghent with their British counterparts that between twelve and fifteen thousand troops would sail from Ireland in September and invade New Orleans sometime in the winter. Actually a force of about two thousand men under Major General John Keane had left Plymouth and was expected to rendezvous in Jamaica in late November with the expeditionary force from the Chesapeake. This initial British force—supplemented by additional reserves sent at different times—constituted about six thousand men, with Lieutenant General Sir Edward Michael Pakenham given overall command in place of General Ross, who had been killed at Baltimore.

To meet, challenge, and defeat this formidable army about to invade the United States, Monroe assured Jackson that he would send him 7,500 men from Tennessee, 2,500 from Kentucky, and 2,500 from Georgia. He also expected the warriors of all the friendly Indian tribes in the area to join in the effort of defense.[35]

Just when this letter reached Jackson is uncertain, but he had begun to pick up rumors out of Jamaica from his vast network of spies that New Orleans was now the focus for a full-scale British invasion. He found this information hard to believe, since Mobile provided the best route to the great city. Still he could not dismiss the evidence at hand. So he quickly ordered the strengthening of Fort Bowyer, assigned a large contingent of troops to the defense of Mobile, and turned over command of the area to Brigadier General James Winchester. On November 22, together with an army of less than two thousand, he finally set out for New Orleans, still concerned that a blunder or miscalculation on his part might mean the successful invasion of his country by a savage enemy bent on its prostration and the scooping up of "Beauty and Booty" in New Orleans.

Chapter 2

New Orleans

The city of New Orleans sits about 120 miles from the mouth of the meandering Mississippi River in a region of swamps and bayous and tiny creeks leading to Lake Pontchartrain to the north, Lake Borgne to the east, and Lake Barataria to the south. It is protected from the temperamental river by a man-made system of high earthen banks, called levees, that run many miles above and below it. Yet it lives off and receives its lifeblood from the river. Its commerce in the first decades of the nineteenth century consisted of virtually every product grown or made, and immigrants of many nationalities and races were drawn to the city via the great Mississippi. As the city grew it took on the shape of a crescent as it curved around a bend in the river, and was therefore sometimes known as the Crescent City.

Because of its width and ever-changing currents, the river provided New Orleans with maximum protection from any force that might try to invade from the west. To the south, Fort St. Philip, a military post sixty-five miles downstream and garrisoned by regular troops manning twenty-eight 24-pounders, stood guard. Nearer the city, Fort St. Leon watched over a particularly sharp looping bend on the Mississippi known as the English Turn. Sailing ships had to stop at the Turn and wait for a change in wind direction in order to navigate the bend. Warships upon reaching the Turn were directly under the fire of the heavy guns of Fort St. Leon.

Only from the east and north was New Orleans vulnerable to attack—and it was from thence that the British planned to make their entrance.

Louisiana had been explored in the 1680s by René Robert Cavelier, Sieur de La Salle, and named in honor of his sovereign, King Louis XIV. New Orleans was founded in 1718 and named by Jean Baptiste le Moyne, Sieur de Bienville, to honor the Duke of Orléans. It quickly developed into an important port and an essential link in France's great North American empire. But nearly a century of fighting with the British brought an end to that empire when France ceded Canada to England in 1763 and, as compensation to her hapless Iberian ally, ceded all of her territory west of the Mississippi River, including New Orleans, to Spain. Then, in 1800, Napoleon Bonaparte demanded and received the return of Louisiana, the news of which so alarmed President Thomas Jefferson that he initiated a diplomatic mission to purchase it. Napoleon's plans for a restoration of the French empire in North America ended in defeat in Santo Domingo, and so he agreed to sell Louisiana to the United States in 1803. Thus, in just a few decades, the inhabitants of New Orleans fell under the rule of France, then Spain, then France again, and finally the United States, and the official language changed from French to Spanish to English. However, during all these transitions French continued to be the language spoken by most of the inhabitants.

After the defeat of Napoleon's army in Santo Domingo, thousands of white settlers on the island fled to New Orleans. And, no matter the government, French-speaking immigrants continued to be attracted to the city, arriving from Canada, from France, and from the West Indies. Descendants of the original French settlers were called Creoles, but soon the term was used to designate Spanish and Portuguese descendants in the region and even applied to Negroes born in the Americas. French Creoles were not Cajuns. The latter term refers to descendants of the Acadians who were brutally expelled from Nova Scotia in 1755 by the British and fled to Louisiana. They lived mostly along Bayou Lafourche, which extended down to the Gulf of Mexico.

The constant flow of French-speaking whites and black slaves into New Orleans, even after the sale of Louisiana to the United States, can be explained by the presence of privateers operating out of Lake Barataria who smuggled them into the country. The slave trade was of particular importance to the pirates, since they had an eager market in the city. A slave of "good stock" in legitimate trade brought $600 or $700 on the open market. The smugglers offered them for $150 or $200. Small wonder that so many inhabitants of the city looked kindly on their illegal operations.

On July 18, 1809, an official head count showed that the number of new arrivals amounted to 5,754, of whom 1,798 were white French, 1,977 "free colored and black," and 1,979 slaves.[1] By the end of the year the population of New Orleans had doubled and consisted of French, Spanish, Americans, a number of Germans, some Portuguese, Italians, and Irish, along with slaves, mulattos, quadroons, and octoroons from Cuba, Santo Domingo, and the West Indies. In the census of 1810 the total population of New Orleans had reached 24,552, of whom only 3,200 were Americans of Anglo descent. Furthermore, the preponderance of French-speaking inhabitants not only dominated the city, indeed the entire delta area, but engendered fierce resentment from Spanish- and English-speaking residents.[2]

This mixture of races, cultures, and languages enriched the life of New Orleans but also made for a mountain of problems for any government attempting to control, police, and regulate this heterogeneous mass. Rivalry between ethnic groups and social classes was virtually a way of life. It became enshrined in the culture.

Added to the problems was the presence of pirates. They initially controlled an area lying west of New Orleans to Bayou Lafourche and south to the Gulf of Mexico. Their ships sailed out of Lake Barataria, the mouth of which is protected from the Gulf by two islands: Grand Terre and Grand Isle. This entire district, about forty miles due south of New Orleans, became the center of smuggling activities by privateers operating throughout the Caribbean. They numbered about eight hundred and were commanded by the Laffite brothers, Alexandre, Pierre, and Jean.

The brothers were born in Port-au-Prince, Haiti, the children of refugees from the Spanish Inquisition. Their grandmother was Jewish, and from her they naturally enough developed a lively hatred for the Spanish. Alexandre, the eldest of eight children, was born in 1771 and after becoming a privateer assumed the name Dominique You. He was hardly more than five feet four inches tall, rather stocky, hook-nosed, swarthy, with jet-black hair and quick and staring black eyes.

Pierre and Jean Laffite were close in age, Pierre being born in 1779 and Jean in 1782. They were educated in Martinique and at a military school in St. Christopher. They followed their older brother into privateering and were trained in cannoneering and the business of piracy by their second cousin, Renato Beluché, a native of New Orleans, whom they called "uncle," and who used a number of aliases in his various enterprises, including Rigmartin and Pedro Brugman.

Unlike his brother Dominique, Jean was tall, just shy of six feet. Always well dressed and elegant in his manner, he was fluent in English, French, Spanish, and Italian, which made him an extremely able administrator and businessman. Pierre, on the other hand, was slovenly and heavier than his younger brother, although they were about the same height. He also lacked the style and elegance of Jean, not that it ever lessened the attention he received from Creole women, who regarded him as the handsomest of the brothers.[3]

During the Napoleonic Wars these pirates preyed on Spanish and English ships in the Caribbean and brought their prizes to the island of Grand Terre, from whence they were smuggled up to New Orleans. Jean Laffite, by dint of his linguistic and organizational skills—indeed, he was a far better businessman and entrepreneur than he was a seaman—quickly emerged as the leader of the Baratarian pirates. He and Pierre began a blacksmith shop in New Orleans, operated by slaves, and Jean obtained a warehouse and acquired an agent, Jean Sauvinet, in the city to help him dispose of the contraband. Once the goods reached Grand Terre they were loaded on shallow crafts and sailed across Lake Barataria and through bayous and waterways to

Donaldsonville and New Orleans. Where the waterways ended, teams of men and mules were stationed to transport the contraband the short distance to the Mississippi, and it was then ferried to the city. Jean built a warehouse in Donaldsonville and another one in the village of Barataria where the goods could be stored while they awaited shipment to the crescent city. Through this efficient operation the people of the city had a steady and relatively inexpensive supply of dry goods, wine, all sorts of manufactured items, and iron. A dozen pair of silk stockings, for example, could be purchased from them for $9.[4]

The city also received a great deal of its food supply from traders from the north, who moved their products down the Mississippi and either sold them or transferred them to large ships that could navigate the Gulf and Atlantic Ocean and bring them to international markets. Receipts of exports at New Orleans rose from $7 million in 1807 to double that amount within ten years. Most of the goods went to Europe and smaller amounts to the islands of the Caribbean and the ports of South America. Among the nation's principal ports, the city shared a preeminent position with New York. One observer called New Orleans "the Grand depot of the Western States and most of the maritime Towns in the United States."[5]

Not that the city lacked products of its own. Plantations lined the Mississippi to the north and south where cotton, sugarcane, rice, oranges, vegetables, and cattle were grown and raised. But the war brought a steep decline in the commerce of the city. American shippers feared their cargo would be seized by the British fleet patrolling the Gulf, and only the Baratarian pirates provided a modicum of commercial activity. By 1814, warehouses bulged with stored goods waiting to be exported, which the British hungered to seize. Some 10,000 hogsheads of raw sugar and 150,000 bales of cotton lay on the wharves near the center of town.[6]

New Orleans itself consisted of several sections, the most important of which was the old quarter known locally as the Vieux Carré. It originally comprised eight streets: Orleans, Bourbon, Chartres, St. Philippe, Toulouse, du Maine, Ste. Anne, and Bourgogne. Additional streets were later laid out to form a perfect rectangle. All these streets were straight and wide, usually thirty-six feet, and boasted sidewalks. The gutters alongside the sidewalks drained into a canal behind the city which ran to a bayou and then to Lake Pontchartrain. Houses were usually two-story affairs built of brick with graceful balconies ringed by delicate iron latticework and arched entrances that led to courtyard gardens. The interiors of these buildings were tastefully furnished with mostly French imports, and the gardens were radiant with tropical flowers and shrubs. All in all, New Orleans exuded the air of a provincial European town, or, as one visitor later described it, "a French Ville de Province."[7]

The center of the crescent city, facing the river, was the Place d'Armes, a three-sided square—the river formed the fourth side— ringed with shops on the first floor and living quarters above. A half-dozen streets converged on the square, but not as spokes of a wheel, rather in straight and parallel lines. After the devastating fire of 1788 the Spanish rebuilt much of the town and added their own unique style of architecture. At one end of the square they built a cathedral, as well as the Cabildo, seat of the Spanish government, and a presbytery, which the authorities later rented and then sold to the city for use as a courthouse.[8]

After the purchase of Louisiana by the United States, President Jefferson sent William Charles Coles Claiborne to serve as territorial governor. Born in Virginia, Claiborne studied law in Richmond, moved to Tennessee, where he became a judge of the superior court, and was later elected to the United States Senate. He supported Jefferson in the presidential election of 1800, for which he was awarded the Louisiana post. At the age of twenty-nine he relocated and brought with him his wife and daughter, both of whom later succumbed to yellow fever. He subsequently married a New Orleans Creole, Clarris Durale, and upon her death he married a wealthy Spanish lady, Sophronie Bosque.

When Claiborne arrived in New Orleans he found resentful, squabbling clans who represented all ethnicities and nationalities, balked at any attempt to change their way of life or their cultural habits and customs, and resented the rush of Americans who invaded the city from the north and east to take advantage of the economic and political opportunities that had suddenly opened up to them.

The French Creoles as a class particularly resented the Americans, whom they found grasping and lacking in proper manners. Wealthy male Creoles would never appear in public without tie, gloves, and hat. They never chewed tobacco or spat it out as did so many Americans from the frontier. Haughty and excessively proud of their breeding, they were courteous to a fault, kissed ladies' hands, and prided themselves on their reputation for hospitality. Every weekend, plantations came alive with dozens of guests, who passed their time hunting, drinking, dining, dancing, and playing cards. Quite often, weekend guests would remain for months without the host indicating in any way that they had overstayed their welcome. Fortunately for Andrew Jackson's purposes, most of these Creoles were rabid Bonapartists and hated England with a passion. As Bernard de Marigny, a Creole leader, later remarked, "One cannot be French, or of French origin, without detesting the English domination. . . . Our state was free, independent, and was a part of the Union and should we sacrifice such noble privileges in order to become an English Colony? What a horrible idea!"

For their part the newly arrived Americans regarded the Creoles as outrageously pagan, reveling in the "delights of the table, the boudoir, and the gaming board." Men kissing each other on both cheeks when greeting really shocked the newcomers, and outraged some. Rachel Jackson gasped when she later visited the city. "Great Babylon is come up before me," she cried. "Oh, the wickedness, the idolatry of the place! unspeakable the riches and splendor."[9]

At first the Creoles held Claiborne at arm's lengths, but he slowly won their grudging approval by emulating their style, delaying any revision of law and government, and appointing many local men to political office. He was so successful at placating the sensibilities of the natives that he won election as governor when Louisiana was admitted as a state into the Union in 1812.

Not that the populace liked him particularly. His marital alliances obviously helped him a great deal, especially with the French and

Spanish Creoles. But the temperaments of the inhabitants were such that any offensive action on the governor's part could instantly generate bickering, complaints, and a refusal to cooperate. A weak, intriguing, and gutless man, according to Vincent Nolte, a German-born merchant, Claiborne "had not the energy necessary to give a great impulse to the population of Louisiana" and cared only for his popularity and preeminence. When Jackson finally arrived in the city the governor resented his presence. He particularly resented the general's absolute authority and the necessity of having to take orders from a man he considered his inferior. The general quickly took the governor's measure. Claiborne, he said, "is much better qualified for great pomp & show, & courting popularity—quiet life—in civil walks—than militiary achievements amidst peril danger."[10]

Of the many Americans to arrive in the city after the Louisiana Purchase, one of the most notable was Edward Livingston, a New York lawyer who served as U.S. attorney and then as mayor of New York City. He migrated to Louisiana because of a scandal involving a theft by one of his agents. He accepted full responsibility for the theft and to make restitution sold off all his property. With the purchase of Louisiana he recognized the opportunity that had opened up for a lawyer of his ability in this new territory, especially one who could render an experienced hand in the change of government. So he moved. Like Claiborne, he married a Creole lady, Louise Davezac, which aided his progress in New Orleans society. As a lawyer he served this society with zeal and enormous intelligence, and in time acquired a considerable fortune. His connections also helped. His brother Robert, who as minister to France negotiated the Louisiana Purchase, played an important role in introducing steam-driven ships to the country by providing financial aide to the inventor Robert Fulton and was later awarded a monopoly on landing rights at New Orleans for his steamboats.[11]

With the outbreak of war against Great Britain and the developing threat of invasion from the Gulf of Mexico, Livingston, as chairman of the New Orleans Committee of Public Safety, organized the city for defense. At the same time, Governor Claiborne issued orders to raise troops for the state militia.

One of Claiborne's principal problems was the presence of the pirates in Barataria. For a number of years he had been trying to clear the outlaws from their lair. He became so enraged by their brazen actions that on November 24, 1813, he issued a proclamation declaring that "in the name of the state, [I] offer a reward of five hundred dollars, which will be paid out of the treasury to any person delivering the said John Laffite to the Sheriff of the Parish of Orleans." Whereupon the bumptious Laffite offered five thousand dollars out of his treasury "to any person delivering Governor Claiborne to me at Isle au Chat (Cat Island) west of Grand Terre, near the mouth of Bayou Lafourche."[12] Jean's brother Pierre was so indifferent to the governor's proclamation and overt hostility that he nonchalantly walked the streets of New Orleans and was promptly arrested and imprisoned.

Events took a dangerous turn when the British tried to recruit Laffite and his pirates and get their permission to use Barataria as a point of invasion. Colonel Nicholls had been instructed to contact Laffite and obtain his consent to the plan.

Nicholls dispatched a letter to the pirate shortly after he arrived in Pensacola in August 1814. He also issued a proclamation to the people of Louisiana calling on them to assist in their "liberation from a faithless, imbecile government." He said he headed a large body of Indians, well armed and disciplined, who would respect their rights if they cooperated in their "liberation." Property, laws, and the peace of the countryside would be guaranteed. Europe was now "happy and free," he added, and France was Britain's ally, now that the tyrant Napoleon had been exiled to Elbe. Interestingly, Nicholls also addressed his proclamation to the citizens of Kentucky. "You have too long borne . . . the whole brunt of the war," he wrote. "After the experiences of twenty-one years, can you any longer support those brawlers for liberty . . . ? Be no longer their dupes—accept my offers—every thing I have promised in this paper I guarantee to you, on the sacred honor of a British officer."

The letter to Laffite invited the pirate to enter the service of Great Britain, for which he would receive the rank of captain in the Royal Navy plus lands in the area and full protection of his property. In return he must "cease all hostilities against Spain, or the allies of Great Britain." Captain John McWilliams conveyed the letter to the pirate, sailing to Barataria aboard the sloop *Sophie*, commanded by Nicholas Lockyer.[13]

Laffite studied the letter very carefully and then asked for a two-week grace period during which he would think over the offer and discuss it with his associates. So, while the pirates consulted among themselves, Lockyer and McWilliams waited aboard their ship just outside the pass leading into Barataria Bay.

The British invitation was indeed tempting, particularly when a sum of $30,000 was added as an inducement, but it meant abandoning their practice of preying on Spanish shipping, and the pirates just could not bring themselves to agree. Their very professionalism forbade it. So they decided to send the British communication to Jean Blanque, who owned a number of ships the pirates sailed, served in the state legislature, and was a man of some renown and influence, and ask him to contact Claiborne and show him the documents.

In his letter to Blanque, Lafitte admitted that he had evaded the payment of duties in the customhouse but swore that he had "never ceased to be a good citizen." In a separate letter to Claiborne he offered his services in the defense of the country and only asked that "a stop be put to the proscription against me and my adherents. . . . I am the stray sheep, wishing to return to the sheepfold." He said he had never sailed under any flag except that of the republic of Cartagena, and if he could have brought his prizes to the ports of Louisiana he would not have employed the "illicit means that have caused me to be proscribed."[14]

Within twenty-four hours after being dispatched, the letters and papers were in Blanque's hands, even though the trip from Grande Terre to New Orleans normally took three days. Blanque brought the communiqués to Claiborne, who called together the legislature's committee of safety and asked for its advice. Were these documents genuine, he asked, and if so would it be proper for the governor to enter into correspondence with pirates? One member of the committee got so enraged at Laffite's audacity that he jumped to his feet and cried, "These letters are a ruse on the part of Jean Lafitte to get Pierre out of jail and make us look ridiculous." Commodore Daniel T. Patterson, the naval commander at New Orleans, also condemned any cooperation with the pirates. "My instructions from the Secretary of the Navy," he said, "are to disperse the Baratarian association. The schooner USS *Carolina* has been sent here for that purpose." And, he added, he fully intended to "carry out these instructions."[15] General Jacques Villeré, commander of the Louisiana militia, took the opposite tack and defended the Baratarians. "They are not pirates," he insisted, "they are privateers." Unfortunately they could not bring their prizes legally into the country. Their only crime was that they disposed of their prizes in violation of the law. "The United States," he continued, "is their adopted country. They see it threatened by an enemy they hate. These documents are true. We must believe the Baratarians."[16]

After considerable discussion the committee decided, with only Villeré dissenting, that the letters were fake and intended as a ruse to spring Pierre from jail. The committee also instructed Patterson to carry out his mission forthwith and destroy the pirates' lair at Grande Terre.

At about the same time this discussion took place, Pierre escaped from jail with the help of some friends, possibly including the jailer himself, and returned to Barataria. Whereupon Jean, fearing an attack by the British because the two-week delay he had requested from Lockyer had about run out, loaded his ships with all the available arms and ammunition on hand and sailed to an island about forty miles west of Grande Terre. Dominique You was left in command of the pirate's base and was instructed to fire the warehouses and remaining ships in the bay if attacked.

But the attack came instead from the Americans. Patterson dropped down the Mississippi with six gunboats, one launch, and the USS *Carolina*, ready for battle and carrying a large contingent of regular soldiers. When Dominique You realized that it was the Americans, not the English, who were initiating an assault, he could not and would not fire back. Instead he ordered the torching of the warehouses and the ships in the harbor. About five hundred Baratarians made their escape just as the Americans landed on Grand Terre and occupied it. You himself surrendered, and eighty Baratarians were captured. Despite You's attempt to destroy his ships, Patterson seized a number of vessels of varying sizes along with some of the booty that had not been consumed in the warehouse fires. Then the Americans burned the Baratarian establishment. In his report to the secretary of the navy, Patterson claimed to have captured all the ships in port together with twenty pieces of cannon mounted on them. He also reported that the pirates and their allies had been dispersed; he then returned to New Orleans, where You and the captured Baratarians were imprisoned in the Cabildo.[17]

The twenty-nine-year-old Patterson was one of the most important and valuable figures in the defense of New Orleans. Born in 1781, he joined the navy at the age of nineteen, served against the Barbary pirates in Tripoli, and was posted to the New Orleans Naval Station in 1806. He married a New Orleans girl (an American, not a Creole), commanded a flotilla of twelve gunboats out of Natchez for a year, and was finally assigned as commandant of the New Orleans station. A superb naval officer, he was diligent, energetic, intelligent, and quick to size up a developing military situation.[18]

Meanwhile the British realized that their mission to enlist Laffite and his pirates had failed. Having waited in vain the full two weeks for a response, Lockyer decided to wait no longer nor venture ashore to scout the area and find out what had happened. Swallowing his pride and sense of failure, he angrily turned his back on Barataria and hoisted sail for Pensacola.

A few days after Lockyer left Louisiana, a letter fell into Laffite's hand from an unnamed source in Havana which confirmed that a massive invasion was underway and that the population in the Gulf area had better prepare for it. Laffite promptly sent it to New Orleans, where it and the earlier letters of Nicholls and Laffite were made public. Edward Livingston used them to rouse the people of Louisiana to the impending danger. Meanwhile Claiborne sent copies to General Jackson.

For the past several months, both Claiborne and Livingston had been in communication with Old Hickory, informing him of conditions in the city and the questionable loyalty of its inhabitants. Claiborne had faith in the Americans and Creoles, but, he added, there were "others much devoted to the Interest of Spain, and whose partiality for the English, is not less observable than their dislike to the American Government." He acknowledged that the city had a battalion composed "of chosen men of Colour" but added that there was much concern about arming them, although they were duly subservient to whites and took every advantage of the privileges accorded them. They were considered loyal to the country and had little inclination toward inciting the slaves to revolt. In fact, many free blacks found employment as overseers on the plantations and in patrolling the swamps in search of runaways. "In the hour of Peril," Claiborne assured the general, he could rely on their "valour and fidelity to the United States." Of the approximately six hundred free men of color living in Louisiana the governor felt that a corps of three or four hundred could be organized for service for a period of six months, and he wondered whether Jackson would be agreeable to accepting them.

In his response Jackson enthusiastically welcomed the services of the free blacks and lectured Claiborne about how they should be treated. "Our country has been invaded and threatened with destruction," he replied. "She wants Soldiers to fight her battles." The free men of color were inured to the southern climate and "would make excellent Soldiers." If you distrust them, "you make them your enemies, place confidence in them, and you engage them by every dear and honorable tie to the interest of the country who extends to them equal rights and privileges with white men." He wanted a regiment of free blacks organized who would be officered by whites and placed on the same footing with other volunteers.[19]

Jackson also enclosed a proclamation to the people of Louisiana in response to the Nicholls proclamation and one to the free men of color, both of which he wanted published. To the people of the state he described the defeat of the British at Fort Bowyer and how the enemy had enlisted a "horde of Indians and Negro assassins" but forgot, in their stupidity, that the fort was defended by citizen soldiers in a free country. Then Jackson summoned the citizens of Louisiana to rally in defense of their country.

"*Louisianians!* The proud British, the national and sworn Enemy, of all Frenchmen, of all Americans, and of all freemen, has called upon you by proclamation; to aid her in her tyranny, and to prostrate the Holy Temple of our liberty. Can Louisianians, can Frenchmen, can Americans ever stoop to be the Slaves or allies of Britain?" No! Never! Can we place any trust in so-called men of honor who courted an alliance with "pirates and Robbers . . . this hellish Banditti?" We are engaged in a just and honorable contest and "I know that every . . . Louisianian, either by birth or adoption will promptly obey the voice of his Country" and "rescue it from impending danger, or nobly die, in the last ditch in its defence."

In his proclamation to the free blacks he called them "brave fellow citizens" who as "Americans" had been summoned by their country to participate in the "Glorious struggle for National rights." As intelligent men they should not be deceived by the promises of the British. "Your love of honor" forbade it, he said. If they would enroll as volunteers, he continued, they would be paid the same amount as white soldiers, namely $124 and 160 acres of land. And he promised that they would not be "exposed to improper comparisons or unjust sarcasm" with white soldiers but would "undivided receive the applause, reward, and gratitude of your Countrymen."[20]

With respect to the "hellish Banditti," Jackson wanted no part of them. He told Claiborne that the pirates should be "arrested and detained, until further advice." Indeed all the "wretches, the refugees from Barataria and its dependencies," should be "scrutinized under existing vagrant laws." Unless proper precautions were established with regard to them, "you will have to lament your country ravaged, and your city reduced to ashes by these incendiaries."[21]

In their several communications with Jackson, Livingston and his Committee of Public Safety informed him that "this Country is strong by Nature, but extremely weak from the nature of its population." It was important that Jackson fully realize the divisiveness among the city's inhabitants. They also expressed their concern about the fact that in the Louisiana area on both sides of the river there were sugar plantations that averaged twenty-five slaves to every white inhabitant. Under the circumstances, they said, it was impossible to call any of the planters to military service. "From you sir," they told Jackson, "we ought not to conceal, that the only hope of preserving this place in case of a serious attack lies in an efficient force to be furnished by you." In other words, Jackson could not count on the population of New Orleans to provide adequate numbers of volunteers to hold off a large force of invading British regulars.

Furthermore, they thought that the most likely point of attack would come by way of a water route from the Gulf to Lake Borgne and Lake Pontchartrain, which were connected by a narrow, shallow strait called the Rigolets, about fifteen miles northeast of the city. Fort Petites Coquilles, a small unfinished fortress, guarded the pass at the Rigolets and provided a degree of protection by virtue of the cannon mounted there. Once through the pass and into Lake Pontchartrain a ship could sail to Bayou St. John, which was a mile and a half north of New Orleans. Fort St. John provided a watch and some protection at this point, but between it and Forte Petites Coquilles only ten cannon were functional. It did not take much knowledge of military strategy to figure that this route seemed the most likely route for an army to reach New Orleans. Five small gunboats protected this pass, each one of which carried a twenty-four-pounder and two small carronades. But the greatest difficulty for an invader in obtaining access to Bayou St. John was a sandbar at the pass, making it impossible for ships of more than five feet draft to get through. Any attempt to reach New Orleans via water routes from Lakes Borgne and Pontchartrain required shallow-bottomed landing craft, something the British failed to bring with them. It proved to be an important factor in their ultimate defeat. The water depth in both lakes varied from six to twelve feet.

Another way of reaching New Orleans from Lake Borgne was a narrow road connecting the Rigolets to New Orleans via the dry land of the Plain of Gentilly and known as Chef Menteur. A landing at Chef Menteur would put the British only "five leagues" or approximately fifteen miles from the city. At the moment the road was totally unfortified, but a small force strategically positioned could easily hold off a large invading army.[22]

This, then, was the situation Jackson would face when he arrived in the city. And one of his most difficult problems would be figuring which avenue of entrance the British would take.

But time was fast running out, for on September 18, 1814, the British launched an armada from Plymouth, England, of sixty ships— frigates, sloops, gunboats, and other transports—carrying several thousand troops under the temporary command of Major General John Keane, who replaced General Ross, killed during the attack on Baltimore. Keane, the son of a member of Parliament, rose rapidly in the ranks and served in Egypt under Ralph Abercrombie, in Sicily under Sir John Murray, and in Spain under the Duke of Wellington. Promoted to the rank of major general in the spring of 1814, he was given command of the troops sent to reinforce General Ross. But the entire invading force was under the immediate command of Admiral Cochrane, who directed operations from aboard his flagship, *Tonnant.* On October 4, 1814, he withdrew from the Chesapeake area and headed straight for Jamaica.[23]

The rendezvous of British warships, matériel, and men occurred on schedule on November 24. After much discussion and planning, a general review of the troops and ships took place in Negril Bay. Rarely had England massed a more powerful fleet. There was everything from huge triple-deckers to small pinnaces, each armed with from eighty guns, such as the *Tonnant* boasted, to six aboard a schooner. All told these sixty-odd ships carried more than a thousand guns.

On November 26 this extraordinary fleet with its enormous and well-disciplined army, which had been "detailed from the grand army of the duke of Wellington" and was known as "Wellington's heroes," sailed out of Negril Bay and headed into the Gulf of Mexico. "It is impossible to conceive a finer sea-view than this general stir presented," wrote nineteen-year-old Lieutenant George Robert Gleig of the Brit-

ish 85th Regiment, who had participated in the siege of Bayonne in France and the attacks on Washington and Baltimore. "Our fleet," he wrote, ". . . gave to Negril Bay an appearance of bustle such as it has seldom been able to present." Within half an hour all canvas had been set and the headlands cleared. The ships caught a fair breeze and "bounded over the water with the speed of eagles, and long before dark the coast of Jamaica had disappeared."[24]

Four days before this grand parade of British might got underway, Jackson finally rode out of Mobile and headed for New Orleans. It took eleven days to reach the city. He deliberately moved at a leisurely pace in order to get better acquainted with the terrain and figure out what were the most likely places for the British to land and begin their invasion. But he needed additional troops. He had urgently pleaded for them from Tennessee and Kentucky. William Carroll, who succeeded Jackson as the major general of the Tennessee militia, was frantically recruiting volunteers and said he would join Old Hickory as soon as possible.

Arm your recruits in Tennessee, Jackson told him in reply, as arms and ammunition were in short supply along the Gulf Coast. Carroll succeeded in raising three regiments and immediately began a descent of the Mississippi River. Unfortunately, strong headwinds slowed his progress.[25] He reached Natchez on December 13; there he rested his men and set up a hospital to care for the sick. John Coffee was also active in finding recruits and upon arriving in Louisiana had positioned his troops in Baton Rouge to cut off any attempt by the British to take the crescent city from the north.

A wildly anxious and excited crowd of people in New Orleans waited expectantly for the arrival of the man who had pledged to save their city from capture or die in the attempt. They were impatient for his appearance because they knew what had happened in Washington when the public buildings and private homes had been burned, and they had also heard gruesome stories of rape and looting that had taken place in Hampton, Virginia, on June 25, 1813.

Finally, on December 1, Jackson rode into New Orleans, accompanied by Colonel Robert Butler, his adjutant general; Major John Reid, an aide and future biographer; and Major Howell Tatum, the chief topographical engineer. The crowd was startled when they saw this frail-looking man. He seemed emaciated and his complexion was sallow and ghostly. The effects of the long months of campaigning in the wilderness, his gunfight with Jesse and Thomas Hart Benton just before leaving Nashville to fight the Creeks, and the dysentery he had recently contracted were plainly visible. He was forty-seven years of age, his hair iron-gray, his face long and gaunt. Still his general manner, "his military reputation, his well known firmness of character," and the set determination of his jaw projected confidence and authority. He was described as "erect, composed, perfectly self possessed, with martial bearing." According to one observer the crowd instinctively knew that the right man had arrived to save them.[26]

With him came fewer than fifteen hundred volunteers and militiamen from Tennessee and Kentucky, a number of whom had served with him in the Creek War. This "feeble force," to quote Vincent Nolte, carried nothing but their guns, cartouche boxes, and powder horns and "had no idea whatever of military organization and discipline." They knew only one thing: how to pick out a target, draw a bead on it, and drop it to the ground.[27] Which proved to be more than enough for the days ahead.

The Creoles were very courteous toward their visitors from the north and even invited them to their homes for dinner. But they were shocked when some of these mountaineers put their feet on the table while having a brandy after the meal. One woman complained to her husband about it. "But what can you expect?" the husband responded. "It is the custom of their country."[28]

Jackson was greeted on his arrival by Governor Claiborne, followed by Mayor Nicholas Girod, a pleasant but garrulous old Creole. He was escorted to 106 Royal Street, a three-story building with a gallery on the second floor, which became his headquarters. As he entered the building the street filled with people who called to him in a continuous roar and demanded he speak to them. Finally Jackson appeared on the gallery to salute them. But none of the general's entourage spoke French, so Edward Livingston volunteered his services and acted as translator. Jackson and Livingston had known each other since 1796, when they had both served in Congress. They shared the dubious distinction of having voted against a congratulatory reply to President George Washington on the occasion of his farewell from public service. For his part, Jackson faulted Washington for the disgraceful Jay Treaty, signed with Great Britain in 1794. Since Old Hickory and Livingston had been in correspondence for the past weeks it did not take long for them to renew their acquaintance. Because of their friendship, Livingston's legal talents, his political skills in working with the legislature, his keen intelligence, his position in society, his good relations with the inhabitants, and of course his linguistic abilities, Jackson decided to appoint him his personal aide, private secretary, and confidential adviser.

Jackson spoke to the crowd through his interpreter and gave them his pledge to "drive their enemies into the sea, or perish in the effort." He used this phrase repeatedly, or words quite similar, in both his written and verbal communications. And he meant what he said. He would literally sacrifice his life in the defense of New Orleans. "Good citizens," he declared, "you must all rally around me in this emergency, cease all differences and divisions, and unite with me in patriotic resolve to save this city from dishonor and disaster which a presumptuous enemy threatens to inflict upon it."[29]

Unite such a disparate and constantly feuding population? A seemingly impossible task but one Jackson was determined to achieve. In some ways, New Orleans was a microcosm of the entire country. The social, economic, and ethnic diversity of the city was matched by that of the United States with its sectional differences, its quarrels over states' rights, its party squabbles, its seeming inability to knit the several states into an American nation. Already Massachusetts had sent memorials to other New England states to elect delegates to attend a convention in Hartford, Connecticut, to discuss their grievances on

account of the war and propose amendments to the Constitution to re-
dress them. There was even talk that the convention might attempt to
bring about New England's secession from the Union.

For Jackson there was never any doubt that he was a citizen of the
United States and that that designation meant something real and con-
crete. Just two years earlier when Congress had authorized the enlist-
ment of fifty thousand troops, he, as general of the Tennessee militia,
had issued a proclamation in which he asked the people of the western
country a simple question: *"Who are we?"* He then proceeded to answer his question. "Are we the titled Slaves of George the third? the
military conscripts of Napoleon the great? or the frozen peasants of
the Russian Czar? No—we are the free born sons of america; the citizens of the only republick now existing in the world; and the only people on earth who possess rights, liberties, and property which they
dare call their own."[30]

This credo was something he fervently believed and something he
insisted the citizens of New Orleans understand and acknowledge,
whether they be French, Spanish, Creole, Cajun, whatever. But as it
worked out it took a great victory over the British and the rescue of
their city to convince them.

After this opening ceremony, Jackson immediately began planning
strategy. While still in Mobile he had sent Colonel Arthur P. Hayne
ahead to examine the defenses of New Orleans, and he now sat down
with Hayne to hear his report.

What of the possibilities of a direct assault up the Mississippi from
its mouth at Balize? he asked. Could it be defended? No, replied
Hayne, not from Balize. The only defense possible began at Fort St.
Philip. Very well then, that would be the first point of defense if the
British sailed up the river. As for Lake Borgne, Commodore Patterson
informed him that he had stationed a fleet of five gunboats consisting
of twenty-three guns and 182 men under the command of Lieutenant
Thomas Ap Catesby Jones to take station in Pass Christiana and guard
the area. Jones was instructed to retire if attacked so as to draw the
British into the Rigolets in front of Fort Petites Coquilles.

For the moment, after hearing these reports, Jackson felt no other

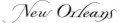

action was necessary, except, of course, to be certain that all the bayous and streams that connected the lake with the city were choked off. For this task he ordered small detachments from the Louisiana militia, under the command of Major Gabriel Villeré, the son of General Jacques Villeré, to undertake this task and block these water routes with shrubs and felled trees.

The general also assigned troops to guard Chef Menteur and man the forts to the north, with both groups instructed to pay particular attention to the possibility of an invasion from Lakes Borgne and Pontchartrain to Bayou St. John. The speed and decisiveness of Jackson's actions delighted everyone who watched him over the next several days. Said one: "At once all was bustle at New Orleans—Jackson was untiringly active."

And the people of the town caught some of his energy. "From all the parishes the inhabitants could be seen coming with their hunting guns" because "there were not enough guns in the magazines of the United States to arm the citizens." In addition, "the ladies formed committees to provide all that was necessary for the wounded and to care for them; private hospitals were established. From the houses of the citizens came bed linen, lint and clothing, in fact everything that could be useful under such circumstances."[31]

The next day the general reviewed the New Orleans uniformed battalion of volunteers in the Place d'Armes—about 287 men. Major Jean Baptiste Plauché commanded the five companies, most of whom were Creoles of good families, except for the Louisiana Blues, a regiment of Irishmen for the most part, commanded by Maunsel White, an expatriate who had married the daughter of a rich Creole planter. The locals watched the activity from their windows and balconies fronting the square and signaled their pleasure with the performance with loud bursts of applause and cheers.

At the termination of the review, Jackson dropped down the river and inspected Fort St. Philip to see for himself its condition and determine whether he thought it could withstand a frontal attack. Accompanied by Patterson, his engineers, Major Arsène Lacarrière Latour, and Tatum, he ordered additional batteries erected and additional men assigned to the fort and at the English Turn. He also appealed to Governor Claiborne and the legislature for "such aid as will enable me to have those works completed, in the Shortest possible time—It will require considerable labour to erect the various Batteries contemplated, and this Labour in a great measure must at this rainy season be performed by your slaves."[32] The legislature immediately approved funds to complete the work on the batteries and invited planters to send as many male slaves to help in the project as they could spare. Jackson also ordered the demolition of the wooden barracks within the fort, and he wanted several pieces of additional artillery mounted on the rampart. Once satisfied that the fort and the fortifications at the English Turn would be brought to the level of defense he required, he took off to inspect all the other possible entrances to the city. He sent Major Plauché's troops to Forts St. John and Petites Coquilles and the battalion of free blacks to guard Chef Menteur. When an assistant district paymaster dared to question Jackson's right to enlist men of color into the service, Old Hickory reared back and blasted him. "Be pleased to keep to yourself your opinions upon the policy of making payment of the troops with the necessary muster rolls without inquiring whether the troops are white, black or tea."[33]

For over a week he labored to cover all possible points of entry and strengthen those most likely to attract an invading force. But it was an almost impossible task. "Indeed, never was a city so defenceless, so exposed, so weak, so prostrate, as New Orleans in the fall of 1814."[34] There were an infinite number of water routes possible, and the troops at hand could not possibly cover them all—or even construct obstructions in these routes. All Jackson could do with the men he had on hand was spread them carefully and wait and see what happened. Once the British made their presence known, he could concentrate everything he had at the point of entry and meet the invader head-on. Jackson was fortunate in that he possessed the extraordinary ability to maintain a high degree of mobility. He could move his troops at top speed so that within a limited time he could present a massive posture of defense to meet the advancing foe.

This high level of energy helped reassure a nervous, fractious,

undisciplined populace who could only imagine the worst possible result if Old Hickory failed. Jackson spent so much time out of the city
on personal reconnaissance that he was criticized for neglecting his
primary responsibility. But he knew what he had to do and simply
turned a deaf ear to all entreaties to act otherwise. He particularly ig-
nored the New Orleans Committee of Defense, which repeatedly argued with him about accepting the assistance of Laffite and his
"hellish Banditti." With respect to the pirates, most New Orleans citizens took a very liberal attitude. *"Ces gens là,"* they said, *"font leurs
affaires, pourquoi gâter leur métier?"*—Those people have their own
pursuits, why interfere with it?[35]

Finally Edward Livingston tried his hand at changing the general's
mind. As both the attorney for Laffite and a friend and confidant of
Old Hickory he scored important points about how the pirate could
provide men to sail Patterson's sadly undermanned ships. There were
insufficient sailors to man the USS *Louisiana* and the USS *Carolina*,
the only two real fighting ships on the river. Still Jackson would not
yield. Bernard de Marigny de Mandeville, a Creole leader, the son-
in-law of the Spanish governor of the Floridas and chairman of the
legislature's defense committee, assured Jackson that the pirates were
devoted to the United States and could be trusted. But "the General
was inexorable," declared Marigny. "He told us that these men are being prosecuted by the civil officers of the United States . . . and that he
neither would nor could do anything in the matter."

Not to be deterred, Marigny and his committee went to the federal
district judge, Dominick Augustus Hall, "a man of learning, loved and
respected by the old Creoles of the country as well as by the Americans," and related to him what Jackson had said and asked for his help.
The city was in dire straits and needed every man it could raise to
serve in its defense. Hall responded immediately. "I am general in
these circumstances," he declared. "Present at once a resolution in the
Legislature demanding that the procedures against these men be suspended for four months and I will immediately give my orders to the
District Attorney of the United States."

Without wasting a moment the committee reported back to the

legislature, and the resolution was immediately adopted by unanimous consent. Informed of the action, Hall then ordered the prosecution of the pirates to cease and released Dominique You and the rest of the Baratarians from the Cabildo on condition that they enlist in the defense of the city. He also granted safe conduct to Jean Laffite so he could return to New Orleans and plead his case directly to Jackson.[36]

But would Old Hickory accept the Laffite brothers and their "Banditti" into his ranks? He could be stubborn and pigheaded, especially if he thought he was being manipulated. Jean Laffite returned to the city and together with his brother Dominique decided to face the general personally and make their case.

They met him accidentally on the corner of St. Philip and Royal streets sometime in early December and immediately plied him with reasons why the general should utilize their talents. They proved to be extraordinary advocates for their cause. Their enthusiasm, their aggressiveness, their bravery, their genuine desire to fight in defense of their city greatly impressed Jackson. Here were some of the very virtues Jackson wished all the citizens of New Orleans possessed. And this direct confrontation was the sort of thing that the general could not resist. It had happened before when Chief Red Eagle of the Creek Nation boldly walked into his tent after the defeat at Horseshoe Bend and surrendered himself. Most commanders would have executed the Indian on the spot or held him for civil trial. Not Jackson. Impressed by the man's courage and boldness, and anxious to enlist his service in subduing other Red Sticks, Jackson released Red Eagle and sent him off on a mission of bringing the Indian War to a complete halt. If nothing else, Jackson was a realist and a pragmatist. He needed Red Eagle, needed him desperately, so he released him. He also needed the pirates in the present situation, and Jean and Dominique kept telling him how much they could assist him in his efforts to save the city. They offered crews for the ships, powder, shot, flints, cannon, and the men to fire them. Ammunition was especially hard to come by in New Orleans, and it was unlikely that a fresh supply would arrive in the foreseeable future.

As the pirates argued, Jackson stared at them, studying them as he

made up his mind. Their offer was irresistible, and after several moments he finally accepted it. He ordered Jean Laffite to assist in the defenses between Barataria and the city. Meanwhile the pirate sent his agents to gather and deliver the war matériel he had promised, and he placed maps and other useful documents at the disposal of the general. At the same time Dominique and Renato Beluché began work on organizing three companies of artillery.

Once the privateers held in the Cabildo were released, other Baratarians volunteered their services to Commodore Patterson, and before the officer realized what had happened he found he had two fully manned ships ready for action. Jean helped with supervising obstructions of bayous west of the city and directing the transport of arms and ammunition to Jackson's headquarters. The general found Jean so useful that he added him to his personal staff to take advantage of his extraordinary knowledge of local geography.

But what Jackson really needed was the fresh troops that he had requested, the troops Monroe had promised. So he waited and watched, still trying to predict from which direction the invasion would come.

Then, on December 12, 1814, the British fleet was sighted near Cat Island at the entrance of Lake Borgne. The final invasion of the United States was about to begin.

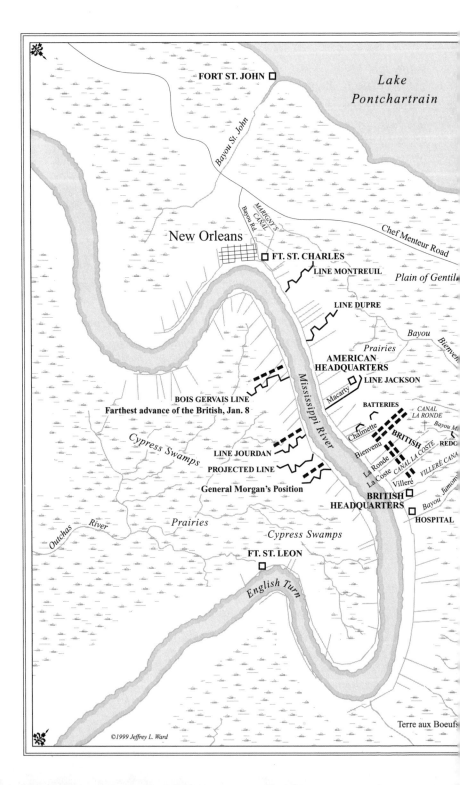

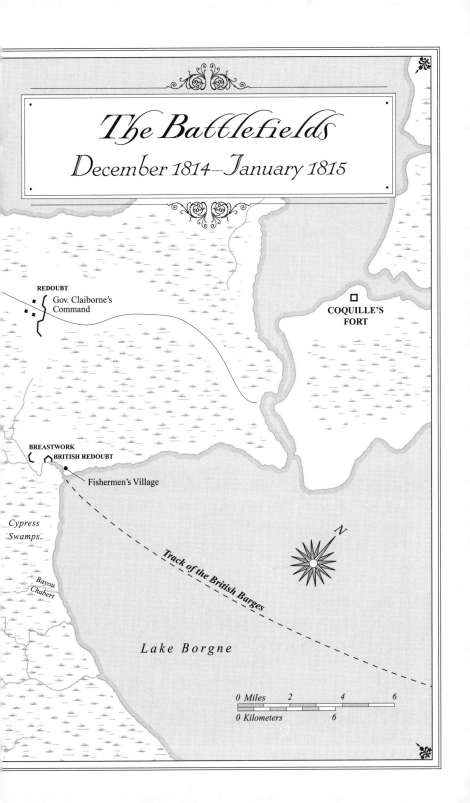

The Battlefields
December 1814–January 1815

REDOUBT
Gov. Claiborne's
Command

COQUILLE'S
FORT

BREASTWORK
BRITISH REDOUBT

Fishermen's Village

Cypress
Swamps

Bayou
Chabert

Track of the British Barges

N

Lake Borgne

0 Miles   2   4   6

0 Kilometers   6

Chapter 3

✤

The Invasion Begins

The principal British expedition force to invade from the Gulf of Mexico had once been assigned to General Ross, but upon his death outside Baltimore on September 12, 1814, it went to Lieutenant General Sir Edward Michael Pakenham, the brother of the wife of the Duke of Wellington. Pakenham was an able officer who had risen rapidly through the ranks. An unfortunate neck wound sustained at St. Lucia had given him a decided cock of the head. But he received a second wound at Martinique that corrected the defect rather neatly. During the Peninsular War against Napoleon he achieved distinction when he tore open the enemy line in a daring but costly attack. At the age of thirty-seven he was regarded as one of the very best officers in the army, and so to him went the command of the military invasion. Upon receiving his orders, which were identical to those given Ross, he set out immediately for Jamaica, but he did not catch up with his troops until after they had reached the American continent.

As Admiral Cochrane sailed from Negril Bay with his enormous armada, the mood aboard the ships was lighthearted and merry. Music, dramatic entertainments, and dancing livened the time spent crossing the Gulf, thanks to the efforts of the officers' wives who accompanied the expedition. The wife of Lieutenant Colonel Thomas Mullens, for example, abandoned the comfort and luxury of an aristocratic home to "share the glory and trials of her husband." Little could she imagine what would befall her husband and herself.[1]

It was keenly expected that the combined operation of the British army and navy would soon disperse whatever troops the Americans managed to assemble and capture the city. After all, these were "Wellington's heroes," and about as professional in discipline and military skill as could be found in Europe. Moreover, they fully expected the citizens of the town to greet them enthusiastically.

Admiral Cochrane understood the importance of flatboats and shallow-draft ships in any invasion of the Gulf around Mobile and New Orleans, and he had ordered such craft to accompany the troop transports. What he proposed was an attack on New Orleans through Lake Pontchartrain. But when the light-draft boats failed to appear, he was forced to alter his plans. There was no way he could get through the Rigolets in force with his deep-draft ships. He was obliged to take a longer and more complicated route, one fraught with uncertainties and peril.

On December 8 the armada reached Chandler Island and then moved toward Cat Island with the expectation of transporting the troops in small boats over very shallow waters into Lake Borgne. But the Americans had five gunboats poised to give battle, and they had to be eliminated before a landing operation could begin. The British fleet therefore anchored just south of Cat Island near the mouth of Lake Borgne about seventy miles from New Orleans and began their preparations to transfer the troops into lighter craft so they could be taken over the bar into the lake. Meanwhile Cochrane ordered forty-five barges and three gigs mounting forty-three guns, commanded by Captain Lockyer and manned by a thousand sailors and marines chosen from the crews of the other ships, to pursue the American gunboats.[2]

On the afternoon of December 12, after a pull of thirty-six hours against wind and current, this flotilla came within sight of the gunboats. At first the commander of the gunboats, Thomas Ap Catesby

Jones, thought the barges were engaged in a landing operation, but when he realized they were coming directly at him he retreated toward Fort Petites Coquilles, as Patterson had ordered. The British were decidedly superior in number and firepower but they relied on rowers to change direction or swing about, which made them vulnerable to the broadsides of the more maneuverable sailing ships.[3] Then, during the night, the wind died and the strong ebb tide pushed Jones and his gunboats toward land, forcing him to anchor between the mainland and Malheureux Island. He therefore lost his greatest advantage in drawing the enemy under the guns of Fort Petites Coquilles.

The British first pursued the tender *Seahorse*, which had been protecting supplies onshore. The *Seahorse* fought off the attackers for thirty minutes before its captain was forced to blow up his ship and destroy the supplies onshore to keep them out of enemy hands.

The following day, December 14, after resting from their exhausting rowing and after taking breakfast, the British again headed for the gunboats. An unbroken line of barges, six oars on each side pulling hard, with stubby-nosed short-range cannon erected over the bows, charged into the American flotilla. Jones drew up his boats across the channel in a close line formation and anchored at the stern to take the fire head-on. He faced a mass of barges bearing down on him. As soon as the British came within range, the gunboats opened up on them. Another American tender, *Alligator*, which was attempting to join Jones, was captured by the British and its guns turned against the other gunboats. For forty-five furious minutes of fighting, and despite the loss of two gunboats that got stuck in the mud, the Americans fought until overwhelmed by superior numbers. During the engagement Jones was wounded in the left shoulder and surrendered command to a master's mate. In his report to Patterson, Jones later boasted that "in this unequal contest our loss in killed and wounded has been trifling, compared to that of the enemy." Indeed, the British lost a number of barges and launches with nineteen killed and seventy-five wounded, including Lockyer, and a relatively large number of officers. The Americans lost six killed, thirty-five wounded, and eighty-six captured.[4]

Once they had swept away the opposition on the lake, the best route for the British to take for their landing operation involved sailing through the Rigolets into Lake Pontchartrain and landing at Bayou St. John immediately north of New Orleans. But without shallow-draft ships it meant rowing a tremendous distance to reach the landing site, and that made little sense because of the guns mounted at Fort Petites Coquilles. The easiest and best route to the city therefore had to be discarded. After several consultations the commanding officers finally decided to land at the extreme western end of Lake Borgne at a place called Bayou Bienvenu, which drained the area east of New Orleans into the lake, a place both Cochrane and General Keene agreed was probably now the only feasible route to advance into the city. And the plan had a single merit: surprise. It called for a speedy landing, "and pushing on, to take possession of the town [New Orleans], before any effectual preparation could be made for its defence." The two men took the precaution to have Bayou Bienvenu scouted to assure themselves that it could lead to the crescent city.[5]

But getting to Bayou Bienvenu created another problem. The warships and heavy transports could not sail into Lake Borgne, so the troops had to be ferried from the anchorage off Cat Island to Pea Island at the mouth of the Pearl River and just east of the Rigolets. Such an operation would at least advance the British army about thirty miles into Lake Borgne. From Pea Island the troops would then have to be transported another thirty miles to Bayou Bienvenu. The rowing alone would be horrendous. But no one aboard the ships doubted for a moment that British sailors could do it.

The victory over the gunboats was a disaster for Jackson. It completely opened up to the enemy the navigation of the lakes and provided them with additional transport to ferry their troops to the mainland. More important, it extinguished Jackson's eyes on the lakes. Now he had no way of knowing where the British would land or what route they would take to reach the city. But at least he knew indisputably that the invasion would take place here.

Word of the battle reached New Orleans just as Jackson was returning from an inspection of the Chef Menteur road. Aware that the British had arrived and were located near the Rigolets, he immediately summoned all his forces into the city. He sent off a dispatch on December 16 to General Coffee in Baton Rouge and ordered him to New Orleans. "I need not say to you, to reach me by forced marches, it is enough to say, that [Co]chrane is on our coast with about [sixty sa]il great & small, and report says has t[ake]n all our gun Boats in the lakes." In another dispatch to Coffee he instructed him to send an express to Carroll with instructions to "proceed without delay to this place." "You must not sleep until you reach me or arrive within striking distance." In an order to the commander of Fort Petites Coquilles he directed him to "defend the post to the last extremity. At the last extremity, spike guns, blow up fort, retire to the Chef-Menteur, and fight again."[6]

Fortunately General Carroll notified Jackson of his presence in Natchez on December 14 before receiving the express from Coffee. He had with him "about 1400 stand of arms and ammunition" in a keelboat that accompanied him. After a few days he said he would drop down to Baton Rouge to link up with Coffee. Meanwhile he was dispatching a messenger "to learn your pleasure."

Jackson responded immediately and ordered Carroll "to proceed night and day" until he reached New Orleans. He told him of the defeat of the gunboats and their loss to the enemy. "The conflict was dreadful," he wrote, "and in their fall they have nobly (from the report of the Spectators) sustained the american Character."[7]

For his part the ever-reliable Coffee assured Jackson that although some of his men were dispersed on a foraging operation that he would round them up and depart for New Orleans and reach him in four days. Not surprisingly, he arrived a day earlier, on December 20, from a distance of 135 miles, and was joined the following day by Carroll and about three thousand Tennessee recruits, along with a regiment of Mississippi Dragoons under the command of Major Thomas Hinds.

Jackson could now sigh with relief. At least he had an army to command and not fragments of militia and volunteers to meet the overwhelming numbers of soldiers the British would land. In addition, a "considerable number of Boat-men from the upper States & Territories" also arrived and tendered their services. Now Jackson had virtually all the men he would command for the coming battle—with the exception of the Kentuckians who would arrive on New Year's day. Although the evidence is contradictory it is probable that Jackson ultimately had between 4,000 and 5,000 men in and around New Orleans.[8]

The information that the British had landed and would presently storm the gates of the city sent shock waves through New Orleans. Although the inhabitants had great confidence in Jackson's personal ability, they still had doubts about his troops and nightmares about what might happen if the British entered the town. And a city run wild with hysterical people could produce chaos. What was needed was discipline, and the thought immediately crossed Jackson's mind that he should declare martial law. So he issued a statement to the "New Orleans Citizens and Soldiers" on December 15 alerting them to the possibility. "The Major-General commanding," he wrote, "has with astonishment and regret learned that great consternation and alarm pervade the city." True, he continued, the enemy had reached the coast and threatened an invasion, but it was equally true that with "union, energy, and the approbation of heaven, we will beat him at every point his temerity may induce him to set foot upon our soil." Their spies and agents, he continued, are attempting to spread sedition and discord to put you off your guard that you may fall prey. "Then look to your liberties, your property, the chastity of your wives and daughters" and remember the conduct of the British at Washington and Hampton. Jackson said he was confident that all good citizens would be found at their posts with guns in their hands and a determination in their hearts to fight for every inch of ground. "But should the general be disappointed . . . he will separate our enemies from our friends."[9]

A short time before Jackson agreed to accept help from the pirates, Commodore Patterson wrote a letter to the governor in which he complained about the shortage of seamen to man his two warships on the Mississippi, the *Louisiana* and the *Carolina*. He therefore suggested the necessity of suspending the writ of habeas corpus in order to round up enough sailors in the city to man these ships. The governor took the letter to the legislature, but it refused its consent. Perhaps mindful of the atrocities of General James Wilkinson during the Aaron Burr conspiracy in 1806, a joint committee of the upper and lower houses, chaired by Louis Louaillier, recommended against a suspension and instead urged an embargo on ships leaving the city and a bounty of $24 to be paid each seaman who would enter the service of the United States for three months. The full legislature agreed to the recommendation and authorized a budget of $6,000 to cover the cost.[10]

Disgusted with the feeble actions of the legislature and conscious of the immense danger looming before the city because of the capture of the American gunboats on Lake Borgne, Jackson finally decided to place New Orleans under martial law. His officers also urged him to take this action. On December 16 he issued a general order to the citizens of the city: "Major General Andrew Jackson commanding the 7th U. States Military District declares the city and environs of New Orleans under strict martial law—and orders that in future the following rules be rigidly enforced." First, anyone entering the city must report to the adjutant general's office. Failure to do so invited arrest and detention. Second, no one might leave the city without permission in writing signed by the General or one of his staff. Third, no vessel of any kind might leave New Orleans or Bayou St. John without a duly signed passport. Streetlights were to be extinguished at nine o'clock in the evening. Anyone on the streets after that hour without permission would be arrested as a spy.[11]

What the order did in effect was force every able-bodied man of whatever color or nationality, except those born in England, to serve as a soldier or sailor. Even the old and infirm were enlisted for police duty to make certain the rules of the order were obeyed. Judges closed their courts and discharged without bail many of the prisoners awaiting trail so that they might serve, and criminals who had less than two months remaining to their sentences were also released if they promised to enlist. The order had the good effect of bolstering confidence among the people and diminishing the sense of panic that had arisen with the news of the British victory on the lake. In a city so socially active and alive the curfew imposed was tolerated out of a sense of duty. But the rule about extinguishing streetlamps really offended the citizens, and Jackson rescinded it on January 2, 1815, at the request of the mayor.

At the same time, Governor Claiborne ordered "the Local Militia *en mass*" into service, including a "Valuable Riffle Company composed of the most prominent characters in the City," several of whom were widely known as expert marksmen. They were commanded by Captain Thomas Beale.[12]

To further bolster the people's confidence, Jackson decided to stage a grand ceremony in the Place d'Armes on Sunday, December 18, with a review of the city militia commanded by Major Plauché and part of the regiment of free men of color. As he knew they would, the people turned out in throngs to watch the ceremony and hear Jackson's address. New Orleanians loved nothing more than a carnival parade, and the brilliant, balmy weather lent a kind of Mardi Gras atmosphere—the celebration just before the impending Lent of invasion and battle. The uniformed companies, the militia, the volunteers, and the marines, all clad in their best attire and "decorated with bouquets" provided by wives, sisters, and mothers, formed under the walls of the ancient Spanish cathedral and "gave memorable brilliancy to the scene." Then they paraded before their general. The color, the pageantry, the music, and the excitement were everything Jackson could have wanted to inspire the watching crowd with confidence that their city would be saved by these brave men.[13]

When the ceremony ended, Edward Livingston stepped forward and read in French the statements Jackson had prepared for each group of the city's heterogeneous mass of citizens and soldiers. Old Hickory appealed to the native-born, to Frenchmen, to Spaniards, to men of color, to citizens of Louisiana, and to "fellow citizens of every description" in this "opulent and commercial town" to show their true worth and heroism for a "country blessed with every gift of nature—for property, for life . . . and for liberty, dearer than all" against an enemy "who vows a war of vengeance and desolation, proclaimed and marked by cruelty, lust, and horrours unknown to civilized nations." Jackson praised them for their courage and strength and promised them "the prize of valour and the rewards of fame."[14]

Confidence among the citizens of New Orleans was further bolstered when Coffee and his troops arrived, along with Hinds's regiment of Mississippi Dragoons. The dragoons had come 230 miles by forced marches from Woodville in Mississippi. Then, on the following day, Carroll and his men came floating down the river into town with their supply of ammunition. Suddenly what had seemed hopeless now looked promising and encouraging. The city teemed with soldiers. "All classes of society were now animated with the utmost zeal. The young, the old, women, children, all breathed defiance to the enemy." Soon the town resounded with "Yankee Doodle," the "Marseillaise" the "Chant du Depart," and other martial airs, and the people prepared for battle "as cheerfully as if it had been a party of pleasure."[15]

Still there were not enough arms and ammunition in New Orleans to satisfy Jackson, and when he heard that ships bringing these supplies had halted at Natchez and feared to sail farther south because of the invasion he wrote a pleading letter to Governor David Holmes of Mississippi. "I must . . . entreat you to use the most effectual means in your power to oblige vessels . . . to hasten hither with all dispatch. This is a critical moment; in which a stoppage of supplies may be attended with the most ruinous consequences."[16]

As these events transpired in town, the British were beginning a landing operation from their anchorage off Cat Island. The plan involved rowing the troops to Pea Island, where they would stay until transported another thirty miles due west to Bayou Bienvenu. And it was an agony. For at least ten hours the seamen rowed the distance one way, carrying only two thousand soldiers on each trip. It took at least three round-trip excursions of sixty miles just to move the troops from the ships to the island. Additional trips were necessary to bring up equipment and supplies. And that was only the first leg of the operation.

The massive move began on December 16—the wives of the officers and the other women, of course, remained aboard the larger ships at the anchorage south of Cat Island—and it took five days to complete. Lieutenant Gleig said that like everyone else he packed his usual supply of linen: a spare shirt and pair of stockings, three days of provisions, and as much rum as the quartermaster would allow. When the word came to embark, every man buckled on his knapsack and haversack and grabbed his musket. Within half an hour two hundred men boarded each of the barges and headed for the island. Nearly one hundred boats of various sizes covered the surface of the lake.[17]

Pea Island was hardy more than a swampy sandbar, virtually stripped of all vegetation and singularly unfit for an army encampment. A British officer kept a diary and recorded the following: "*16th.* Disembarked on a small Island, the whole of which except about 6 Acres was a compleat swamp, passed a cold night." Lieutenant Gleig noted that "it is scarcely possible to imagine any place more completely wretched." To make matters worse, a torrential rain pelted the troops as they disembarked and almost submerged the island. Gleig confessed that he "had never known what rain, real genuine rain, was." He was thoroughly soaked. There were no tents or shelter of any kind, and that evening they endured a killing frost, freezing clothes to bodies. The second night was colder than the first, and the following three days were even worse. Unused to such dreadful climate and living conditions, many West Indian troops sickened and later died.[18]

And more torment lay ahead. They needed to be rowed another thirty miles to Bayou Bienvenu before they could begin an advance on New Orleans.

Just as the ferrying operation to Pea Island got underway, Cochrane dispatched two officers, Lieutenant John Peddie, an assistant quartermaster to the army, and Captain Robert Spencer of the navy, son of the Earl of Spencer, to Bayou Bienvenu to scout the area and determine the best place for the troops to land. The bayou, one of the most important in the area, flowed in a southeasterly direction, draining the waters of several other bayous and canals. It was navigable for vessels of one hundred tons and ranged from 110 to 150 yards wide. Its principal branch, Bayou Mazant, ran southwest toward the Mississippi

River and received the waters of the canals from the plantations of Jacques Villeré, Pierre Lacoste, and Denis de Laronde, located alongside the river just below the city.[19]

Peddie and Spencer traveled across Lake Borgne from Pea Island and arrived at the mouth of Bayou Bienvenu without difficulty. On a tongue of land just a short distance inland they discovered Fishermen's Village, which consisted of twelve very large cabins. About thirty or forty Spanish and Portuguese fishermen lived there. Disguising themselves as fishermen in blue shirts and tarpaulins, Peddie and Spencer procured a pirogue from two locals, who also served as rowers and guided them up the bayou. They then turned into Bayou Mazant, which took them to the canal of the Villeré plantation. From that point they walked to the Mississippi River, sampled the water, and surveyed the surrounding area. The banks of Villeré's canal afforded firm footing, and the plantation itself was protected from the river by a four-foot levee. It made an ideal staging area for the army. Once the troops had landed at Bayou Bienvenu they could head for the river and then move quickly north along the Mississippi to the city, which was less than ten miles away. What seemed extraordinary and very encouraging was that during the entire time the two men took to reach the river, no one discovered who they were, although at one point they came close to detection.[20]

The two officers returned to Pea Island with several fishermen and gave their report. The bayou was navigable, they said, and if the troops could be ferried to its mouth and then sail to the Mazant they could reach the firm road that would take them to the Mississippi. New Orleans lay just a short march away. Several of the fishermen were quizzed about Jackson's strength, but they gave conflicting evidence. Some contended that the Americans had only a few thousand men under arms; others insisted that the number reached twenty thousand. Prisoners taken from the gunboats seemed to corroborate the larger number, but no one could be sure.

General Keane, still in command of the army, immediately gave the order to begin transporting the troops to Bayou Bienvenu. Because of the limited number of barges, only a portion of his men could be ferried at one time. So he divided his command into three brigades. The first consisted of the 85th Light Infantry and 95th Rifles, part of the 4th Light Infantry, a troop of rockets, and two light three-pounders under Colonel William Thornton of the 85th, who had led the successful assault on Bladensburg in the Chesapeake. They went first, a total of sixteen hundred men. The other two brigades would follow when the boats returned. Accordingly at nine o'clock in the morning of December 22, 1814, the first brigade entered the boats. General Keane, who would make all the wrong decisions for the expedition, accompanied them, along with his staff and heads of the engineering and commissariat departments.

The morning was dark, chilly, and uncomfortable. But "the ardor of the excited and enthusiastic Britons, intent on so grand a design, the conquest of so rich a city," wrote Alexander Walker, could not be dampened.[21] "From the general down to the youngest drummer-boy," agreed George Gleig, "a confident anticipation of success seemed to pervade all ranks; and in the hope of an ample reward in store for them, the toils and grievances of the moment were forgotten." Several American deserters told the British about the "wealth and importance of the town," the "large quantities of government stores" available, "and the rich booty which would reward its capture." They also swore that the people of the city "were ready to join us as soon as we should appear among them." They said that Jackson was personally hated because of his "tyranny and violence" and that not a single Louisianian would "adhere to his standard" when they "beheld the British flag fairly unfurled." Later when the British realized the truth they treated these informants like spies, not deserters.[22]

It seemed to take an eternity for the barges to cross the thirty-some miles to the bayou. The barges were so overloaded that the men could not change position or stretch their legs. They were packed in like a "bundle of logs in . . . a cord of wood." A mile out from Pea Island a sudden storm drenched them to the skin. It was as if a "thousand shower-baths" had opened up on the flotilla. Charcoal fires were lighted in the sterns of the boats and were permitted to burn as long as daylight lasted. But as soon as it grew dark they were extinguished for fear of attracting attention and setting off an alarm. Ever since they left their ships at the anchorage these men had encountered hostile elements, as though to drive them back. But their blood was up. They would not be denied. They knew that total victory over the Americans would atone for all their present misery.

The boats moved ten abreast. Two light cutters served as vanguard, two more protected the flanks, and three others brought up the rear of this flotilla. At the same time, Admiral Cochrane in a small schooner stayed just far enough away to watch the operation and superintend it. By the afternoon the rain eased up and the clouds dissipated, but a cold, driving wind lashed the huddled troops. Each boat had ankle-deep water at the bottom. There was so much suffering aboard these boats that an order was passed to cease rowing, cast anchor, and hoist awnings.[23]

But after an hour or so, when it started getting dark, the order was passed to haul anchor and resume rowing. Soon the dim outlines of land could be seen. As they drew closer the men could discern a wide, flat swamp, covered with a sheet of reeds eight or nine feet high and intersected with stagnant pools and narrow creeks of immense depth. Not a house or any sign of life was visible. "It was as wild as it is possible to imagine," said Gleig. The boats continued along the coast looking for the mouth of the bayou. Not much later they found it. And, as far as they could tell, no one had seen them. They had succeeded in moving a considerable distance in complete secrecy. Not Jackson nor anyone else in New Orleans knew that they had arrived just over a dozen miles from the city.

It should never have happened. The bayous should have been clogged, the soldiers spotted. Jackson had given specific orders on December 19 to Major Gabriel Villeré to act "without delay" and obstruct the bayous and passages connecting the lakes with the Mississippi. In addition he directed Villeré to station a guard or post of observation at every important point and report regularly to headquarters anything that looked suspicious.[24]

Just why Bayou Bienvenu was not obstructed remains a mystery, but a detachment of the militia consisting of a sergeant, eight white men, two mulattoes, and one negro was in fact sent by Major Villeré to Fishermen's Village to discover whether the enemy might invade via that water route. They reached the village early in the evening, found only one fisherman in residence, occupied the cabins, and posted a sentinel. Shortly after midnight the sentry heard a noise and alerted his comrades. They all rushed out to discover what he had heard and observed: five barges coming up the bayou. It was an advance party of the main British army. Against such overwhelming odds they knew they did not have a chance, so they darted about looking for a boat by which to escape. But the British saw them and captured four of them. The others scrambled away on land. Three of them wandered around for a day and finally returned to the village and surrendered. The fourth spent three days of terrible hardship in the prairies, swamps, and canebrakes, swimming in the bayous, eating snakes and roots, and finally stumbling into an American camp on the road leading from Gentilly to Chef Menteur.

The prisoners were locked up in the cabins of Fishermen's Village. One of them, a man named Duclos, was interrogated at length about the size of Jackson's army. Duclos reported that it was from twelve to fifteen thousand in the city and another three thousand at the English Turn. That was disquieting news indeed. Nonetheless Cochrane ordered the advance party to proceed with all deliberate speed so that the invasion could be accomplished quickly.[25]

The boats carrying the main British army finally pushed into the bayou. Alligators as plentiful as bullfrogs popped their heads up and down, observing the intruders as they glided by. The putrid smell of the swamps hovered like a canopy over the creeks and stagnant pools. And it was cold and damp.

Cochrane took up a position onshore to see that the operation moved along swiftly. Rowers were urged to increase speed. The boats continued forward five abreast until the stream became so narrow that they had to proceed single-file. When they reached Bayou Mazant, oars could no longer be used and the boats had to be moved by "punting," that is, employing a long pole or oar and pushing from the stern of the craft. Finally they grounded. The sailors jumped out and went scouting for solid ground. They reported back that there was a path next to the bayou that was solid enough to bear heavy traffic. The soldiers, almost entirely light troops, disembarked single-file, going from boat to boat and reaching the shore at one point only. They then rested until Keane and Rear Admiral Pultney Malcolm, who had stayed behind to hasten stragglers, could catch up. It was now 4:00 A.M. on December 23.

When Malcolm and Keane arrived, a brief consultation was held and engineers were sent ahead to cut away obstacles and bridge the many narrow streams that emptied into the bayou. At 10:00 A.M. the troops were ordered into formation. A column quickly lined up with Thornton in command and American deserters and guides posted at the head. Then they marched along the narrow defile, taking care not to wander into a quagmire. The whole operation slowed because of the thick vegetation and the necessity of cutting cane and reeds and building bridges to cross the numerous streams.[26]

Soon the ground grew firmer and the path wider and more distinct. The marsh thinned out; reeds gave way to woods and the woods to enclosed fields. The soldiers quickened their pace and moved rapidly through the low, stunted cypress woods into the open and cultivated fields that formed the plantation of General Jacques Villeré. The sugarcane had been harvested months before, and what remained was stubble. Soon a grove of orange trees appeared and then two or three farmhouses. Forming his troops into companies, Thornton stole rapidly along Villeré's canal at double-quick time and surrounded the buildings.

Major Gabriel Villeré, son of the general, was sitting on the porch of the house smoking a cigar and talking with his brother Célestin. Suddenly he saw a flash of red as men dashed through the orange grove and headed toward the river, which was only a thousand yards away. In a moment he realized they were British soldiers. He sprang from his chair and raced through the house to escape by a rear door. He ran into several armed men, one of whom was Colonel Thornton. Easily captured, as was Célestin, he was taken to another room under guard to await the arrival of General Keane. It was then 11:30 A.M., December 23.

With the British arriving in force on the plantation, Gabriel Villeré realized he had to get free and sound the alarm; he had to get back to New Orleans and alert Jackson. He decided on a desperate act. He suddenly sprang from his captors and jumped out the window, knocking down several soldiers who stood in his way. Soldiers fired at him, and Thornton screamed, "Catch him or kill him!" Villeré dashed across the yard, hurdling a high picket fence. Other soldiers pursued him and fanned out so as to surround him. He plunged into the cypress forest that fringed the swamp with the British in close pursuit. There is a story, perhaps true, that he hid himself in the dense foliage of a live oak tree and was compelled, "with tears in his eyes," to kill a favorite dog that had followed him in his flight and might reveal his presence. Villeré finally eluded his pursuers and made his way to the plantation of his neighbor Colonel Denis de Laronde. The two men rushed to the river, boarded a boat, and rowed to the opposite bank. There they met Dussau de la Croix, a member of the New Orleans Committee of Public Safety, and together they galloped up the west side of the Mississippi, recrossed the river, and hastened to the city to inform Jackson of the arrival of the British army.[27]

It is quite possible that Villeré's courage was prompted by the fact that he had failed in his responsibility to obstruct the bayous and thereby had allowed the British to reach his father's plantation. It is also possible that he deliberately neglected to carry out his duty because of the damage to the property that would result from the operation. Perhaps he relied on the pickets to warn him in sufficient time to summon the militia. In any event he could now only hope that he would reach New Orleans in time for Jackson to meet and stop the invasion.

When Villeré met with Laronde he was told that on the previous day Laronde had sent word back to headquarters that several ships had been sighted near Bayou Terre aux Boeufs to the south. On receiving this news, Jackson ordered Tatum and Latour, his engineers, to investigate and to examine "very particularly" all the bayous between Bayou

Terre aux Boeufs and Lake Borgne. The two men left New Orleans at 11:00 A.M. on December 23 and headed south. No sooner did they get to Laronde's plantation than they met "several persons flying toward town" who told them that the British had captured the Villeré house and Villeré's son. Tatum immediately turned around and rushed back to New Orleans to inform Jackson, while Latour got as close to the Villeré plantation as safety allowed in order to observe the enemy's movements. Latour was a man of heroic stature with a helmet of black hair, black eyes, and darkened skin. He was forty-five years of age, intelligent, a graduate of the Paris Academy of Fine Arts and a most astute engineer and architect. He carefully crept forward and got within rifle range of the British before taking a hidden position. He waited and watched, absorbing all he saw.[28]

In the interim, General Keane joined the advance column and ordered the troops into battalion formation. He wheeled right along the levee road paralleling the Mississippi and marched past Villeré's house for about a mile to the northernmost line of the Villeré plantation, where he halted between the river and a cypress swamp. Thornton urged Keane to continue the march and seize the obviously defenseless city that had no idea of his presence or location. It seemed to him that New Orleans could be taken with the troops at hand, that it was unnecessary to wait for the remainder of the army to catch up with them. And he was probably right. Jackson was presently blind to Keane's whereabouts. He could never defend the city against a surprise attack. The resulting street fighting and guerrilla warfare would have had devastating effects on the people and the city.

But Keane dismissed the advice. He was a cautious man and chose to halt the advance, thereby committing a major blunder. The captured pickets at the entrance of the bayou had informed him that Jackson had about twenty thousand men. It seemed ridiculous, but the figure was substantiated by sailors taken prisoner after the gunboat fight. Both pickets and sailors may have believed what they said or may have fabricated the number to deceive the enemy. It is impossible to tell for certain. In any event, Keane hesitated. He also worried about his lines of supply and communication with the fleet. They were tenuous at best.

He therefore decided to wait until the main body of the army reached him. Consequently the troops "piled" their arms and formed a regular bivouac.[29] That decision unquestionably saved the city from capture.

Still the high command was convinced the army would take the city whenever it was ordered to advance. Admiral Cochrane boasted that he would eat Christmas dinner in New Orleans and even "spend the carnival" there, meaning Mardi Gras. Later he arranged to have his boast circulated in the city, and when Old Hickory heard it, he allegedly responded, "Perhaps so, but I shall have the honor of presiding at that dinner."[30]

By this time Latour had estimated that the British at Villeré's plantation numbered about sixteen hundred to eighteen hundred men, and he noted their exact position. There were three regiments in place— they were the 4th, 85th, and 95th—and they took positions at the boundary of Lacoste's plantation while Keane set up headquarters in the Villeré house. A detachment of about a hundred men was sent to guard the rear. All of which made Keane extremely vulnerable. The riverbank was unsecured from attack; the right rested in a swamp that they knew nothing about; the rear was inadequately protected; and lines of communication ran through bayous and swamp water. Lieutenant Gleig summed up things exactly: "It must be confessed that our situation hardly deserved the title of a military position." Added to which the troops were exhausted and hungry and anxious to lie down and sleep. Latour took mental note of all this and then stealthily withdrew and raced back to New Orleans to report his information. It was then 1:30 P.M.

At exactly that time, General Jackson was sitting at his headquarters reading documents when he heard the clatter of horses come to a stop outside his door. A sentry reported that three men urgently wished to speak with him.

"Show them in," the General ordered.

Villeré, Laronde, and de la Croix rushed in, stained with mud and breathless because of their tiring ride.

"What news do you bring, gentlemen?"

"Important! Highly important!" gasped the exhausted de la Croix.

"The British have arrived at Villeré's plantation, nine miles below the city, and are there encamped. Here is Major Villeré, who was captured by them, has escaped, and will now relate his story."

Villeré told his story in one great rush. Because he spoke French, his words had to be translated by de la Croix. When Villeré and de la Croix finally stopped speaking, Jackson drew himself to his full height, his eyes smoking with anger. He struck the table with his clenched fist and exclaimed, "By the Eternal, they shall not sleep on our soil!" Then he turned to his secretary and aides and said, "Gentlemen, the British are below, we must fight them to-night."[31]

Unlike Keane, Jackson was spoiling for a fight—and the sooner the better. "I will smash them," he reportedly said, "so help me God!" He realized he must stop the British in their tracks and not let them step another foot closer to New Orleans. He must rush to the head of the invasion front and meet it head-on. The decision was a wise and ultimately successful one.

Still, could this be a ruse or decoy by the British? When Latour returned from his mission and gave the general his estimate of British strength at the Villeré plantation, Jackson knew at once that this force constituted only the advance of the main army. Could it be then that this advance was meant to distract him and draw him down the Mississippi when the main assault would come along Chef Menteur in the Plain of Gentilly? He could not be sure. All he knew was that the British had been sighted to the south and he must instantly respond.

Acting with desperate speed, Jackson issued a flurry of orders. The alarm gun was fired. The volunteer companies commanded by Major Plauché now stationed at Bayou St. John were summoned to the city on the double. The troops responded with enthusiasm and ran all the way back. The Louisiana militia and Carroll's Tennessee troops were left behind to guard Chef Menteur in case the British were in fact only feinting as they moved up the Mississippi. A detachment of artillery with two six-pounders, along with a detachment of marines, mustered along the levee road beside the Mississippi and moved south.

The city came alive with sound and excitement. Soldiers poured through the streets. The people waved and shouted them on. But a crowd of women were seen weeping openly in the streets because of the persistent rumors of what would happen to them once the British occupied New Orleans. Later it was argued that the women should have fled New Orleans. But that remark provoked Marigny into declaring that "in a city threatened by all the horrors of conquest by a large army, no lady fled from the city. Fly? That thought never came to the mind of the Louisiana ladies." And if, by some misfortune, the line of Jackson's defense had been carried, he went on, "more than one young lady would have assumed an Amazon costume and taken the lance," just like Joan of Arc. Still they were terrified and they wept. Jackson saw them, turned to Livingston, and instructed him to tell them that "he was there, and the British should never get into the city, so long as he held the command."[32]

But the ladies were taking no chances. They armed themselves with daggers instead of scissors, just in case. They had recently seen Jackson's vaunted Tennesseans under Coffee's command, and they had serious doubts about the ability of these men to stand up to British regulars. There was absolutely nothing military-looking about them. They wore woolen hunting shirts of "dark or dingy color" and "copperas-dyed pantaloons," both made at home by wives, mothers, and sisters, with slouching wool hats made of raccoon and fox skins and belts of untanned deer skin into which they stuck hunting knives and tomahawks. Their long, unkempt hair and bewhiskered faces might scare a Creole lady but hardly the troops of His Majesty's army. But what the ladies did not know was that most of these men could bring down a squirrel from the highest tree with a single rifle shot. Their many years living in the Tennessee wilderness had made them expert marksmen, and their many months of military service in fighting Indians under the command of Coffee and Jackson had converted them into disciplined soldiers.

Jackson also asked Commodore Patterson to order as many armed vessels as he had ready to drop down the river and take a station opposite the enemy. At 7:30 P.M. they were to open fire, which would be the signal for the start of a general attack. Meanwhile he directed General David Morgan, commanding the troops at the English Turn, to create a diversion from the rear.

Patterson had two armed vessels available, the USS *Carolina* and the USS *Louisiana* anchored in the river near New Orleans. But only the 230-ton schooner *Carolina*, with its fourteen mounted guns, captained by John D. Henley, was ready for action at this time. Since there was no wind, the sloop-of-war *Louisiana* could not steer in the very erratic currents of the Mississippi. Patterson boarded the *Carolina*, now manned to a large extent by the Baratarians, and ordered Lieutenant C. C. B. Thompson to follow him aboard the *Louisiana* as soon as the wind returned.

Just before three o'clock in the afternoon, Jackson mounted his horse and rode to a position just south of the city to review the troops as they headed to the front and give final orders to their commanders. Around him gathered his aides: Livingston, Reid, Davezac, Duplessis, Captain Butler, and Captain Chotard. First came the two regiments of regulars, the 44th Infantry, the 7th Infantry, sixty-six marines, and twenty-two artillerymen hauling two six-pounders, followed by Captain Thomas Beale's company of New Orleans rifles composed of merchants and lawyers, Major Plauché's battalion of uniformed companies, the battalion of blacks under Major Jean Dacquin, eighteen Choctaw Indians under Captain Pierre Jugeant, the Mississippi Dragoons, and Coffee's cavalry—in all about sixteen hundred to two thousand men, although Latour calculated 2,131. As they passed they saluted the general and headed down the road. When Jackson saw Planché's battalion, which had literally run from Fort St. John to New Orleans, he turned to his aide Davezac and said, "Ah! Here come the brave Creoles."[33]

The city emptied. No more tramping troops through the streets. No more reviews on the public grounds. No more sounds of bugle, drum, or martial band. The silent town housed only anxious women and men too old and feeble to serve at the front.

Hurriedly the troops made their way to a position on the Laronde plantation, north of the British encampment. Only Lacoste's plantation separated the two armies. It was then five o'clock in the afternoon, but the December day had already darkened.[34]

As Jackson completed his review of his troops, he turned and stared at the river. Through his telescope he saw the *Carolina*, armed with five six-pounders and two long twelves on pivots, sailing down the Mississippi. It finally anchored opposite the British encampment and within musket range. It had taken its position and waited. Seeing it, the British did nothing. In fact they mistakenly thought it was a merchant vessel that regularly plied the Mississippi or one of their own cruisers that had passed the fort unobserved. A number of the troops walked on the levee to wave and look at the ship close up. So sure were these invaders that their presence was unknown and so confident and secure did they feel that they lighted large fires and started cooking their suppers in kettles belonging to the slaves of the plantation. They had entered every house in the area and "brought away quantities of hams, fowls, and wines of various descriptions." Other soldiers were resting in their bivouacs hoping to get some sleep.[35]

And then it happened. At seven-thirty the *Carolina* opened up with a deadly fire right into the center of the encampment—and continued firing for ten minutes without letup.

"Flash, flash, flash, came from the river," reported Gleig; "the roar of cannon followed, and the light of her own broadside displayed to us an enemy's vessel at anchor near the opposite bank, and pouring a perfect shower of grape and round shot, into the camp." And the British distinctly heard someone cry out in a commanding voice, "Give them this for the honour of America."

The shots rained down "like so many thunderbolts amongst the astounded troops." Whole piles of guns were scattered, and kettles were knocked from the fires. Soldiers toppled over wounded or sent "whence no traveller returns."

The troops scrambled for their guns. The fires were extinguished. Officers buckled on their swords. Bugles sounded and commands were shouted over the din.[36]

The battle for New Orleans had begun.

Chapter 4

The Night Attack

When Jackson formed his line at Lacoste's plantation it was done so silently that the enemy pickets five hundred yards away never heard the troops getting into position. He stationed Coffee and his eight hundred men along with the Mississippi Dragoons and the New Orleans rifle company on the extreme left, with orders to advance along the swamp when the signal was given until they reached the boundary line between the Lacoste and Laronde plantations. They were expected to turn the enemy's flank and crowd them to the river. Coffee had his cavalry dismount, leaving one hundred men to guard the horses and keep them ready if needed. On the right, commanded by Jackson himself, the artillery and marines, the two battalions of volunteers, the regulars, Plauché's battalion, Dacquin's free men of color, and Jugeant's Choctaw Indians were stretched from as near the river as possible across the plain to Coffee's position. These forces were the main fighting strength of the army and were to engage the enemy directly once the signal came.

Coffee, a man of few words, gathered his Tennessee backwoodsmen and spoke to them very quietly: "Men, you have often said you could fight; now is the time to prove it. Don't waste powder. Be sure of your mark before firing."[1]

Jackson waited patiently for the sound of the cannon roar from the *Carolina*. Then at seven-thirty the thunder of the broadsides from the ship broke the silence of the night. Still he waited, ten long minutes, so that the *Carolina* could pour shell after shell on the unsuspecting enemy, hoping to draw their complete attention away from his position.[2]

When the shelling began, Colonel Thornton, a far more able British officer than Keane, came running toward the levee. He immediately ordered additional troops to the support of the pickets along the river and to the outposts stretched across Lacoste's plantation. The 85th Regiment took a position along the levee and opened fire on the *Carolina*. But the army's heavy artillery had not yet arrived, and muskets had no real effect. All the British had was three-pounders—useless against the hull of a warship. In desperation they fired Congreve rockets, but they too failed to inflict any damage.

The guns of the *Carolina* flashed again and again, and "a deadly shower of grape swept down numbers in the camp." The pounding became insistent.

Finally, Jackson gave the order to advance. A company of the 7th Infantry rushed forward as far as the boundary of Lacoste's plantation and were met by brisk fire from a British outpost consisting of eighty men. In a volley that was "absolutely murderous," the Americans drove them back to a defense line along a ditch and a fence. Additional British troops rushed to support the outpost, and their heavy fire proved very destructive.[3]

The American artillery also advanced. Covered by the marines, it moved up the high road alongside the river and blazed away at the enemy's outpost. It was met with such heavy return fire that the marines fell back. In a bold move, a reinforced British contingent made a rush for the artillery guns. At that moment Jackson and his staff rode by amid a shower of bullets, and when he saw what was happening Old Hickory called out, "Save the guns, my boys, at every sacrifice." The marines rallied, and with the help of a company of the 7th Infantry they hustled the guns to safety.

It was later reported that Jackson was complimented on his ability to bow at social occasions with extraordinary grace. Supposedly he replied that he learned the art on the night of the 23rd when he bowed and ducked as British bullets whistled around his head.[4]

Toward the center of the line the 7th advanced and opened fire on a strengthened British position. To their left the 44th joined in the attack, and the engagement became general with steady shooting on both sides. In the flash of the muskets many Americans saw for the first time the red coats of the English and their "peculiar method of firing." The British still kept up their old custom of forming their position three deep: one row of men kneeling on one leg, and the two other ranks firing over their shoulders. As a consequence, reported Vincent Nolte, most of the enemy bullets went whizzing "over our heads."[5]

Brandishing his sword and cutting and thrusting at the Americans, Gleig cried out to his men, "Let us cut our way through." He no sooner spoke than a frontiersman grabbed him around the waist, another seized his arm, and a third was about to plunge his bayonet into him when the frontiersman realized he might inadvertently stab one of the other Americans and so backed away. The Englishman was thrown to the ground and was about to be bayonetted when his friend Lieutenant Charlton arrived with ten men and rescued him.[6]

As the fighting continued, the British received additional support, and their line rapidly extended beyond Jackson's so that they nearly outflanked him. Fortunately, Plauché's battalion of Creoles and Daquin's free men of color arrived in time to prevent the disaster. Together they opened a heavy fire upon the enemy and forced them back. Hand-to-hand fighting ensued, and Plauché was about to order a bayonet charge when Colonel George Ross, who commanded the volunteer battalions, spiked it by ordering Plauché to stand fast. Some historians of the battle argue that if Plauché had given the order an entire regiment of the British army might have been cut off and forced to surrender.[7] Even so, the Americans were fighting with a distinct disadvantage. "The moon shone on the back of the enemy," reported

Major Tatum, "and gave them a decided advantage in discovering our situation, when it was difficult to see them from our lines."[8] This fact, he argued, contributed to the "confusion and derangement of our lines." In any event the British pulled back to their original position on the boundary line between the Lacoste and Villeré plantations, which they were able to do successfully because a thick fog rolled in from the river, extinguished the moonlight, and obscured the battlefield.

On the extreme left, Coffee and his troops rushed forward at the sound of the signal and drove the British back to the Villeré boundary line. Coffee wheeled his troops to the right and headed toward the river. Many of his rifle troops swarmed over the Villeré plantation and penetrated to the very center of the British camp. A portion of the British 85th Regiment arrived to halt the Americans, and the two sides engaged in heavy hand-to-hand combat. The Tennessee sharpshooters armed with long rifles and hunting knives brought down many sentinels, firing faster and with greater accuracy than the enemy. "Not a man discharged his piece without doing execution," reported Latour. Officers of both armies hastily collected a group of their men and pursued detachments of the other side, causing sudden and deadly confrontations on the field. The fighting became so intense and the two sides so intermingled that mass confusion best describes what the engagement was like. "The annals of modern warfare," declared Lieutenant Gleig, "furnish no parallel" to what took place. Indeed, Captain Cooke declared that as far as he knew there was no instance on record "since the invention of gunpowder . . . of two opposing parties fighting so long muzzle to muzzle." In the dark it was frequently impossible to tell friend from foe, particularly since they both spoke the same language. Not a few men were killed by friendly fire.[9]

The British posted several groups of riflemen in the slave cabins on Lacoste's plantation and these soldiers kept up a running fire on the right side of Coffee's position. But the "long and deadly instrument of the western hunter and Indian fighter" in the hands of the skilled Tennesseans easily dislodged the British, whose short rifles were no match for the weapons of the Americans.[10] These redcoats hid behind the cabins, and when the Tennesseans came to search the huts they rushed out and engaged them in hand-to-hand combat. And where the British used swords and bayonets the majority of Americans countered with tomahawks and hunting knives. Within minutes a large number of British were killed or taken prisoner as they attempted to escape into the woods. Because many of Coffee's men were dressed in hunting shirts, which, in the dark, could be mistaken for the shirt the 93rd Highlanders wore, it sometimes happened that as a British soldier advanced and saw what looked like a Scot he called out, "Are you the 93rd?" A bright and resourceful Tennessean replied, "Of course," and proceeded to step forward, tap the unsuspecting soldier on the shoulder, and announce, "You are my prisoner."[11]

In the confusion one segment of Coffee's brigade, consisting of two hundred men under Colonels Dyer and Gibson and a company of riflemen under Captain Beale, became separated from Coffee's command. In their search for Coffee they soon discovered a large force of soldiers in front of them and hurried toward it. They were ordered to stop and identify themselves. "Coffee's brigade," they responded. When they realized the name meant nothing to their interrogators, they turned around and ran. The enemy fired on them, and Gibson fell. Before he could move, a British soldier pinned him to the ground with a bayonet. With a mighty heave Gibson jumped to his feet, threw his assailant to the ground, and made his escape. Meanwhile Dyer had retreated fifty yards when his horse fell over dead from a gunshot. Entangled in the fall and slightly wounded, Dyer nonetheless summoned his men to attack. They forced their way through the enemy position but lost several men in the engagement. Beale also charged the enemy and took a number of prisoners but lost a few of his own men. Then they retired to their original position and joined Hinds's dragoons.[12]

The rest of Coffee's brigade continued to push the enemy flank back and at length reached a position in front of the old levee, where they continued to keep up a destructive fire. But the heavy smoke from the shooting, the increasing fog from the river, and the likelihood of endangering his men by exposing them to the belching broadsides of the *Carolina* convinced Coffee he must withdraw. He sent a dispatch to

Jackson about his situation, and the general ordered him to rejoin the main army.

It was now 9:30 P.M. The conditions on the field forced Jackson "to content himself for the present with having convinced the British that Americans were not to be intimidated by the martial renown of the heroes of Wellington," and he withdrew to his original position at the Lacoste plantation line, where his troops passed the night without fires.[13]

At 11:30 P.M., shots were heard in the direction of Jumonville's plantation, south of Villeré's. When some 350 militiamen stationed at the English Turn under Brigadier General David Morgan learned that the British had arrived at Villeré's plantation, they wanted to march north and engage the enemy. But Morgan refused to permit it until he received orders from Jackson. Then, when the night battle began and the men could hear the firing, Morgan relented and gave the order to march. They tramped through the darkness and arrived at Jumonville's plantation. At 11:30 P.M. they discovered the British outposts and fired upon them. They were unable to advance or inflict any real damage to the British position, so they reconnoitered in a neighboring field, and waited until daybreak before retreating to the Turn.[14]

Although the British had nearly captured his artillery, Jackson could be proud that his men had advanced deep into the British encampment, perhaps 350 to 500 yards. This nighttime engagement lasted about two hours over a square mile of plantation fields and ditches. British casualties in the battle amounted to 46 killed, 167 wounded, and 64 missing. The Americans lost 24 killed, 115 wounded, and 74 missing or captured.[15] The British were amused when they found that a number of those captured were lawyers and merchants, not in any way professional soldiers or men used to combat. "To do them justice," wrote Lieutenant Gleig, "the poor lawyers, as soon as they recovered from their first alarm, joined heartily in our laughter."[16]

But it says something about the determination of the Americans that they fought as well as they did despite the fact that many of them were inexperienced in the art of war and had never acted together as an army. This was the first time they had fought as a unit. Their remarkable showing demonstrated again that when men are beating back an invasion of their homeland they can achieve heights of success not ordinarily possible under normal wartime conditions. "The heroes of Wellington," reported Latour in his *Memoir*, were made "to appreciate the prowess of those warlike sons of the western country."[17]

More important, the ability of the Americans to hold their own against well-trained, experienced troops reinforced General Keane's fears that he was facing an army that vastly outnumbered his own. He was now certain that Jackson had at least fifteen thousand troops. As a consequence he resisted any argument about renewing his advance. Not until his entire army had been landed—several barges had run aground coming from Pea Island to Bayou Bienvenu—and had reached his camp would he consider making any further advance. The British troops arriving at Bayou Bienvenu heard the battle and tried to hurry their progress, but the dark and fog and swampy terrain greatly slowed their forward movement. Not until the next morning did they begin to arrive at Villeré's plantation. Fresh, disciplined troops would have given Jackson's unseasoned men a real fight and would have greatly outnumbered them. Quite obviously, Jackson needed to back away and end the battle.

In some respects this was an American victory, although the British claimed it as theirs and Jackson himself was disappointed that he had not destroyed the British advance guard. In fact, Old Hickory's attack had been repulsed, but he had taken the offensive, returned a surprise invasion with a surprise counterattack, and in the process paralyzed the British for the next several days. He actually attacked them in their own camp, something they hardly expected. Always aggressive, Jackson stopped the invasion in its tracks and probably saved New Orleans. Had he not acted so promptly and decisively and with such "impetuosity," the British might have marched directly to the city. And if they had they would undoubtedly have taken it.

Furthermore, Jackson now had an army of veterans. They had sustained their first action, and sustained it magnificently. They had been under fire and had not flinched or turned and run—except for a few when they realized they were outnumbered. More important, they were eager and anxious to renew the fight.

In addition, the British learned several painful lessons. Instead of an easy victory, they encountered determined opposition. Instead of natives "ready and eager to join us," they found the houses deserted, cattle and horses driven away, and "every appearance of hostility." No one welcomed them. The many people living in the surrounding plantations had fled. To march to New Orleans by the only road available was impossible because it was commanded by the armed vessels in the river. "In a word," lamented Gleig, "all things had turned out diametrically opposite to what had been anticipated; and it appeared that instead of a trifling affair [which would] fill our pockets . . . [it] presented difficulties not to be surmounted."[18]

One of those difficulties was the unwillingness of the Americans to abide by the rules of modern military behavior. They refused to station a regular chain of outposts, either night or day. Instead each morning during the ensuing days some five hundred mounted riflemen charged around the open field and, said Gleig, "watched our movements in a very irregular and unsoldierlike manner." In addition, during the night small bands of Tennesseans wandered around the field looking for the enemy and engaging them in battle—"in which General Jackson appeared to take so much delight," claimed Gleig—much to the annoyance of the British, who believed that when the principal fighting ceased that was the end of it for the day. They did not expect to have to continue fending off pesky frontiersmen who did not know when to stop fighting. It was all most improper.[19]

Once Jackson withdrew to his original position and the situation seemed relatively quiet, Gleig went searching the battlefield for a missing friend, a man named Grey. When the *Carolina* first began to fire its cannons, Gleig and Grey had been enjoying a meal of "a couple of fowls taken from a neighbouring hen-roost" along with a few bottles of "excellent claret, borrowed from the cellar of one of the houses nearby." As a matter of fact, within a few days the British had cleaned out whatever food and drink they could find in the numerous cabins and houses on the surrounding plantations. At the sound of gunfire,

Gleig and Grey instantly ran forward to join their men and check any advance the Americans might attempt. They separated and never met again.

After the battle, Gleig hunted for his friend. He admitted that while wandering over the area "the most shocking and most disgusting spectacles, everywhere met my eyes," men with "wounds more disfiguring, or more horrible" than he had ever witnessed; men shot through the head or heart, or stabbed to death from bayonets, hunting knives, or sabers; men dead from heavy blows to the head from the butt ends of muskets. Not only were the wounds "exceedingly frightful," said Gleig, but the faces of the dead "exhibited the most savage and ghastly expressions." In several places he saw an English and American soldier with "the bayonet of each fastened in the other's body," attesting to the deadly closeness of the engagement.

Gleig finally found his friend shot through the temple by a rifle bullet, but the hole was so small as to leave hardly any evidence of its entrance. When he came upon Grey lying in a pool of blood behind a dunghill he threw himself to the ground and wept like a child. They "had known and loved each other for years," having suffered many hardships and dangers together. Then he carried the lifeless body to Villeré's home, which had been converted into a field hospital. Every room in the house was crowded with "wretches mangled, and apparently in the most excruciating agonies." Some attempted to sit up, shrieking with pain. One man's appearance "was too horrible ever to be forgotten." He had taken a bullet through the windpipe, "and the breath making its way between the skin and the flesh, had dilated him to a size absolutely terrific." His head and face were particularly shocking, every feature enlarged while his eyes were totally hidden between his cheeks and forehead so "as to destroy all resemblance to an human countenance." Gleig went down to the garden of the house, dug a grave, and buried his friend in his uniform.[20] Grey was not yet nineteen.

The scene on the American side was no different. The wounded were gathered from the field and taken to the city, where they received as much medical care as was then available. Virtually every house became a hospital of sorts. Women searched among the wounded for fathers, husbands, brothers, or sons. The arrival of prisoners caused a stir, especially when some of them revealed the arrival of reinforcements to General Keane's army and the information that even more troops were expected in the morning. The news sent a shudder through New Orleans, especially among the women, who had been reminded repeatedly about the reputations of British soldiers and how they ravaged a city and its women after they had captured it.

General Jackson was also told about these reinforcements, by deserters and scouts as well as prisoners.[21] It was information he could hardly dismiss, although he desperately wanted to dismiss it and continue with his plan to renew the battle the following morning. At midnight he held a meeting with his aides and a group of officers. Livingston was particularly vehement in advising against another attack. Did it make any sense to risk the city and his army of a few thousand men without bayonets against what appeared to be a vastly strengthened British army of at least six or seven thousand highly trained and disciplined soldiers who had bayonets and knew how to use them?

It was against Jackson's nature to back off, but all his life he had been a pragmatist and he knew when to pick a fight and when to call it quits. The moment had come to back away from his present position. As the meeting ended, Jackson announced that on the following morning, December 24, 1814, he would pull his army back two miles and set up his defense behind an old millrace called Rodriguez Canal between the Macarty and Chalmette plantations. As he later reported, he feared the consequences "under the circumstances, of the further prosecution of a night attack with troops then acting together for the first time."[22]

Jackson understood that a single line of defense could prove fatal if the British breached it. So he erected a second line a mile behind the Rodriguez Canal at the Dupré plantation, and a third line a mile and a half farther north on the Montreuil plantation. Jackson figured that if he was forced to abandon the Rodriguez Canal he would withdraw with the help of Coffee's cavalry to the Dupré line and defend it. To reassure his troops he stationed a considerable number of men at the

Dupré line, even though they were unarmed, hoping it would provide "as great a show as possible of strength and intended resistance to the enemy." All communication between the two lines was forbidden to keep the fact of its "want of preparation" a secret not only from the enemy but also from his own men.[23]

As he pulled back to the canal, which was a little less than ten miles southeast of New Orleans, Jackson left behind at Laronde's plantation the Mississippi Dragoons and Captain Jedediah Smith's Feliciana troops of horse to observe the movements of the enemy and keep him posted.

On December 24, Christmas Eve, the day the American peace ministers in Ghent, Belgium, signed a treaty with their British counterparts that ended the War of 1812 on the basis of *status quo ante bellum,* the American army withdrew to its new position behind the Rodriguez Canal. It was a ditch four feet deep and ten feet wide that ran at a right angle from the east bank of the Mississippi into a "thick, and almost impenetrable" cypress swamp about three-quarters of a mile inland. Jackson chose this position because it provided the narrowest front to defend between the river and the swamp and made an excellent barrier to defend against an advancing enemy. Shovels, pickaxes, saws, spades, hoes, carts, wagons, and slaves were brought from the city, and the work begun of widening and deepening the canal and building a rampart along the northern rim (closest to the city) from the mud and debris dredged out of the grass-grown bottom of the ditch. "A number of negroe men were now procured from the citizens," said Major Tatum, "to ease the labour of the soldiery and preserve their health and activity for more important service."[24] In addition, Jackson directed Livingston to order a search of every store and house in the city for muskets, bayonets, and cartridge boxes and press them into public service. Receipts for these necessary items would be given except to those serving in the militia or volunteer corps.[25] Also it was generally believed that many young men had failed to volunteer, so orders were sent out to prepare a register of every male in the city under fifty in order "that measures might be concerted for drawing forth those, who had hitherto appeared backward, in engaging in the pending contest."[26]

Over the next several days the soldiers erected an earthen rampart and installed artillery pieces at regular strategic intervals. The men competed to see which group could build the highest mound in front of their position. They spent the entire Christmas Eve building this rampart and finally raised it at least three or four feet high. But as they dug deeper they struck water and the excavated dirt began sliding back into the canal. So cypress logs were cut and laid crib-fashion to anchor the mud. Additional soil was then brought in from surrounding areas to thicken the watery mass and strengthen the wall of the rampart. After a week's work they finally succeed in erecting a parapet that was at least seven and in some places eight feet high from the bottom of the ditch. This front line was now called "Camp Jackson."[27]

On the extreme right of Camp Jackson next to the river the two six-pounders were mounted so as to command the levee road. Latour was instructed to cut the levee and flood the ground in front of the canal. But this operation proved useless when the temporary swell of the Mississippi receded and dropped to the level of the road. At the same time, Jackson ordered the *Carolina*, now joined by the sixteen-gun *Louisiana*, to regularly pump cannonballs at the enemy to keep them from initiating an attack. These two floating batteries took their position and constantly pitched fire and metal into the enemy encampment. Although they inflicted no serious damage, the incessant bombardment had a devastating effect on the morale of the redcoats. It also succeeded in keeping three British battalions pinned down alongside the levee. But once it became dark these troops were withdrawn, slowly and carefully, company by company.[28]

Jackson established his headquarters in Edward Macarty's plantation house approximately one hundred yards behind the ditch. Each day he first watched the movements of the British troops from a dormer window on the top floor and then went out and rode his horse among the troops as they dug the canal wider and deeper and mounded the rampart higher, assuring them of ultimate success. "Here we shall plant our stakes," he cried, "and not abandon them until we drive these red-coat rascals into the river, or the swamp."[29]

And all this labor was expended without any annoyance from the British advanced posts. Every five minutes gained by the Americans, argued Captain Cooke, "was of vital importance," and each hour lost by the British in waiting for reinforcements "was the coming death-blow to their final hopes of success."[30]

Jackson also sent a dispatch to General Carroll at Chef Menteur and told him that if he detected no sign of the enemy in his area to join the main army at the Rodriguez Canal immediately. General Morgan, who was stationed on the east bank of the Mississippi at the English Turn, now realized that his position made no sense, since it had been established to guard against an invasion coming north from the mouth of the river. He suggested to Jackson that he abandon his post and rejoin the main army. The general responded by directing him to move his troops and cannon across the river to Fort St. Leon, leaving a sufficient number of men to guard the Turn, and then march to a position on the west bank opposite the British encampment. But before leaving, Morgan was instructed to cut the levee below the enemy camp, as near as possible to them, "without being discovered." The following day, Morgan reported that "last night, within gun shot of the Enemy's Centinel—I succeded in cutting pretty effectually the Levey—It was a most favourable spot, at this season of the river—This morning I reconnoitered . . . and found [the enemy] with a strong party busily occupied in stopping the Cut."[31]

Besides repairing the damage to the levee the British completed ferrying their troops from Pea Island to the encampment. By the end of the day, December 24, all the soldiers and guns, including twelve field pieces and three brass howitzers, and related equipment and stores, had been brought into position. But the 1st and 5th West India regiments had been badly depleted because of exposure to the cold and rain, for which they were unprepared. No attempt had been made to provide them with warm clothing. About two hundred men died or were so ill that they could not be transported from Pea Island.

The location of the British camp, seriously defective from the very start, now lay in a likely crossfire with Jackson's army straight ahead, two floating batteries in the Mississippi, and Morgan's troops directly opposite on the west side of the river. It was a certain recipe for a British disaster.

The day after Jackson's withdrawal, Christmas, at 11:00 A.M., there was a stir in the British encampment. Salvos were fired into the air and the troops shouted their welcome on "the unexpected arrival" of their new commander, Lieutenant General Sir Edward Michael Pakenham, who had finally caught up with his army. He "was admired and beloved by both officers and men," said Gleig. On the eve of the Battle of Salamanca during the Peninsular War, Wellington ordered him to lead the 3rd Division and "take the heights in front and drive everything before him." Pakenham turned to Wellington with the cry "Give me one grasp of that all-conquering hand . . . and I WILL." And with that pledge he charged forward and completely routed the defending French.[32] Nothing less was now expected of him by both his officers and men. Notwithstanding all the recent hardships these troops had endured, "the city of New Orleans, with its valuable booty of merchandise," said Captain Cooke, "was craved for by the British to grasp such a prize by a *coup de main*."[33]

It was rumored among the troops that Pakenham had the commission to serve as governor of Louisiana once he captured it and had been promised an earldom when he completed his assignment. It was also believed that a lady waited aboard one of the ships in Lake Borgne and expected to become the general's wife once the battle had been won.[34]

Not only would the conquest of Louisiana enrich Pakenham but to the English mind it "would have proved beyond all comparison the most valuable acquisition that could be made to the British dominions, throughout the whole western hemisphere," claimed Gleig. "In possession of that post, we should have kept the entire southern trade of the United States in check; and furnished means of commerce to our own merchants, of incalculable value."[35]

Serving with Pakenham as second in command came Major General Samuel Gibbs, who had also distinguished himself in the Peninsular War. The two men were considered the ablest lieutenants of the famed Iron Duke, the two men most likely to imitate the success of their great chief. Best of all, three thousand additional soldiers arrived with him, including a squadron of dragoons "with their saddles and bridles, and other cavalry gear, ready to place upon the backs of American horses, so soon as they should be fortunate enough to obtain them."[36] For the British soldiers standing on the cold and wet ground alongside the Mississippi this change of command was indeed heartening, and they demonstrated by their cheers how much they welcomed Pakenham's leadership. They knew how desperate their situation was and they prayed that he would make it all come out right.

On this Christmas Day a number of slaves from the surrounding plantations entered the British camp seeking their freedom, and they were immediately put to work under the direction of the commissaries. They were dressed in rudely fashioned clothes: horse cloth with loose sleeves and a hood, their shoes made of bullock hide undressed with the hair on the outside. One of them approached an officer and in perfect French begged to have a collar of spikes around his neck removed. The collar had been put on him as punishment for his attempt to run away. And it was a torture. He could not lie down to sleep because of the spikes, and in piteous tones he begged the officer for deliverance. "This ingenious symbol of a land of liberty," the officer sarcastically commented, was immediately removed at the farrier's forge.[37] True, it was a frightful contradiction of the American commitment to freedom, but it says something equally squalid about the British character that in printed notices stuck on plantation fences by English agents the citizens of New Orleans were assured by the invaders that "YOUR SLAVES SHALL BE PRESERVED TO YOU, AND YOUR PROPERTY RESPECTED. WE MAKE WAR ONLY AGAINST AMERICANS!"[38]

Pakenham immediately set about inspecting his troops out of the range of the *Carolina* and then surveyed the ground and his position, cursing the stupidity that had fashioned such an abomination. He was caught in a narrow defile between a swamp and a river, and it would take an enormous effort to punch his way out of it. It was "a sort of *cul de sac,*" and Pakenham's fulminations and prediction of "an ominous result" were "heard by every officer and soldier in the bivouac." Nevertheless he assured his troops that he would "do his best to get them out of this Jeopardy in which he had found them by persisting in the attack."[39]

Pakenham next called a meeting of his staff and stated flatly that with the size of the force available the entrance into New Orleans should have been swift and easy. "I regret the defeat of our forces due to the error made on the 23rd of December," he snapped. "Our troops should have advanced to New Orleans immediately on taking Villeré's plantation."[40] He pondered his option of withdrawing the entire operation and beginning again at another point. But Admiral Cochrane, who was utterly contemptuous of American military prowess, angrily interrupted. "We were not defeated," he thundered, "and there is nothing wrong with our position. If the army shrinks from the attack here, I will bring up my sailors and marines from the fleet. We will storm the American lines and march into the city. Then the soldiers can bring up the baggage."[41]

Possibly stung by this taunt but more probably anxious to capture New Orleans without further delay, Pakenham decided against a withdrawal and chose to stand his ground. The following day, December 26, he and his staff rode out to reconnoiter the American lines. As he looked over the flat plain that lay stretched out in front of him he could see no evidence of any regular army to oppose him. All he saw was Hinds's horsemen galloping around the field in a most unmilitary fashion, apparently watching any movement in the British camp and occasionally taking potshots at the pickets and sentinels. These horsemen screamed their defiance, fired, and then wheeled around and made a hasty retreat. To Pakenham these men gave the "appearance of snipe and rabbit hunters beating the bushes for game" and certainly not soldiers engaged in a military operation. Pakenham had never seen anything like it, not on any battlefield that he had ever experienced.

Apparently there was no American army worthy of the name opposing his own. Obviously it would be an easy matter to smash ahead and rout whatever hostile force put up a fight.[42]

But first he must do something about the dangerous warships that "vomited iron harbingers" into his camp. He had to get rid of this "watery dragon." Strange to relate, commented Captain Cooke, "Sir Edward failed to make an instantaneous advance, and set himself down to lay siege to the American schooner."[43] To Cooke, Sir Edward was wasting precious time. An immediate advance was surely the proper move, according to the captain. In any event, the general directed that a battery of two nine-pounders, four six-pounders, two 5.5-inch howitzers, and a 5.5-inch mortar, including furnaces to heat the balls, be hauled from the ships at anchor to the bayou and through the canebrakes to the camp. After dark they were to be erected at the river's edge. Sailors under the direction of Cochrane and Malcolm endured most of the incredible exertions involved in transporting these monsters a distance of over sixty miles. In the wet and cold of day and night the sailors succeeded in positioning these cannons on the riverbank.

At 2:00 A.M. on December 27, the gunners lighted fires to heat the shot that would be aimed directly at the *Carolina*. Then, shortly after 7:00 A.M., the guns opened fire. This was the first indication to the Americans that the British now had heavy artillery. The nine-pounders belched hot shot, the six-pounders shrapnel, and the heavy howitzers cold shot and shell. Almost immediately the skilled gunners found their range and brought down the ship's rigging, spars, and bulwarks. On the second round of hot shot the *Carolina* caught fire. Because the shot lodged in her main hold under her cables and could not be removed, the fire soon raged out of control.[44]

The captain ordered the crew to abandon ship, since it was obvious that it would explode within minutes because of all the gunpowder in the cabins. The men clambered over the sides into boats and pushed off to the opposite shore. At 9:30 A.M. the ship blew up with a tremendous roar, shaking the ground for miles and raining burning fragments in every direction. "In itself," reported Gleig, "the sight was a fine one, but to us it was peculiarly gratifying, for we could not but experience something like satiated revenge at the destruction of a vessel from which we had suffered so much damage." The British gunners cheered their success with shouts loud enough to be heard by the Americans, and then they turned their attention upriver, to the *Louisiana*. Now it was the only warship left to harass them.

Jackson, watching from the Macarty house, sent orders to get the ship out of range. But wind and current made it impossible. So one hundred intrepid Baratarians piled into boats, attached hawsers to the *Louisiana*, and rowed like men possessed. While hot shot fell hissing into the water around them the sailors with a mighty effort at the oars hauled her to safety. Only one British shell fell on the deck of the ship, wounding several crewmen.

This was a victory for the British but also a very small victory for the Americans. For if Pakenham had directed his fire first at the *Louisiana*, which was farther away, he most likely would have destroyed both ships. To escape the devastating fire the *Louisiana* had to move only half a mile, while the *Carolina* had at least two miles to sail to reach safety.

The *Louisiana* now took station across the river, firing one last defiant round at the British. Her anchored position allowed her to rake lengthwise any column of troops that advanced on Jackson's rampart. Except for one killed and six wounded, the remainder of the *Carolina* crew were saved to join the American line, where they helped man the artillery.

After celebrating the victory of eliminating a nuisance that had made life miserable for his troops, Pakenham reorganized his army. He formed it into two brigades. Major General Gibbs commanded the brigade on the right, consisting of the 4th, 21st, and 44th and the 1st West Indian, while Major General Keane commanded the 85th, 93rd, and 95th and one black corps of the 5th West Indian on the left. Of artillery Pakenham now had ten pieces in the field.

On the evening of December 27 the British moved forward and by the superiority of their numbers drove back the American advance guard. Within minutes they occupied the Bienvenu and Chalmette plantations. For the remainder of the night, Pakenham had several batteries set up next to the river. When the task was completed he had his men rest in their places. But the Americans peppered any man who showed himself, and the intermittent shooting throughout the night made sleep impossible. Once more these rabbit hunters crept up stealthily in squads and fired at the British pickets, a most improper action according to "civilized" warfare as practiced in the early nineteenth century. According to the rules, "looked upon as, in some degree, sacred," sniffed Gleig, two forces facing each other who remain inactive for the night were not to have their outposts molested, not unless a direct attack upon the main body of the army was intended. But the Americans did not conform to "civilized" warfare. "No such chivalric notions" informed their conduct. To the British their actions "appeared an ungenerous return to barbarity." They acted more like assassins than soldiers, said Gleig, and murdered sentinels in "cold blood."[46]

Gleig himself was assigned to an outpost on the left front of the army. Every half hour he visited his sentinels to see to their needs and make certain they were awake. Shortly after one o'clock in the morning he had passed a thicket when suddenly his dog, who accompanied him, started barking fiercely. He froze. And in that instant a half-dozen muskets roared from the thicket; he would have been killed had he taken another step forward. The bullets whizzed past his head as he returned the fire. Charging with sword in hand into the thicket, he found the rabbit hunters gone. His life had been saved by the alert warning of his dog.[47]

Meanwhile Jackson had the two six-pounders that had escaped capture the night of the 23rd positioned on the levee, together with a twenty-four-pounder. He stationed a twelve-pound howitzer to command the road with another twenty-four-pounder to the left of the howitzer. Altogether Jackson had twenty-four pieces of artillery arranged in four batteries. They were placed on wooden platforms that rested on cotton bales laid three deep to prevent them from sinking into the mud. Openings for these guns were formed with six or eight cotton bales and fastened to the main body of the redoubt by iron rings and covered with dirt. Some of the bales caught fire in the ensuing action and created a "most intolerable and persistent smoke," so all the cotton was eventually removed from the lines. When Vincent Nolte recognized the marking on several bales as his own, he complained to Livingston that his expensive cotton, worth from ten to twelve cents a pound, was being used, and cheaper cotton worth only seven or eight cents would have been just as effective. Without missing a beat, Livingston responded, "Well, Mr. Nolte, if this is your cotton, you, at least, will not think it any hardship to defend it."[48] Jackson then ordered this artillery to blow up all the buildings on the Chalmette plantation and the Bienvenu plantation to the north of it within six hundred yards of the American line in order to prevent the enemy from using them for protection.[49] Combustibles of various kinds had previously been hidden in these buildings so that when hit by the artillery they exploded.

Jackson's line was weakest on the left. At first he extended it no farther than the cypress woods, leaving a good bit of dry land undefended. But Jean Laffite warned him of this flaw and the general immediately extended his line to the swamp. In all the line ran about three-quarters of a mile.

Old Hickory was tireless in his efforts to prepare his defenses. He worried about Chef Menteur, never knowing for certain whether that would be the focal point of the British invasion. He rode constantly among his men, encouraging them, offering suggestions about strengthening the rampart, making swift judgments about plans offered by his engineers, and getting reports from the dragoons about the enemy's movements. For five days and four nights he went without sleep and never once sat at a table to take a regular meal. Food was brought to him in the field, and he would pick at what was offered without dismounting. When begged to take some rest he replied, "No, sir; there's no knowing when nor where these rascals will attack. They shall not catch me unprepared. When we have driven the d—d red coat villains into the swamp, there will be time enough to sleep."[50]

As the sun came up on December 28 and burned away the mist rising from the river—it turned out to be a bright, crisp, and clear day—Pakenham ordered a general advance of the British army. From the window of the Macarty house, Jackson watched the brilliant array of soldiers marching smartly toward his mud rampart, one column close to the river, the other near the cypress swamp. The "red coats," as Jackson invariably called them, were about to test the metal of the "dirty shirts," as the British called their American foes. To the "dirty shirts," who had never seen professionals in action, never seen smartly dressed and perfectly controlled soldiers responding so quickly and so precisely to the orders shouted at them, "it was certainly a formidable display of military power and discipline." And a little intimidating too.[51]

Drums began their incessant beat. Bugles sounded over the plain. And pickets rushed back to the line. Then the British army began to move. Under a shower of Congreve rockets and continual fire from their artillery, the column near the river under Keane crossed the open plain in front of Jackson's ditch. Pakenham and his staff rode near the center of the line so he could watch both columns advance. Just at that moment several groups of dirty, bewhiskered Baratarians under Dominique You and Renato Beluché arrived at the Rodriguez Canal, having run the distance from Fort St. John, where they had been stationed since their release from prison. Most likely Jean Laffite had convinced Jackson that Dominique and Renato were the best gunners available and should be summoned from sentinel duty to man the line. Jackson immediately assigned the two men to the twenty-four-pounders with other Baratarians, including Vincent Gambie, Louis Chighizola, and Raymond Ranchier, among the crew. Then the sailors from the *Carolina* appeared in two groups, one under Lieutenant Crawley, who took over the howitzer, and the other under Lieutenant Norris, who manned the twenty-four-pounder.[52]

When the redcoats got to within six hundred yards of the Rodriguez Canal, the American batteries opened up on them in a stupendous roar of cannonading, supported by the deadly fire from the *Louisiana*. The ship could easily sweep the road with her fire, because the Mississippi was hardly half a mile wide at that point. For seven hours the ship kept up a steady fire and poured upward of eight hundred shot on the right column. One single ball from her killed fifteen British soldiers.

For their part the enemy maintained a steady fire and constantly launched Congreve rockets at the Americans, wounding a number of them. These rockets were the newest weapon in the British arsenal, and the frontiersmen had never seen them before. They rose with a great swooshing sound and seemed to dart from one side to another, and when they fell to the ground they would slither through the cane stubble like snakes and finally explode with a sharp report and a gush of acrid smoke. It was hoped that their noise and erratic flight would strike terror into the Americans and send them fleeing.[53]

Rockets were first used in India against the British in the eighteenth century, and Sir William Congreve became interested in this recoilless weapon and improved it. Wellington reportedly fired more than twenty thousand Congreve rockets during his siege of Copenhagen in 1807. They were introduced into America at the Battle of Lundy's Lane in July 1814, but their most remembered use came during the bombardment of Fort McHenry when Francis Scott Key watched "the rockets' red glare, the bombs bursting in air."[54]

Although these rockets did frighten the Americans at first, their novelty soon wore off and their value proved very limited. They could not be directed with any accuracy; they might have been more effective against a cavalry by frightening horses.

On the other hand, the crossfire between ship and ditch proved extremely devastating as they raked the advancing redcoats, so devastating in fact that the enemy soldiers dove into any ditch or cavity they could find for protection. "That the Americans are excellent marksmen, as well with artillery as with rifles," Lieutenant Gleig allowed, "we have had frequent cause to acknowledge; but, perhaps, on no occasion did they assert their claim to the title of good artillerymen more effectively than on the present. Scarce a ball passed over, or fell short of its mark, but all striking full into the midst of our ranks, occasioned terrible havoc."[55]

The screaming of the wounded, the explosion of houses hit by artillery, the tremendous cannonading that moved down British ranks, and the smoke that blinded the advancing column caused some panic. Two English fieldpieces and one mortar were dismounted and several gunners killed. With the advance going nowhere and the carnage mounting, Pakenham finally ordered a halt and issued a command to take cover. But the beleaguered redcoats, crouching on the ground for protection, had to wait until nightfall before they could withdraw, abandoning several batteries as they fled. Regiment after regiment stole away, not in a body but one by one. Those troops farthest from the river retreated as best they could.[56]

Near the swamp, out of the range of the *Louisiana* and the American artillery close to the levee, the British column under Gibbs might have turned Coffee's flank, gained the rear, and reached Jackson's barricade at its weakest point—the mud rampart on the left was extremely thin and hardly protected the men from musket fire—had Pakenham not ordered a general retreat. He probably thought that the devastation on his column near the river was matched by an equal devastation on his right along the swamp. With all the smoke and fire raging around him it was impossible for him to see clearly what was happening at both ends of his line.

The retreat demoralized his troops. "There was not a man among us," wrote Gleig, "who failed to experience both shame and indignation, when he found himself retreating before a force for which he entertained the most sovereign contempt."[57]

In the engagement the Americans lost seven killed and ten wounded. That night three British deserters managed to reach the rampart without injury and reported that their side had lost 152 men killed, wounded, or taken prisoner, although officially the English admitted to only sixteen killed and forty-three wounded or missing.[58]

So the first encounter of the proud Pakenham with American rabbit hunters ended in disaster. The enthusiasm that had greeted him on his arrival on Christmas Day turned to disappointment and chagrin just a few days later. Here the mighty British army had arrived to demonstrate military power at its highest, here these soldiers had waited eight long, miserable days and nights within less than a dozen miles of the alluring city, and yet they were stopped dead in their tracks. It was baffling. It was also downright humiliating.

As darkness descended it concealed the mortification felt by the British from the prisoners and slaves—and from the two hundred Chickasaw and Choctaw Indians who had accompanied them. The Indian prophet who had predicted victory managed to "get gloriously drunk" in order to escape censure from his tribe. Earlier Gleig had asked several Cherokees why they supported the British and the Indians replied that "they had come over to the side which they believed to be the strongest, perfectly satisfied that there was no force in Louisiana capable of offering to us any serious resistance."[59] Perhaps now they had their doubts.

During this assault Jackson was told by one of his volunteer aides that some members of the Louisiana legislature were so concerned about the possibility of British capture of New Orleans that they were prepared to offer terms of capitulation and surrender, provided the city was spared destruction. The general immediately alerted Governor Claiborne to this report and instructed him to keep a close eye on the legislators and at the first sign of their contacting the enemy to arrest them and hold them subject to his further orders. He added that he really did not believe the information, but if it proved true he told Claiborne to "blow them up." The governor went further and closed the legislature and put a guard at the door of the capitol. Outraged, a committee of the legislature confronted Jackson and demanded to know what he would do in the event that he was forced to call a general retreat.

Angrily, Jackson tongue-lashed them. "If I thought the hair of my head could divine what I should do," he said, "forthwith I would cut it off; go back with this answer: say to your honorable body, that if disaster does overtake me, and the fate of war drives me from my line to the city, they may expect to have a very warm session." As the committee turned away the members knew exactly what he meant.

In a calmer moment when his aid John Reid posed the same question about what he would do if the British broke his lines and forced his retreat, he was more precise and the answer more frightening.

"I should have retreated to the city," Jackson replied, "fired it, and fought the enemy amidst the surrounding flames. . . . I would have destroyed New Orleans, occupied a position above on the river, cut off all supplies, and in this way compelled them to depart from the country."[60]

Ralph E. W. Earle's portrait of Andrew Jackson, painted shortly after the Battle of New Orleans, was widely circulated around the country and helped enhance Old Hickory's reputation as a military and national hero.

William Carroll

John Coffee

Philemon Thomas

Jacques Villeré

Jean Baptiste Plauché

Michael Fortier

These officers shared with Jackson the great victory over the British on January 8, 1815.

Commodore Daniel Todd Patterson, painted here by John Wesley Jarvis, stationed ships in the Mississippi River to protect Jackson's front lines and regularly bombarded the British position.

The rash, arrogant, but highly talented Major General Sir Edward Michael Pakenham, brother-in-law of the Duke of Wellington, suffered defeat and death below New Orleans as he desperately tried to rally his troops to renew their assault on Jackson's front lines.

In a rather fanciful representation of what the Battle might have looked like, John Landis depicted the death of Pakenham. On the left side of the rampart are Generals Keane, Pakenham, and Gibbs; on the right side are Generals Coffee, Adair, Jackson, and Livingston.

These portraits of the Laffite brothers Jean and Dominique You could easily serve as "wanted" posters for outlaws, and perhaps they did.

William Claiborne was appointed territorial governor of Louisiana Territory by Thomas Jefferson and later won election as governor after Louisiana was admitted into the Union as a state. Jackson thought he was "much better qualified for pomp and show" than for "military achievements amidst peril." He was painted in 1840 by E. B. Savary.

Each day from the top floor of his headquarters at the Macarty house Jackson carefully observed British troop movements on the field.

On the grounds of the Chalmette plantation American forces destroyed the Duke of Wellington's army of "military heroes" and earned the lasting gratitude of the American people.

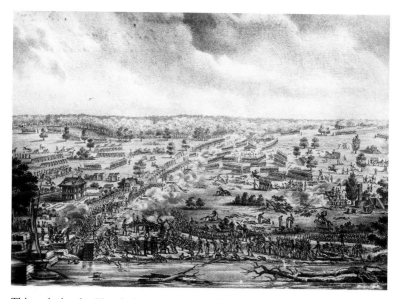

This painting by Hyacinth Ladotte, one of Jackson's engineers, is an attempt to represent visually to the American people the supreme moment when raw "defenders of freedom" vanquished a resplendent British army.

The two battle scenes on this page, and many more like them that regularly appeared in books and magazines for decades after the Battle, helped the American people to realize and appreciate the heroism and magnificence of their first great military victory over the British.

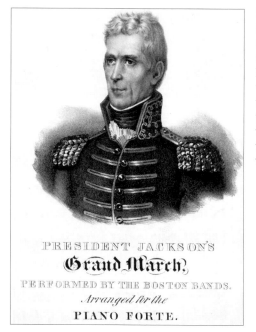

PRESIDENT JACKSON'S
Grand March,
PERFORMED BY THE BOSTON BANDS.
Arranged for the
PIANO FORTE.

This advertisement poster for "President Jackson's Grand March" was another example of how his image and career were constantly presented to the American people to remind them of his towering contribution to their freedom and advance toward democracy.

The caption of this portrait reads: "The presence of the English before N.O. flung terror among the women of the city. 'Tell them,' said Jackson to Livingston, 'I am here, the British shall never reach the city.' Riding along the line he would exclaim, 'I will smash them so help me god.' No man living ever did so much to humble England as Andrew Jackson."

Chapter 5

The Artillery Duel

The frustrations the British high command endured during these last days of 1814 necessitated another reevaluation of what would be necessary to smash the American defense and capture New Orleans. Attempting to storm Jackson's lines again was out of the question. So Pakenham called a council of war with his generals and the admirals of the fleet and solicited their opinions. Cochrane, Malcolm, Gibbs, Keane, and several others attended. The final consensus was that they really had no choice but to treat the enemy's fieldworks as a walled and fortified city and erect breaching batteries against them and thus silence them. Therefore heavier artillery was needed. The guns brought earlier could not do the job effectively. More were needed. So orders went out to the fleet to send in thirty more pieces of cannon of the largest size possible.[1]

Over the next several days the British army took a position two miles south of Jackson's line while naval personnel attended to the horrendous task of hauling the artillery across Lake Borgne and up the bayou to the army's present position. They were still confined to a plain, intersected with narrow ditches, between a swamp and a river. No wood or cover of any description concealed their position or movements. However, their outposts were positioned several hundred yards from the American rampart, while the sentinels went even closer. And the headquarters for the army was established near the place where the action of December 23 had been fought.

Over a period of three days the British sailors succeeded in landing ten eighteen-pounders and four twenty-four-pound carronades and hauling them into position under the cover of night—these in addition to those guns already stationed on the field.[2]

Jackson used this respite of three days to strengthen his own line, particularly the segment of it that bordered the cypress swamp where the British almost broke through on December 28. He also added a number of heavy guns provided by the *Louisiana*. In all he set up eight batteries.

Battery No. 1 was stationed about seventy feet from the bank of the river and was commanded by Captain Enoch Humphrey of the U.S. artillery. It consisted of two brass twelve-pounders and a six-inch howitzer, all on field carriages. Soldiers of the regular artillery manned the two twelve-pounders, while members of the Dragoons of St. Gème's Company worked the howitzer. Battery No. 2 was commanded by Lieutenant Otto Norris of the navy and stationed ninety yards from No. 1. It was elevated and consisted of a twenty-four-pounder manned by part of the Baratarian crew of the *Carolina*. No. 3, commanded by Dominique You and Renato Beluché, consisted of two twenty-four-pounders manned by the Baratarians. It was positioned fifty yards from No. 2. Battery No. 4, commanded by Lieutenant Charles Crawley of the navy, had a thirty-two-pounder and was located another twenty yards from No. 3. Battery No. 5, commanded by Colonel Perry and Lieutenant William C. Kerr of the artillery, had two six-pounders and stood 190 yards from No. 4. No. 6, commanded by General Garrigues Flaujeac, who was one of the four members of the legislature at the front lines, consisted of a brass twelve-pounder and was placed thirty-six yards from No. 5. It was served by a company of Creoles under Lieutenant Etienne Bertel. No. 7 boasted a long brass eighteen-pound culverine and a six-pounder manned by gunners of the U.S. artillery under the direction of Lieutenants Samuel Spotts and

Louis Chauveau. It was located 190 yards from the No. 6 battery. The eighth and final battery consisted of a small brass carronade whose undercarriage was in such bad condition that it provided little service. Located on the edge of the woods, it was commanded by a corporal of artillery and served by militia men of General Carroll's army. It was positioned some sixty yards from No. 7.[3]

At this point the line bent left where the woods began and extended a short distance into the swamp to meet any flanking action the British might attempt. But because the ground was so low and almost impossible to drain, the troops were literally encamped in water and had to walk knee-deep in mud. Small islands in this muck provided enough space to pitch a tent, but the soldiers were living and sleeping in a watery morass.

The weakness of the left side of the line, demonstrated so clearly on December 28, caused Jackson to bunch up Batteries 6 and 7 to correct the weakness. Later an eighteen-pounder was added to Battery No. 5 to further fortify this section. He also directed Carroll's and Coffee's men to heighten and strengthen their section of the rampart. But perhaps Jackson's concern was needless, for the British tended to keep as far away as possible from the swamp and from the deadly accuracy of the Tennessee sharpshooters.

The British watched as Jackson worked zealously to enhance his position. They watched as more and more tents were erected to accommodate the strong reinforcements that seemed to arrive daily. But so many of these incoming troops lacked weapons that Jackson requested the ladies of New Orleans to search their closets, cellars, garrets, and drawers and bring to him every pistol, old musket, flint, sword, gun barrel, and ramrod they could find. He also made certain that his men were well fed. The city was stocked with meat, vegetables, fruit, flour, and meal, something the British sorely lacked once the plantations they "plundered" had been completely emptied of food and wine. In fact they were eating horse meat to keep from starving. Prisoners taken by the Americans had "horseflesh" in their knapsacks. Each man received one and a quarter pounds of the meat and it was meant to last four days.[4]

While all these preparations were under way, Jackson continued to harass the enemy by elevating his guns high enough to reach their new bivouac. If nothing else, this constant cannonading proved extremely annoying. In addition, each morning at dawn the *Louisiana* would drop down to the position she occupied on December 28 and fire on every group of redcoats that dared to show itself. At nightfall she returned to a safe anchorage above the lines. Jackson also sent Major Latour to erect batteries on the opposite side of the river, from where a flanking fire could be thrown across the entire front of his line. Thus if and when the British advanced in a frontal attack they could be caught in a crossfire. One hundred and fifty slaves labored for six days to execute Latour's plans. Commodore Patterson landed two twelve-pounders from the *Louisiana* and the following night erected a twenty-four-pounder right beside the other two. These pieces with several others that were later added constituted the marine battery and were manned entirely by sailors from the *Louisiana* who had enlisted or had been pressed into service when spotted on the streets of New Orleans. "Every man who smelt of tar was seized and compelled to serve."[5] These sailors came from so many different countries that hardly a third of them spoke English. This marine battery was a proverbial "Tower of Babel"; still, Lieutenant C.C.B. Thompson established such excellent discipline among them that "it may be justly said that never were guns better served."[6]

Back on the east side of the river, Jackson made several attempts to penetrate into the woods on the right end of the British line to discover a path through the swampy terrain by which to turn the enemy's flank. But these efforts were largely unsuccessful.

Concerned about spies and deserters who might try to communicate with the British, Jackson lined the banks of the Mississippi with sentinels who regularly kept "watch-boats" running up and down the river. To test their efficiency the general set adrift two empty flatboats from the levee one night. The two small craft had not floated far toward the lines when they were spotted by boatmen, who challenged them and then gave the alarm when they heard no response. The *Louisiana* immediately roared into action and destroyed the empty decoys before they could reach the lines. Jackson was now satisfied that no one could float up or down the river without discovery.[7]

And, of course, every night a group of Tennessee dirty shirts went on a hunting expedition. On one occasion they stole from the line toward a British sentinel and concealed themselves in the brush as they waited for him to walk by. When he appeared there was a sudden and deadly shot, and the sentinel fell to the ground. A rabbit hunter hardly ever missed when he drew a bead on a target. The dirty shirts then stripped the sentinel of any valuable equipment, especially his arms and accouterments. These were temporarily hidden from view. When it came time to relieve the sentinel the corporal of the guard found him lying dead on the ground. Another sentinel was immediately posted. Minutes later another shot rang out and the second sentinel collapsed in a heap and was immediately divested of his equipment. Still a third sentinel shared the fate of his predecessors before the corporal of the guard realized he had lost three men in the one position and that it was too dangerous a place to patrol. The spot was abandoned and the American sharpshooters returned to their camp with the spoils of their hunting party.[8]

This boldness, this risk-taking, this exuberance, seemed to pervade the entire American army. The events of December 23, 25, and 28 had imbued them with "a spirit of personal daring and gallant enterprise." They knew that they had the British at their mercy and could defeat them. It was a heady feeling, a feeling of superiority that Americans desperately needed. Such a feeling freed them at last from any sense of subservience to British might and power.[9]

Night after night this reckless pursuit of adventure kept the field between the two hostile camps alive with American soldiers wandering about looking for prey. A small number of men from each corps, having received permission to venture outside the line, would converge at a central point in front of the lines and proceed to attack the nearest British outpost. These assaults kept the enemy in a state of alarm and nerve-racking tension.

Even the Choctaw Indians terrorized the British camp. Organized by Pierre Jugeant, son of a Creole French trader and a mixed-blood

Choctaw woman, they patrolled the edge of the swamp and caused much concern among the enemy. Their agility as they leaped from log to log, shooting at any redcoat that came within sight, made them a formidable addition to Jackson's army. They killed or wounded no fewer than fifty British soldiers during these nightly forays. They too enjoyed the sport of the evening, and their screams and shouts of success with each killing frequently paralyzed the young recruits in Pakenham's army.

Sometimes at night the dirty shirts charged into the very mouths of British cannon and drove off the pickets. It was even reported that on one occasion the Tennesseans dragged a six-pounder forward of the American line and fired it point-blank at the sentinels guarding an enemy outpost, causing "terror to the whole British camp." It was great fun, great sport, and buoyed the spirit of these "defenders of freedom." Even before the final battle took place an entire army of Americans recognized in their own minds that they had achieved a personal emancipation, a genuine independence from their nation's former sovereign. Most of them, of course, had been born after the American Revolution. Still, over the past thirty years they had experienced the insults of British policy toward the United States and worried over British intentions toward American freedom. Like Jackson as a youth, they had undoubtedly heard from their parents what it meant to be subjects of George III, the still-reigning king. Now, fighting below New Orleans and smiting British military power day and night, they were, in a very real sense, declaring once again their country's and their own independence from monarchical tyranny.

About midnight these revelers in freedom would return to their camp and try to get some sleep before the next dawn. They would lie down on beds of brush gathered from the swamp; the Tennesseans, who were positioned on the extreme left of the line, had to content themselves with gunwales or logs raised a few inches above the soft mire of the marsh.

Shortly after daybreak the camp would come awake. Drums beat out a regular rhythm and several bands played lively martial tunes, the liveliest of which, as might be expected, came from the Orleans battalion of Plauché, which could be heard in the "gloomy camp of the British," where not even a bugle sounded unless as a warning. The "Marseillaise" was a favorite, but the frontiersmen preferred "Yankee Doodle." There was marching and countermarching in the American camp as the excitement of martial music roused the men to their duty. Gleig admitted that the music entertained not only the American troops but the British as well. Some of the music Gleig described as "spiritless," since the "Yankees are not famous for their good taste in anything;—but one or two of the waltzes struck me as being peculiarly beautiful; the tune, however, which seemed to please themselves the most, was their national air known among us by the title of 'Yankee doodle'; for they repeated it at least six times in the course of their practice."[10]

How different the British camp. The army sat around without tents, without parade, without show of any kind. A dozen little huts had been erected, and these consisted merely of planks torn from houses and fences nearby and provided no protection from the cold, damp, inclement weather. No band played and the soldiers marched in complete silence.[11]

On the night of December 31, American sentinels came alert to the fact that the British had advanced within five or six hundred yards of their ditch and could be heard digging and hammering. They peered intently into the night and could vaguely discern that the enemy were completing the preparation of gun emplacements for their big cannons. The artillery and engineering officers had persuaded Pakenham to give the artillery and the navy the opportunity of breaching Jackson's line. They said they could silence the enemy's batteries in three hours. So Pakenham set his soldiers to work completing the construction of several redoubts or temporary fortifications behind which the gunners could fire their guns in comparative safety. Half of the army had been marched forward and halted about three hundred yards from Jackson's line. These troops had stacked their guns and with picks and shovels were busily finishing fieldworks from which they fully expected they would demolish the American position. They knew, said Gleig, that they "worked for life or death."[12] The 85th and 95th covered the working parties in front and on the flanks, and the entire operation was conducted as quietly as possible.

But the engineers faced one problem: the lack of solid materials with which to build the redoubts. They used whatever they could find in the houses on the plantations they had ransacked. Anything that could slow or stop a bullet or cannonball was thrown onto the mounds. They even rolled the hogsheads of sugar that lay around the ruins of the sugar houses of the plantations nearby and placed them upright beside the parapets of the batteries. They mistakenly believed that the sugar would be as effective as dirt in stopping bullets and cannonballs. Several thousand dollars' worth of American sugar was expended in the operation.

By dawn, six batteries were completed in three separate crescent-shaped formations, one on the right, one in the center, and one on the left, spaced at nearly equal distances from one another. These batteries, consisting of thirty pieces of heavy ordnance with enough ammunition for six hours of continued cannonading, were capable of throwing over three hundred pounds of metal per salvo. And they were manned by skilled gunners of the fleet and the artillery, men who were veterans of the Napoleonic Wars and had fought with Lord Nelson.[13]

Sounds of hammering, dulled by distance, alerted the Americans to the approaching danger. The outposts also sent back word that the British were engaged in some activity, probably the building of gun emplacements. Then the hammering ceased and all was silent. But veterans of the American army knew there would be action the following morning.

New Year's Day dawned on a plain so thick with fog that nothing could be seen beyond twenty yards. Dead silence. By eight o'clock the fog was still impenetrable and the silence deafening. By nine the American troops began to suspect that another day of waiting was in the offing—just as well as far as the Creoles were concerned. This was New Year's Day, a day to celebrate.

Jackson conceded that indeed the day was special, and since the

British were obviously not about to attack he called off the work schedule and ordered a grand review of the entire army on the open ground between the defensive lines and his headquarters at Macarty's house. And the *Louisiana* stayed safely anchored above the lines, for Patterson had received information the night before from a deserter that the British had established two enormous howitzers in a battery along the levee where cannonballs were kept scorching hot to fire on the *Louisiana* the next time she came within range. He therefore ordered crew members to remove two additional guns from the ship and add them to the marine battery.

So, as the morning progressed, the American troops behind the Rodriguez Canal prepared for the grand review. Clean clothes and uniforms were the order of the day. Regimental and company flags and standards were unfurled; officers rode back and forth through the ranks, looking proud and eager. Local citizens with permission from the commanding officer had entered the camp to visit with friends and relatives and help them celebrate the beginning of a new year. They walked nonchalantly from tent to tent and across the field. "All was animation, confidence, security and joviality in the American camp."[14] So let the redcoats come. They would finally get what they so richly deserved and what had never been properly administered before by an American army: a thorough and humiliating thrashing.[15]

At ten o'clock the fog began to dissipate and the sun shone brightly on the colorful American scene, one the British could see very clearly from their position just three hundred yards away.

And then it happened, suddenly, unexpectedly, devastatingly. At a signal from the central British redoubt, thirty large cannon belched forth their tons of fiery missiles at almost point-blank range. At the same time dozens of Congreve rockets shot into the air and "filled the firmament with flaming orbits and rained meteoric showers" upon the American camp.[16]

In the flash of cannon fire the festive scene behind the Rodriguez Canal dissolved. Taken totally by surprise, the Americans were thrown into confusion. Ranks came apart; lines of smartly dressed troops disintegrated; order degenerated into confused crowds. "The ranks were broken," Gleig joyfully reported, "the different corps dispersing, fled in all directions, while the utmost terror and disorder appeared to prevail." Oh, moaned Gleig, *"Oh, that we had charged at that instant!"*[17]

Indeed. Had they charged, or had antipersonnel ammunition rather than demolition ammunition been used, the British might have cracked Jackson's lines and marched on to New Orleans.

During the first ten minutes of the bombardment, the Macarty house, which the British knew was Jackson's headquarters, was hit with one hundred balls, rockets, and shells. These missiles shattered bricks, furniture, and plaster and propelled the pieces in every direction like shrapnel. At the time Jackson and his staff were finishing breakfast, and when the rockets struck they rushed from the house. Fortunately, everyone escaped injury. Before long the porticos of the house were blown away "and the building made a complete wreck."[18]

Once the initial shock of the attack wore off, the American troops rushed to their posts, knowing that they were safe standing behind the rampart. By the time General Jackson reached the front of his line the artillerymen were waiting with breathless anxiety and some degree of apprehension but with lighted matches to open fire once the smoke and haze surrounding their batteries completely dissipated.

Jackson first turned to see if Humphrey's battery was ready. Standing erect with his men was their commander, his teeth pronged around his usual cigar, calmly surveying the scene and preparing to direct his men to fire.

"Ah!" Jackson exclaimed. "All is right; Humphrey is at his post, and will return their compliments presently."

Old Hickory, together with his aides, Reid and Butler, and the two lawyers, Grymes and Davezac, then walked the entire length of the line, pausing at each battery to inspect its condition and waving his hat in response to the cheers of the artillerymen.

"Don't mind those rockets," he told them, "they are mere toys to amuse children."

But the constant roar of the cannon, the blaze from their mouths, the frightening hissing and crashing of shells, the screaming rockets and the red glare they emitted as they circled, and the shaking of the entire delta from the pounding action of thirty huge monsters of destruction terrified the soldiers. The visiting citizens from New Orleans scurried madly to find shelter, crying out their alarm and invoking God Almighty to save them.[19]

Finally the Americans counterattacked. Humphrey's battery led off with his twelve-pounders, firing several volleys in quick succession, followed almost immediately by the larger guns of the batteries commanded by Dominique You, Beluché, Norris, and Spotts. With each salvo the Americans vomited 224 pounds of metal. Soon it became a steady, unrelenting fire being thrown up from the ditch. And the marksmanship was impeccable. The phlegmatic Humphrey called out through his teeth without disturbing the position of his cigar, "Let her off," which was the command to fire. He gave this command after carefully lowering and elevating his guns several times to get the proper range. The agile, fiery, quick-witted You, standing defiantly on the very edge of the embankment and exposed to the "storms of British shot," shouted to his grim-faced men in French to speed their firing and cram their guns to the mouth with cable shot, ship canister, and any other destructive material they had at hand. He turned to peer at the enemy through his spyglass, and in that moment a cannon shot grazed his arm. "I will pay them for that," he promised, as he quickly bound up the wound.

The refined, well-mannered, and serene Lieutenant Norris was an altogether different commander. He spoke so matter-of-factly to his men that it almost seemed as though he were conducting a drill. Garrique stirred his artillerists with reminders of their past heroics under Napoleon and how their ancient foe was waiting just a few hundred yards away to feel once more the might of Gallic wrath.

At first, reported Lieutenant Gleig, the American batteries remained silent, but then several minutes after the firing began, they "recovered confidence, and answered our salute with great rapidity and precision."[20]

As Jackson strode down the line, he continued encouraging his men not to be afraid and endeavoring by his words to infuse spirit and courage in them. Several times he had to dodge the rockets, and on one or two occasions he saw brains splattered over the ground and prostrate bodies twisted in a heap. Throughout the engagement Jackson constantly moved from one extreme wing of his line to the other.[21]

At one point the British sent a contingent of soldiers to attack Jackson's left along the edge of the swamp because of its vulnerability during the engagement of December 28. Coffee ordered his men to drive the attacking enemy into the swamp and then drown them. The intrepid Tennesseans, "leaping like cats from log to log" and wading indifferently through mud and muck, "satisfied the heavy, beef-eating, bog-fearing Britons" that they could easily defeat them in swamp fighting, and after a short skirmish drove them back to their camp.[22]

The British infantry, waiting to rush forward and begin a general assault once the artillery had done its job in pulverizing the enemy's rampart, had trouble finding shelter. Knolls and elevations for protection were few, and the dirty shirts had no difficulty picking off any soldier who dared to show himself. According to one observer, a group of officers of the British 93rd Regiment took refuge in a shallow hollow behind a slight elevation of the ground. It was then suggested that only the married man of the group should lie on the bottom in order to have maximum protection. That meant Lieutenant Phaups, and he laughingly took his position as the others climbed around and on top of him. This activity drew the attention of the American sharpshooters, who began firing at the elevation—and kept firing at it. Phaups could not restrain his curiosity and in a moment of foolishness stuck his head up to see what was going on. He only exposed the top of his head and his eyes, but that was more than enough. A twelve-pound shot smashed into his skull and blew out his brains. The other members of the group later buried him in full uniform on the spot where he died.[23]

For an hour and a half the tempest of fifty or more booming cannons raged, interrupted only occasionally to allow the hot metal to cool off. Men tried desperately to concentrate on loading, firing, and reloading their behemoths and to ignore the tumult and roaring hell around them. Later the British acknowledged that the Americans did not panic as much as they expected. The American army, they admitted, was "the first . . . army that was not thrown into confusion by their rockets." Across the river the marine battery opened up on the British howitzers on the levee, and now the delta really did tremble and shake as though an earthquake had struck.[24]

"I had never before witnessed so severe a cannonade," Tatum reported, "for the time it lasted, as on this occasion (even in the 6 weeks siege of the City of Charleston in 1780) the firing was, almost, without interruption on both sides for nearly three hours."[25]

In this titanic duel it was obvious that the British had several advantages. Surprise for one; larger guns, and many of them, and greater weight of metal for another. In addition they were manned by veterans of Trafalgar, the Nile, the Peninsular War and any number of other ferocious battles over the past few years. And their batteries presented a very narrow front, while the American line ran a little over a thousand yards. In addition, the British batteries were mounted low, while Jackson's were positioned on high platforms that exposed them and made them much more vulnerable. Not surprisingly, the British inflicted more damage on the American position than Jackson could afford. Their largest battery directed its fire against Battery No. 3, manned by the pirates You and Beluché, and caused some but not irreparable damage. You's twenty-four-pounder had its carriage broken, Crawley's thirty-two-pounder was hit, and part of Garrique's twelve-pounder was wrecked. Two powder caissons blew up, one of which contained a hundred pounds of explosives, and made such a resounding blast as to cause the British cannoneers to stop their firing and let out a mighty cheer. These were explosives Jackson could ill afford to lose. In addition, a boat filled with stores and moored on the levee about 200 yards behind the lines was sunk. The cotton bales near the battery by the levee were hit, sending trails of burning cotton flying in every direction. A few of them fell into the ditch and billowed forth heavy smoke that blinded the gunners. Some of Plauché's men voluntarily vaulted over the breastwork and extinguished the blaze, although one volunteer was seriously wounded in the action. After this incident no cotton bales were ever used at the breastwork. Instead good old Louisiana mud and dirt served to strengthen it.

On the levee the British battery tried to sink the *Louisiana* and kept shot constantly heated to hurl at her in the hope of setting it ablaze, but the ship stayed well beyond the reach of British guns. The British battery also exchanged several volleys with the American marine battery on the opposite shore. It fired with great accuracy and a few shots hit Patterson's works but did not inflict serious damage. Once Humphrey and his battery leveled the British redoubt immediately in front of him he turned his guns on the levee, and together with Patterson's guns they demolished the emplacement.

One low-ranking American soldier attached to the Louisiana militia, by the name of Judah Touro, volunteered to help carry ammunition from the magazine to Humphrey's battery. Despite the missiles soaring over his head and on either sides of him he diligently kept at this task, seemingly oblivious to the danger that surrounded him. Then, suddenly, he took a twelve-pound shot in the thigh, which tore off a large mass of flesh. He was removed to a wall of an old building well behind Jackson's lines and nearly demolished by the British bombardment. A doctor dressed the wound but held out little hope for him. Touro's best friend, Rezin D. Shepherd, who had been assigned to Patterson's marine battery but had recrossed the river to find two masons to help complete the building of the battery, heard what had happened to his friend and rushed to the stricken man's side. The doctor told him there was no hope of recovery. But Shepherd would not accept that verdict. He obtained a cart and drove the wounded man to the city, administering brandy very liberally along the way to his prostrate and semiconscious friend. When he reached the city he carried Touro into his house and summoned the women who had been caring for the army's sick and wounded and begged them to attend his friend and provide him with all their nursing skills. He then returned to his assignment.

Touro miraculously survived, and after the war the two men became millionaires, gave freely of their money to many charitable causes, and were regarded as "patriarchs" of the New Orleans community. Touro was known as "the Israelite without guile." When he died in 1854 he bequeathed half of his estate to all the Hebrew congregations in the country and other charitable and religious organizations, and the other half to the man who had saved his life on January 1, 1815. Shepherd used the money to restore a street in New Orleans where the two men had lived most of their lives. Then he had the name changed to Touro Street.[26]

There were many other heroic acts that took place on and off the battlefield during this intense bombardment, not all of which ended as happily as that of Touro and Shepherd.

For hours the two lines continued to belch forth their death-dealing projectiles, the English, surprisingly, taking the worst of it. Not until noon did it appear that the British fire had slackened, an obvious indication that they were hurt, and maybe hurt badly.

The reasons soon became clear. As the smoke and dust of the battle slowly settled the Americans could see the extent of the great damage they had inflicted on their enemy. The embankments of all three formations into which the six batteries had been erected had been knocked apart, the guns exposed, and a great many artillerists killed. Several guns had been smashed or dismounted, and many others damaged. The skill with which the American gunners had picked off the British artillery and shattered their parapets was positively astounding. "Too much praise," Jackson later reported to Secretary Monroe, "cannot be bestowed on those who managed my artillery."[27] Furthermore, the sugar barrels arranged around the gun emplacements had proved utterly useless; American firepower had no trouble shattering them or slicing right through them and killing the men in the very center of the battery. And when these barrels burst, as they frequently did, the sugar in them rained all over the guns and made them impossible to operate. Also, some of the British guns lacked proper flooring and after a round or two drove themselves into the mud and out of action. It was a pitiful sight for the British. Several officers considered the action a monumental defeat and a stain on the honor and reputation of the artillery service. "We were completely foiled," admitted Gleig.[28]

The Americans, on the other hand, were relatively unscathed, despite the damage to several guns and the loss of some ammunition. For one thing, their rampart remained completely intact. Cannonballs simply buried themselves in the thick mud walls without puncturing them or causing them to collapse. "Our fire," noted a British officer, "apparently made very little impression on their works."[29] For another, and far more noteworthy, was the fact that the British could not find the proper range. Instead of imitating the Americans, who took the time to fire a few guns and straddle their targets in order to get the proper range, the British in their haste and desire to achieve maximum surprise started blasting away only to have their cannonballs sail over the heads of the Americans and land in open fields well behind Jackson's lines. A great deal of precious ammunition was wasted in this haste to punch out a barrage of missiles. Finally, and in addition to everything else, the gun emplacements closest to the river were caught in a crossfire and the marine battery on the opposite side of the river succeeded in toppling the British artillery mounted on the levee.

By noon the enemy had slackened their fire. An hour later the guns on the left and center ceased firing, and by three o'clock all the guns fell silent. It was a total disaster for the British. Our "intention in the morning," said one British officer, "was to attack but now it was entirely dropped."[30]

Entirely dropped. What a sickening feeling for the exhausted British soldiers and their Indian allies, who seemed trapped with little chance of escaping except by a frontal attack or by retreating back to their ships. The morale of these heroes plummeted. The Americans, said Gleig, "convinced us, that all endeavours to surpass them in this mode of fighting, would be useless." We were "not only baffled and disappointed, but in some degree disheartened and discontented."

Within moments after the serious firing stopped, the American "fiddlers and the French horn-players from New Orleans struck up their notes within hearing of the British centinels." The merriment only added to the chagrin and embarrassment of the Britons.

The English suffered forty-four killed and fifty-five wounded in the bombardment, while American casualties amounted to eleven dead and twenty-three wounded; and most of the American casualties were civilians who had come to witness the battle at what they thought was a safe distance behind Jackson's lines. Unfortunately for them, the failure of the British to gauge their targets accurately led to their deaths.[31]

One such casualty was the French hatter Laborde. Standing directly in front of him was the notary Philippe Peddesclaux, who would surely have been hit had he not stooped over to let a friend light his cigar. When he stood straight again, there on the ground lay "Laborde's scattered brains and prostrate body."[32]

Toward evening it began to rain, and as the British retreated they abandoned their "heavy guns to their fate." But, surprisingly, Jackson made no attempt to capture them. Was this a ruse? the English wondered. Was the American general deliberately waiting for his enemy to come forward to take them so he could then riddle them with twelve-pound shot? The British had no way of knowing. So they waited, waited until dark, and when the Americans failed to secure the guns, working parties from the British line were sent out and those that had not been destroyed—five were left behind—were dragged back to camp through the mud. "It was my fortune," reported Lieutenant Gleig, "to accompany them. The labour of dragging a number of huge naval guns out of the soft soil into which they had sunk, crippled, too, as most of them were in their carriages, was more extreme by far than any one expected to find it; indeed, it was not till four o'clock in the morning that our task came to a conclusion, and even then it had been very imperfectly performed."[33]

Jackson made no effort to seize these guns, which he might have done successfully without endangering his troops. Nor did he attempt to drive the enemy away from them when they came forward to reclaim them. Perhaps he felt it was not worth the effort, since many of the guns were damaged or broken. He acted with extreme caution and probably feared that the enemy might launch another attack once he exposed his men to their fire. He had no idea what the British would do next or whether they would renew their offensive the next day. All he knew was that he had held his own against a very powerful enemy. But he also knew that he desperately needed more arms and ammunition. And he needed them immediately.

Daily Jackson had kept up his pleas to the secretary of war to send more supplies, warning that otherwise the consequences could be catastrophic. "Again I must apprise you," he wrote Monroe, "that the Arms I have been so long expecting have not yet Arrived." All he had heard was that the supplies were on the river above at Natchez but had been halted so that the captain in charge of them could attend to his "private speculations. Depend upon it," he lectured the secretary, "this supineness, this negligence, this criminality, let me call it, of which we witness so many instances in the agents of Government, must finally lead, if it be not corrected, to the defeat of our armies, and to the disgrace of those who superintend them."

At least the Kentucky troops had finally arrived. General John Adair, the adjutant general for the detachment, presented himself at Jackson's headquarters on the evening of January 2, announcing the speedy arrival of the Kentucky militia, whom he had left the day before at Bayou Lafourche, connecting the Mississippi above New Orleans near Donaldsonville. But only one-third of them were armed, he said, "and those very indifferently."

Jackson sighed his disappointment. "I have none to put in their hands," he complained to Monroe, "and can therefore make no very useful disposition of them."[32] Fortunately batteries along the mud rampart at the Rodriguez Canal were relatively safe, because the gunners had plenty of ammunition, thanks to the Baratarian pirates. Indeed, Jean Laffite had once boasted to Jackson that he could furnish ammunition for an army of thirty thousand. At the moment the gunners at the ditch had over 3,000 cannon cartridges, filled and empty, over 56,000 pounds of gunpowder, over 28,000 cannon shot of different sizes, over 21,000 musket cartridges, and over 12,000 flints.[35] Perhaps this was another reason Jackson made no attempt to seize the British guns after the battle. And because the American artillerymen were so well supplied they could keep up a constant bombardment night and day. In fact, reported Latour, "whenever a group of four or five men showed themselves, they were instantly dispersed by our balls or shells. The advantage we derived from that almost incessant cannonading on both banks of the Mississippi, was that we exercised our gunners, annoyed the enemy to such a degree that he could not work at any fortification, nor, indeed, come within the reach of our cannon by day, and was deprived of all repose during the night."[36]

Still, Jackson needed men at the front line fully armed with guns and ammunition. When arriving troops showed up without guns he was obliged to join them to the unarmed Louisiana militia on his second line at the Dupré plantation. At least "by the show they might make [they] would add to his appearance and numbers, without at all increasing his strength."[37]

Jackson kept hoping that the ship at Natchez with supplies would reach him before the main attack began. But he did not know what to expect next or when. Neither did the British. All their plans, all their hopes, all their dreams of easy conquest had come to nothing. Even this last effort on which they had placed "so much reliance" proved abortive. Officers and men alike begrudgingly admitted that "General Jackson had shown himself a general of the first class both in attack and defence, since his first surprise." Even so, they knew they were better troops, "the very elite of His Britannic majesty's dominions." Finally, said Gleig, "something like murmuring began to be heard through the camp." Justifiably so, he added. This army had cheerfully endured great hardships in landing and had dragged itself through swamps and muck and wilderness. It had been fed "false reports" as to the practicability of this invasion and now found itself trapped in a place from which there was no escape except by victory. Twice foiled in its attempts to puncture the enemy's entrenched position, it now discovered that its highly vaunted artillery was "greatly overmatched." This seemed like the final blow to its pride and endurance.

To make matters worse, the invaders' food now had to come from the fleet, since they had stolen and consumed everything eatable in the neighborhood, and fleet fare was both "scanty and coarse," consisting of salt beef, a sea biscuit or two, and a small amount of rum. When the pork and beans ran out it was not uncommon for the officers and men to appease their craving for food by eating sugar taken from the casks and molded into something resembling cake. Even worse, there was no rest—only constantly broken attempts at sleep. Not only did the artillery from Jackson's front line play unremittingly upon them both by day and night, but they were also exposed to a deadly fire from the opposite bank of the river, where no less than eighteen pieces of artillery were now mounted and "swept the entire line of our encampment." And so the murmurs were quite understandable. Only they were not the murmurs of professional soldiers anxious to escape a disagreeable situation, Gleig assured himself. "On the contrary, they resembled rather the growling of a chained dog, when he sees his adversary and can not reach him."[38]

Admiral Cochrane growled as well in his report. And it was curt. The batteries had failed their mission. There was nothing more to be done at present. The final attack would have to be deferred until the arrival of additional troops, momentarily expected under the command of Major General John Lambert.[39]

At one point during the artillery battle of New Year's Day, the American Batteries No. 1 and No. 2 ran out of ammunition, and Jackson, in a raging tempest, summoned Claiborne, who was in charge of these supplies. "By the Almighty God," Jackson screamed at Claiborne, "if you do not send me balls and powder instantly, I shall chop off your head, and have it rammed into one of those field-pieces."[40]

The desperate need for men and ammunition preyed on the commander's mind, for he knew that one day soon the British would launch the major assault, and if they broke through his lines and forced him to retreat he would be obliged to burn New Orleans.

Chapter 6

✤

Final Preparations

What next? Jackson wondered. What further plans did the British now have to capture New Orleans? And was the main invasion before him? Or would the enemy, as he constantly feared, steal up Bayou Bienvenu by way of its northern branch, swing around behind him, and reach the city via the Gentilly Road?

He needed information. He needed spies. And one of the most fascinating men he met, who proved to be indispensable in obtaining information, was Reuben Kemper, a tall, rawboned backwoodsman who loathed Spanish rule of Louisiana and Florida and had engaged in many assaults against his enemy in a lifelong struggle to win freedom for the southwest. And in Kemper's mind, the British were no better than the Spanish. So when the call went out for soldiers to defend New Orleans against invasion, Kemper joined the Feliciana Dragoons, and because of his daring exploits and courage, Jackson employed him as a spy. Frequently Kemper, in ill-fitting and badly worn clothing, would scout the enemy lines with a group of bush fighters and report to Jackson any movement or activity of the enemy.

Because of the constant fears and rumors that the British would get behind the American line and approach the city from the north, Jack-

son sent Kemper with twenty men to reconnoiter the English position
at the juncture of Bayou Mazant and Bayou Bienvenu, where the redcoats had first disembarked. If any attempt was made to swing behind
Jackson it could be spotted at this point. The juncture was an important link in the line of British communications, and it was well guarded.
In addition, a breastwork had been built at the end of the bayou to protect the invaders' principal magazine. Sentinels were posted at the tops
of trees to observe the approach of anyone moving across the prairie.
They also burned the prairie grasses to prevent the Americans from
creeping stealthily into position and cutting off the army from the fleet
and this depot.

It was a dangerous assignment that Jackson had given Kemper,
since the group would be separated quite a distance from the American outposts and would have to take great risks to secure the information the general needed. But the tough old backwoodsman relished it.
He and his men reached their assigned position and were able to observe and track the activities of the British over a number of days
without being observed. They reported back the heartening news that
the invasion was indeed in front of the American army at the Rodriguez Canal and that no attempt was under way to take another route
to reach New Orleans. Kemper and his bush fighters were Jackson's
eyes, ears, and hands in the outlying region. "No individual in Jackson's whole army," declared one historian, "performed more efficient
service."[1]

At the same time that Jackson sent Kemper on his assignment he
also ordered Major Davis, an assistant inspector general, to take two
hundred men from Coffee's brigade and check the area around Chef
Menteur for any sign of a British presence. Davis and his men lost no
time in getting to the Gentilly Plain, even though they had to endure a
heavy rain, bad roads, and mud up to their ankles. When they finally
reached their destination they found not a single British soldier, which
again confirmed that the invasion was indeed stationed alongside the
Mississippi River below New Orleans.

There were many other Louisianians besides Kemper and Davis
who could claim considerable credit for their contribution to the de-

fense of their city. General Jean Humbert, for example, performed any number of strange, possibly mad, and undoubtedly heroic acts in the name of freedom. A stout, compact, squarely built man, neatly dressed and thoroughly military in his bearing, Humbert never appeared in public without wearing his old uniform as a general of the French Republic. In the days before the invasion, he could be seen marching toward the square in New Orleans at noon each day, singing the "Marseillaise," wearing a French Revolutionary hat on his head, and carrying a large, brightly shining sword under his arm. He headed for a favorite café on the levee near the French market, where he would greet old comrades, lay his sword on the table, call for a glass of cognac, and begin a game of dominoes.

When Jackson arrived in town, Humbert was one of the first men to volunteer his services. Without a regular command, he nonetheless accepted any and all assignments to obtain information about the enemy, no matter how perilous or difficult. Frequently he would mount a large black horse and saunter along the levee road within range of enemy gunners. He would pull out a field glass, observe the British camp, and then wheel his charger around and leisurely trot back to the American lines, while bullets whizzed around his head. He would immediately report to Jackson the precise condition of the enemy's camp and anything else he had observed.

But Humbert was very punctilious, very military, and the behaviour, manner, and dress of the Tennessee frontiersmen frequently nettled him. He considered them rude, careless, and undisciplined and prone to fighting like savages instead of gentlemen. What particularly infuriated him was their distinctly unmilitary habit of "thinking for themselves." They had the audacity to discuss the merits of their officers and whether certain commands ought to be obeyed. On one occasion he took a contingent of Coffee's cavalrymen for a reconnoiter of the British line. Unmindful of the danger himself, he brought the men under the heavy fire of a British redoubt. The men did not appreciate risking their lives in what they regarded as an idiotic enterprise, so they blandly turned their horses around and headed back to the lines, leaving Humbert swearing and cursing at them and calling them cowards. He reported this cowardice to Jackson, who, understanding the mentality of the Tennesseans, simply smiled and tried to assuage Humbert's anger with assurances that these freemen would prove their bravery in due course. When Jackson later saw one of these cavalrymen he asked him why he had run away.

"Wall, general," drawled the Tennessean, "not understanding French, and believing our commander was a man of sense, we *con*-strued his orders to retire out of the reach of the cannonballs, and so we just kinder countermarched."[2]

Humbert also tried to help Jackson in figuring the enemy's next move. It was the one thought uppermost in Old Hickory's mind. And as he fretted and worried he was somewhat heartened by the arrival on January 4 of two thousand Kentucky militiamen, even though poorly armed, under the command of Major General John Thomas, who had marched from Bayou Lafourche near Donaldsonville above the city. Never were reinforcements more anxiously expected. But they were so ragged as they walked shivering through the streets that they held their pants and shirts together with their hands to keep from disgracing themselves. They had hoped to find in New Orleans "an end to their exposure and destitution" only to learn that Jackson "had not a musket, a blanket, a tent, a garment, a rag to give them." In his anger Jackson ordered a detachment of troops to go up the river to Natchez, find the captain of the ship who had his supplies but had not brought them to New Orleans as his duty required, and bring him back in irons. The words Jackson used describing this hapless captain's parentage, character, and various parts of his body were so "forcible" that they could not be repeated.[3]

Those Kentucky militiamen who were armed—about 550 of them—were sent to the Rodriguez Canal, where they took a position to the rear of the line. The others were assigned to the backup positions closer to the city.

The deplorable condition of these militiamen in such inclement weather prompted Louis Louaillier, a member of the lower house of the Louisiana legislature, to win approval of a proposal to appropriate $6,000 for relief, the money to be distributed by a select committee.

Subscriptions were also put forward in New Orleans, since so many citizens of the city had watched these freezing men as they marched down their streets and had been shocked at their appearance. Another $6,000 was quickly raised in these subscriptions. Surrounding counties also contributed when they heard what these men were suffering. In all some $16,100 was raised and used to purchase blankets and woolens, which were distributed among the ladies of New Orleans to be fashioned into clothing. Within a week the ladies had made 1,200 blanket cloaks, 275 waistcoats, 1,127 pairs of pants, 800 shirts, and 410 pairs of shoes, and a large number of mattresses which were either handmade or purchased. These articles were then distributed among the troops most in need.

With such an expenditure of determination and will there could be no doubt that the battle for New Orleans involved not just generals and officers and soldiers, but every citizen in the entire city and surrounding parishes of Louisiana.

As the city waited each day of the new year to discover the enemy's next move, Jackson took his usual position at the topmost window of the wrecked but still standing Macarty house and watched hour after hour for any signs of activity from the British camp. On Friday, January 6, as an afterthought proposed by his engineers, he ordered the construction of a redoubt or separate fortification in advance of his forward line by a few feet on his extreme right, constructed so as to allow the enemy's front to be enfiladed if it reached the edge of the rampart. It stood alone. Between it and the parapet a single plank was laid over the Rodriguez Canal to provide quick and easy passage between the two positions. A ditch completely surrounded the redoubt, but it did not go deep enough and was unfortunately dry because of the falling of the Mississippi. Jackson had his doubts about the usefulness of the construction, but he yielded to what he considered the better judgment of his engineers. When he inspected the nearly complete structure he shook his head and said to one of his aides, *"That will give us trouble!"*[4]

When the redoubt was finished it was guarded by a company of the 7th Regiment commanded by Lieutenant Andrew Ross, but its artillery was manned by a company of the 44th commanded by Lieutenant Dauquemeny de Marant. Behind it and between Battery No. 1 and the river at the extreme right of the line, Captain Thomas Beale and his New Orleans volunteer company of riflemen, consisting of about thirty men, were stationed.[5] The guns of Battery No. 1, when fired, just grazed the side of the newly constructed redoubt, which may explain Jackson's concern. In addition to the redoubt a powder magazine was built at the same time.

In the assignment of troops to the line, the 7th Infantry Regiment was stationed to cover the section from the redoubt past Battery No. 1 to Battery No. 2 and reaching as far as Battery No. 3. This regiment numbered 430 men and was commanded by Major Henry Peire. Battery No. 2, of course, was commanded by Lieutenant Norris and No. 3 by Dominique You and Beluché.

The line between the battery of the privateers and Battery No. 4, commanded by Crawley, was occupied by Major Plauché's battalion of volunteers, numbering 289 men, along with Major Lacoste's battalion of free men of color, numbering 180.

From Battery No. 4 to Colonel Perry's No. 5 the line was defended by Major Louis Daquin's battalion of Santo Domingo free men of color, numbering about 150, and another 250 soldiers of the 44th commanded by Captain Isaac L. Baker. All the troops from the 7th Regiment on the river to the 44th beyond battery No. 5 inclusively were commanded by Colonel George Ross.

Guarding the next segment of the line from Batteries No. 6 and No. 7 were the Tennessee troops under General Carroll. To the right of Battery No. 7 an additional fifty marines under Lieutenant Francis de Bellevue were posted, and they were the last of the regular troops. When the Kentucky militiamen finally arrived, they were brought up to reinforce the left side of Carroll's position. They straddled Battery No. 8, at which point the swampy woods began. All of these troops numbered about sixteen hundred men.[6]

Coffee and his troops, including the Choctaw Indians and number-

ing between eight hundred and twelve hundred men, guarded the remainder of the line into the cypress swamps, a distance of half a mile.
The line then turned left and ran into the woods so that Jackson's line
was anchored at both ends. Outposts extended about five hundred
yards in front of the line.[7]

Captain Peter V. Ogden's cavalry was stationed behind the Macarty
house along with a detachment of dragoons, the whole numbering
fifty. And Major Hinds's Mississippi cavalry was posted at Jackson's
fallback position at Dupré's plantation, which was a mile behind the
breastwork.

The rampart behind which all these men crouched in anticipation of
the frontal assault varied in height and thickness. Where it was highest, a shelf was formed for the men to stand on when they fired, and
where it was lowest, the men bent to fire and stooped to load. At the
center of the line a tall flagpole had been erected with the Stars and
Stripes flying high enough to be seen by both armies and even on the
other side of the river. Well behind the line was a conglomeration of
tents and shanties where the men could rest and sleep when not on
duty. Each one of these huts had a small American ensign that "Creole
fancy or American ingenuity" had devised.

Behind these tents and shanties at a distance of approximately four
hundred yards a close line of sentinels stretched from the river to the
swamp to prevent anyone from leaving the camp.

As it subsequently developed, the actual battlefield when the main
attack began extended only a short distance. From Jackson's front line
to a position where the British commenced their assault the distance
was a little over four hundred yards. Although the American rampart
extended three quarters of a mile from the river to the swamp, only
seven hundred yards of that line would bear the brunt of the actual
fighting. In other words, the battle was played out in an area of roughly
four hundred by seven hundred yards.

And so the Americans waited and watched. Not until the evening of
Friday, January 6, did Jackson first begin to suspect what the enemy
might do. A sentinel posted at Chef Menteur saw a small English boat
sailing from the fleet to Bayou Bienvenu, presumably loaded with

supplies. Orders were quickly given to send out three American brigs and capture her. It did not take long for the three boats to overtake their quarry, and in the engagement ten British prisoners were seized and hurried to Jackson's headquarters. Interrogated, they revealed that the redcoats were digging a canal from the bayou to the Mississippi. The next morning, Commodore Patterson walked behind the levee on the west side of the river to a point directly opposite the British position and spent several hours observing their movements through his telescope. It soon became clear that the enemy were getting ready to transport soldiers to the west bank and planned an attack from *both* sides of the river by which to enfilade Jackson's position at the Rodriguez Canal.

The general had already reinforced the west bank on January 4 by shifting the 2nd Regiment of Louisiana militia to General David Morgan's command. This line of defense was established about three hundred yards in front of Patterson's marine battery. The original 260 militiamen under Morgan had been augmented with 160 troops from the Louisiana militia. When Patterson reported to the general what he had seen, Jackson then ordered the 1st Regiment to join the 2nd along with the Louisiana militia in reserve and detachments of the Kentucky troops. Unfortunately the four hundred Kentuckians ordered over under Colonel John Davis were poorly armed. At seven o'clock in the evening after a long hard day of labor at the parapet the Kentuckians marched back to New Orleans, where they crossed the river by ferry. About half of them had weapons or found them in the city, so only two hundred men set out to join Morgan. They arrived on the western shore about two o'clock in the morning. They were hungry, chilled to the bone, and exhausted. They moved south to Morgan's position over a rain-drenched road, walking knee-deep in mud and water. Not until four o'clock did they finally reach Morgan's outpost "as unfit for duty involving danger and exertion, as can be imagined."[8]

Morgan had been ordered to take a position opposite the British camp, and Major Latour had constructed a fortified line at Boisgervais's Canal on Dr. William Flood's plantation. A parapet was completed for the entire length of the canal, but a few days later, after the British had pulled back two miles from Jackson's lines, Morgan moved part of his troops forward to the adjoining Jourdan plantation and took a position near the southern boundary of the plantation. This advance consisted of 120 militiamen armed with fowling pieces (a light gun used to shoot birds) and musket cartridges that did not fit. If the advance was meant to bring a force to a spot where it could attack the British as they landed after crossing the Mississippi, it was completely misconceived. For one thing, the force was inadequate even with the addition of the exhausted and ill-armed Kentuckians; for another, the spot was several hundred yards from a likely landing area. The move proved to be totally unwise.

Back at his original position, Morgan had two six-pounders erected on his left under John Nixon of the Louisiana militia and one twelve-pounder under Lieutenant Philibert of the navy. Patterson's marine battery occupied a position to the rear of Morgan's line but could not protect him, since its guns were pointed directly east to flank the front of the Rodriguez Canal. Worse, Morgan had divided his command instead of concentrating his defense on a single line, as Jackson had done. Thus the arrangement of men and arms on the west bank was a disaster waiting to happen. And it came soon enough.

The British plan of attack was indeed as Jackson now understood it. After the failure of the New Year's Day artillery duel, Pakenham had called a meeting of his officers and proposed a two-pronged assault from both banks of the river. It would commence with an attack on the west bank. Jackson's guns would be seized and turned against his lines. Caught in a crossfire, the Americans would be driven from their position by the advancing British troops on the east side of the river. "For its boldness," declared Gleig, the scheme was worthy "of the school in which Sir Edward had studied his profession." With a larger force—he expected reinforcements momentarily—Sir Edward had the advantage of being able to divide his army between the two sides of the river, something Jackson could not do without seriously weakening his line at the Rodriguez Canal. Pakenham expected to ferry fourteen hundred men, along with some artillery, to the west bank, where they would move forward under darkness and attack Morgan's line at daybreak.[9]

To execute his plan Pakenham assigned Admiral Cochrane the task of conveying these troops across the Mississippi. In what one historian has called "a novel, bungling, and exceedingly laborious mode"[10] of transporting the necessary barges from the bayou, Cochrane set sailors and soldiers to work cutting a canal across the entire neck of land from the bayou to the river of sufficient width and depth to permit the boats to sail from the lake to the bayou and then to the Mississippi. The distance from the bayou to the river was approximately two miles. For an army that was already exhausted and dispirited, this was a gargantuan task. The officers and men argued against Cochrane's scheme and suggested that the barges be dragged on rollers just as the cannon had previously been dragged from the bayou to the river. And the cannon were infinitely heavier than the barges.

But Cochrane, a crusty old Scot, held his ground, and nothing the officers said dissuaded him. So the work began. The men were divided into four companies, and they labored night and day, the parties taking turns and relieving one another after a stated number of hours so that the work would go on around the clock. And it was backbreaking. As Gleig reported, "the fatigue undergone during the prosecution of this attempt no words can sufficiently describe."[11]

Unfortunately one disaster followed another in the implementation of this plan. The soil through which the canal was dug was soft because of the constant rain and the banks gave way and choked the canal, preventing the heaviest craft from moving forward. These blocked the movement of boats to the rear, and thus instead of a flotilla of ships made available to convey the troops across the river only a few boats got through. And it took from January 2 to the 6th to accomplish this much. Pakenham did not mind the delay, because he expected reinforcements and did not want to initiate his plan until they arrived.

And just as the work on the canal came to an end, the reinforcements appeared. They consisted of two regiments, the 7th (Fusiliers) and the 43rd Light Infantry, numbering seventeen hundred soldiers in all, with Major General John Lambert in command. Supposedly no two regiments stood higher in the number of laurels they had won in battle. The 7th Fusiliers wore blue facings to their red coats and a brass plate and white tufts in their caps. They also carried a light blue knapsack and used drums when marching. The 43rd had white facings, green tufts, and a curved bugle horn in their caps. They sported a black knapsack and preferred bugles to drums. Each member of both regiments carried sixty pounds of ball cartridge in his pouch as well as a firelock and bayonet with extra flints, picker, and brush. The officers of the 7th carried swords decorated with gold ornaments, those of the 43rd swords with silver ornaments. They were all veterans of recent campaigns in Spain and the south of France. Their commander, General Lambert, though young, had served under Wellington and had won the Iron Duke's confidence as an officer of unsurpassed courage. An Englishman by birth, he had been sent to America, like so many other young British generals, to win fame and fortune.[12]

Pakenham now had somewhere between eight and ten thousand soldiers under his command, a great majority of them well disciplined and highly skilled in their profession. In addition there was a large contingent of marines and sailors, who not only shared camp duty and the physical labor involved in all the daily tasks but stood ready to participate in the forthcoming battle if needed.

The new arrivals jokingly asked the veterans of the past fourteen days, "Why . . . how is it that you have not provided us with good quarters in New Orleans, as we expected. Why, what the d—l have you been about?"

The answer came with a snarl: "Oh! say no more about it."

Privately the veterans complained about the "hesitation" shown for the past two weeks. It was enough "as to make the very military blood curdle in one's veins."

But why the hesitation? What stopped you?

What stopped us? "Bullets stopped us—bullets—that's all."[13]

The arrival of the reinforcements and the completion of the canal gave the officers and men renewed belief in their ability to crush the unkempt, dirty, and untrained frontiersmen who dared to challenge their advance. Pakenham's plan of action also seemed infallible, and the rank and file regained confidence in the capability of their commanding officers to lead them to victory.

As a result there was heightened activity in the bivouac. The constant buzz and excitement of voices could be heard distinctly within the American lines. Several huts accidentally caught fire, adding to the "confusion, revelry, and mirth." Everyone seemed certain that Pakenham would finally rescue them from their entrapment.[14]

What the general planned to do was dispatch fourteen hundred men, consisting of the 85th, a portion of the West Indian regiment, and a number of marines and sailors, across the river under the command of one of the best officers of the entire operation, Colonel William Thornton. They would depart in barges on the night of Saturday, January 7, and carry with them a corps of rocketeers and three carronades.

Facing the main American army at the Rodriguez Canal, Pakenham divided his army into three brigades under Generals Gibbs, Keane, and Lambert. He stationed Gibbs on the right end of his line near the wood with the entire regiments of the 4th, 21st, and 44th along with three companies of the 95th Rifles. Gibbs's force, numbering 2,200 men, faced the segment of Jackson's line that ran from Battery No. 8 to the swamp and was considered by the British the most vulnerable part of the American defense. Gibbs's army constituted the main column of attack and was expected to hit Carroll's troops with tremendous force while a portion of the West Indian regiment created a diversion and attacked Coffee's men near the swamp.

Keane was posted on the left end of the line with about twelve hundred men, consisting of the 93rd Regiment, the remaining companies of the 95th, and the light companies of the 7th and 43rd and the remainder of the West Indian troops. Colonel Robert Rennie headed a column of light troops of less than a thousand men who were to move along the high road next to the river and attack the isolated redoubt that Jackson had just built a few feet in advance of his forward line. It was expected that once Thornton's men on the west bank captured Patterson's marine battery they would wait until a rocket signaled the main attack and then fire on Jackson's line while Keane's troops moved forward and seized the American position alongside the river.

About midway between Rennie's and Gibbs' columns of attack stood the 93rd Regiment, the crack Highlanders in their gorgeously appointed uniforms. They stood tall and proud with blankets rolled and slung across their backs and their bonnets devoid of their usual ornamentation. The sable plumes of real ostrich feathers that normally adorned their hats had been left in England. Colonel Robert Dale led them, but it was here that General Keane chose to command his brigade in person, and he seems to have decided to hold back the Highlanders until summoned or until either the left or right attacking forces appeared most in need of support.

The third brigade, consisting of the fusiliers and light infantry under General John Lambert and numbering about seventeen hundred men, was held in reserve about a mile to the rear. In all, Pakenham had over five thousand men on the line, including the reserves. Adding sailors, engineers, and the men crossing the Mississippi under Thornton, there were at least eight thousand British soldiers poised to seize New Orleans.

Once the main attack commenced, the 44th, an Irish regiment that had seen a great deal of service in America, would rush forward on the right side and hurl heavy fascines or bundles of sugarcane into the Rodriguez Canal to fill up the ditch, after which scaling ladders would be thrown against the parapet so it could be mounted. When their commanding officer, Colonel Mullens, heard what their assignment involved he reportedly said, "My regiment has been ordered to execution. Their dead bodies are to be used as a bridge for the rest of the army to march over."[15] On the left side of the line a corps of black troops was also assigned to carry the ladders and fascines for Keane's brigade.

The plan as Pakenham had devised it was an excellent one in the tried-and-true tradition of European warfare. Whether it would work on the swampy shores of the Mississippi would be tested the following day.

All Saturday afternoon while the British completed their preparation for the general attack, Jackson stood at the high window of the Macarty house and watched what was happening. Later he and General John Adair, who had taken over command of the Kentucky troops, replacing General Thomas, who was ill, made a final round of the lines, inspected each battery, and tested the strength of the parapet. When they reached the battery manned by the Baratarians, Jackson turned to one of his aides and said, "I wish I had fifty such guns on this line, with five hundred such devils as those fellows behind them." He was thinking, of course, of their superb performance during the artillery duel that had taken place on January 1. In fact, during the height of the main battle on January 8, Jackson was heard to say, "If I were ordered to storm the gates of hell, with Captain Dominique as my lieutenant, I would have no misgivings of the result!"[16]

He sampled some of the Baratarians' delicious-smelling coffee during his tour, slyly accusing them of smuggling it in. The pirates laughed and nodded their heads. Trying to hide the smile on his face, the general rode on.

When they had completed their tour, Jackson turned to Adair and said, "Well, what do you think of our situation? Can we defend these works or not?"

"There is one way, and but one way, in which we can hope to defend them," the Kentuckian reportedly replied. "We must have a strong corps of reserve to meet the enemy's main attack, wherever it may be. No single part of the lines is strong enough to resist the united force of the enemy."[17]

There were backup lines of defense at the Dupré and Montreuil plantations, but Jackson conceded that Adair was right and that additional troops were indeed needed as support at the rampart. So he commissioned Adair to take as many of his armed men as necessary to form a reserve corps and station them wherever he thought best.

To meet the British onslaught expected for the following day, Jackson strung out his troops over a line stretching 1,650 yards, 950 of which ran into the swamps and woods. The remaining seven hundred yards fronted an open field covered with stubble or weeds and cut by numerous small ditches. Between the Tennesseans, the Choctaw Indians, the marines, the New Orleans uniformed companies, the battalion of free men of color, the regular regiments, Adair's Kentuckians, Hinds's Mississippi Dragoons, and the Louisiana militia Old Hickory had a total of a little more than four thousand men on the line and in reserve.[18]

When Jackson returned from his tour with Adair he went immediately to his perch atop his headquarters and peered again at the activity of the enemy. With his telescope he could see a great number of soldiers and sailors busily moving something very unwieldy, which he supposed to be artillery. He also noticed soldiers at Laronde's plantation diligently making fascines while others constructed scaling ladders. Officers of the staff were riding from one position to another giving orders. Pickets near the wood had been increased and stationed closer together. Clearly a major attack was in the offing.

While Jackson stared out the high window of the Macarty house, Pakenham climbed a tree in the woods to examine the American line. By evening the Americans could hear the British working on reestablishing their batteries. Hammer strokes signaled the "note of preparation." American officers sent orders down the line that subalterns were to be ready at the first signal. Half of Jackson's troops spent the night behind the rampart, rotating regularly so that everyone could find a few moments of rest. Most of them believed that the next day they would face some "twelve to fifteen thousand bayonets," not counting two thousand additional marines and sailors held in reserve.[19]

By evening, despite their strenuous round-the-clock-labor, the British had fallen far behind in their time schedule. The canal, such as it was, had been completed late in the evening of January 6, but because of the cave-ins only a few boats reached the encampment. Thornton and his fourteen hundred men were supposed to cross the Mississippi immediately after dark on January 7. They arrived at the river's edge on schedule but found no boats. It meant that barges had to be dragged from the canal to the Mississippi. This extremely arduous task of hauling the boats more than two hundred yards delayed Thornton's departure by eight hours. In addition only about 340 men, 50 seamen, and another 50 marines out of the original fourteen hundred planned for the operation could be transported because of the limited number of barges.

Finally Thornton could wait no longer. If the major assault was to begin early Sunday morning, January 8, he and his men had to get moving. So, cursing their luck, they entered what boats were available and began to cross the river about three o'clock in the morning. Unaware of the treacherous currents of the Mississippi River, the British expected to row directly across to the opposite side. They soon learned otherwise. The river's current at this particular point ran at the rate of five miles an hour. When the barges pushed off from land they were seized by the mighty and unpredictable Mississippi and carried a mile and half downstream.

The plan called for these troops to land approximately three miles south of the American position. They were then to move rapidly along the bank, slice through Morgan's line, seize Patterson's marine battery, and turn these guns on Jackson's line, whereupon Pakenham would charge the rampart. Unfortunately, by the time Thornton and his men reached the west bank of the Mississippi, the attack on the east bank had already begun.

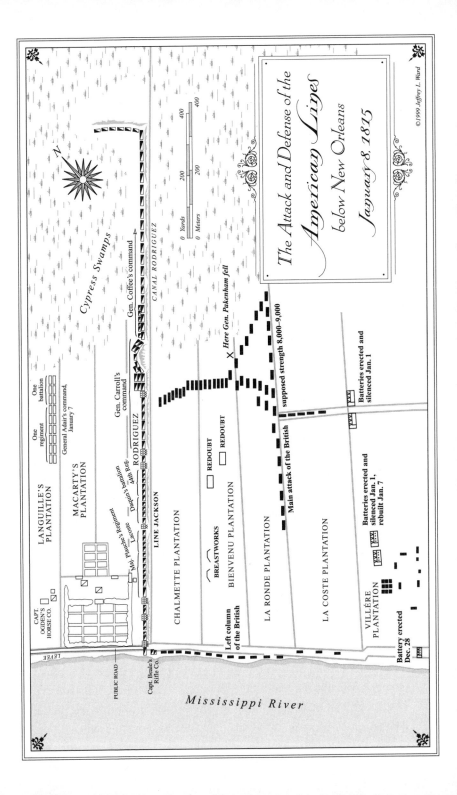

The Attack and Defense of the
American Lines
below New Orleans
January 8, 1815

©1999 Jeffrey L. Ward

Mississippi River

LEVEE

PUBLIC ROAD

Cypress Swamps

N

CANAL RODRIGUEZ

Gen. Coffee's command

General Adair's command, January 7

One regiment   One battalion

LANGUILLE'S PLANTATION

MACARTY'S PLANTATION

Gen. Carroll's command

RODRIGUEZ

CAPT. OGDEN'S HORSE CO.

Maj. Plauché's Regiment
Lacoste   Daquin's battalion
44th Reg.

LINE JACKSON

Capt. Beale's Rifle Co.

BREASTWORKS

REDOUBT

REDOUBT

Here Gen. Pakenham fell
X

supposed strength 8,000–9,000

Main attack of the British

Left column of the British

CHALMETTE PLANTATION

BIENVENU PLANTATION

LA RONDE PLANTATION

LA COSTE PLANTATION

VILLERÉ PLANTATION

Batteries erected and silenced Jan. 1

Batteries erected and silenced Jan. 1, rebuilt Jan. 7

Battery erected Dec. 28

0 Yards   200   400
0 Meters   200   400

Chapter 7

The Eighth of January

Commodore Patterson did not sleep that night. He, like everyone else, knew the main attack would come the following morning, so he again took his regular position on the western bank of the river directly opposite the British camp and watched and listened. His aide, Rezin D. Shepherd, the friend of Judah Touro, accompanied him. It was shortly before midnight. By the light of the campfires the two men could see a string of redcoats lining up along the levee. They heard the shouts of the sailors as they dragged the barges along the canal, fighting against the collapsing walls of the ditch. And they heard their cries of delight as they launched each boat with a loud splash into the Mississippi.

From the unusual activity along the levee and the raucous sound of so many voices it suddenly dawned on Patterson that the British were about to cross the Mississippi in force and launch their invasion from the west bank, not the east bank as expected. The thought nearly paralyzed him. Here was Jackson with thousands of men crouched behind a rampart of mud with eight batteries manned by some of the best gunners available, and here he was behind a redoubt recently built by Latour with an inadequate force poorly armed and a forward line of defense under Morgan, who had committed his army piecemeal.

Patterson's first thought was to order the *Louisiana* to drop down near the barges and blast them out of the water. But that was impossible, as he soon realized. Half the ship's guns and all her gunners had been removed to create the marine battery. To ready this ship to sail and fight would require the return of all the men from the battery. And if the attack actually did come on the east bank, Jackson would need the marine battery to set up a crossfire.

Patterson hurried back to his command post, muttering all the way about the weakness of Morgan's position and dreading the thought that the west bank could be overwhelmed and the enemy could capture New Orleans without a real fight. Unsure of his next move, he instructed Shepherd to cross the river and report personally to the general what they had seen and heard and implore him to send reinforcements. Shepherd hurried away.

General Jackson was sleeping on a couch in the Macarty house, his aides lying on the floor fully dressed except that their sword belts had been unbuckled and their pistols and swords laid to one side. A sentinel stood guard outside the room. When Shepherd arrived he informed the captain of the guard that he had an important message for the general, and he was immediately conducted to the room where Jackson was sleeping.

As the door opened, the commander raised his head. "Who's there?" he barked. Shepherd relayed Patterson's message and added that Morgan too felt that additional troops were needed on the west bank if the impending catastrophe was to be prevented.

"Hurry back," Jackson responded as he rose from the couch, "and tell General Morgan that he is mistaken. The main attack will be on this side, and I have no men to spare. He must maintain his position at all hazards."

Regretfully Shepherd withdrew, recrossed the river, and delivered Jackson's response. It can only be imagined what Patterson and Morgan felt on receiving this rejection of their pleas.

Once awakened, Jackson looked at his watch. It was after 1:00 A.M.

"Gentlemen," he called to his aides, "we have slept enough. Rise. The enemy will be upon us in a few minutes. I must go and see Coffee."[1]

The men roused themselves, buckled on their sword belts, grabbed their firearms, and followed Jackson out of the house. As the hours passed, all appeared to be in readiness. At four o'clock Adair marched his reserve of a thousand Kentuckians to the line and stationed them about fifty yards from the rampart immediately behind Carroll's men.

It was a stroke of pure luck, for this was the very part of the line where the British would concentrate their assault. The spot had been selected because an American deserter had informed Pakenham that it was the weakest area of Jackson's line, not knowing that Adair would bring his reserves to reinforce Carroll's position.[2] Between Coffee's men and Carroll's and now Adair's, the British attack was facing a massed force of well over three thousand men.

As dawn approached, drums thundered an end to sleep and the American troops roused themselves. Some of them fixed a breakfast of bacon and cornbread with either coffee or something stronger.[3] Knowing that the day could bring death or mutilation, any number of Creoles opted to skip breakfast.

Not far away, British troops were also being roused from their sleep. As they fumbled for their knapsacks and muskets they shivered in the cold. No fires were permitted for them to warm themselves or heat some food. Dry biscuits were distributed. Since the moment of their arrival, few had undressed or bathed. Heavy rains had pelted them daily, accompanied by thunder and lightning; the rain usually lasted the entire day and ceased only toward dark when cold frosts took its place. The soldiers were alternately wet and cold: soaked by day, frozen at night. And now they were expected to go into action. Bone-tired and utterly miserable, they nonetheless formed their ranks on the soft, mushy ground and moved through the sugarcane stubble into position, expecting to win a great victory within a matter of a few hours.[4]

Like Jackson, Pakenham had tried to get some rest, in the Villeré house, but he only slept fitfully. Finally he rose and rode to the bank of the river where Thornton had just set sail with his diminished force. This attack group slipped quickly out of sight, and he listened for the sounds that would tell him the progress of the flotilla. But he heard nothing. The swiftly moving Mississippi swept the men far downstream and well out of sight and sound. It is interesting to speculate whether Pakenham in that moment knew that the timing of a concerted attack on the west and east banks was totally askew, that under no circumstances would Thornton get to his designated position by daybreak. If he did, he had no intention of altering his schedule. His men were geared up for an early-morning attack, and any delay in the operation could affect their morale and performance.

Shortly after four o'clock, Pakenham rode away from the riverbank. Turning to one of his aides, he said, "I will wait my own plans no longer."[5] Most probably he hoped to launch his attack while it was still dark and thus surprise his enemy and reduce the effectiveness of their fire. He delayed for a little while in the hope that Thornton could get into position. But once the rising sun began to disperse the darkness he knew he had to act.

Deep in his thoughts and sense of apprehension, Pakenham rode past the Highlanders. Colonel Dale, looking morose and depressed, stood near his men. The regiment's physician, Dr. Dempster, approached Dale and told him about the delay in getting Thornton and his men to the west bank of the river.

Dale did not reply. Instead he took out his watch and a letter he had written and handed them to the doctor and said, "Give these to my wife; I shall die at the head of my regiment."[6]

Pakenham continued riding until he came to Gibbs's column, where the major thrust of the invasion would be launched. Gibbs appeared annoyed and angry. The Irish regiment commanded by Mullens had not taken the fascines and ladders to the head of the column where they belonged. The fascines and ladders had to go first if his brigade was to achieve its objective. He had already sent an officer to discover the reason for the delay and expected a report momentarily.

Impatient to know the cause of the delay, Pakenham sent his own aide, Major Sir John Tylden, to ascertain whether the 44th Regiment could get into position in time. At Mullens's subsequent court-martial,

Tylden testified that when he found the Irish troops he discovered that they had just started to move, and move "in a most irregular and unsoldierlike manner, with the fascines and ladders." All of which he reported back to Pakenham. Tylden supposed that in the time that had elapsed since he left the regiment "they must have arrived at their situation in column." He could not have been more mistaken.

Delay. Delay. Delay. More time had been lost. The entire operation depended for success on coordination of several segments of the attack, with each one moving according to a predetermined schedule. And none of it was developing as planned.

The attack should have been aborted, right then and there. But Pakenham had no intention of calling a halt. "I will wait my plans no longer," he had said, and he meant it. Impatient, if not reckless, he would not wait to have absolute proof that the 44th had reached its position at the head of the main column of attack. Their being in position was critical. Pakenham simply dismissed the seriousness of the problem. Arrogant and overconfident, he undoubtedly assumed that he was facing an inferior force of undisciplined frontiersmen who would run as soon as charging infantryman with fixed bayonets came barreling at them. Despite the previous incidents of American ability and courage he could not conceive of a rabble, a ragtag collection of misfits, defeating the greatest army on the continent if not in the world.

Pakenham's impetuosity in the Peninsular War had brought victory. Here outside New Orleans it would bring devastating defeat.

He looked across the field. He looked at his columns of soldiers. Without another moment's thought he gave the order:

"FIRE!"

He hardly moved a muscle as he commanded "that the FATAL, *the ever-fatal rocket* should be discharged as a signal . . . to begin the assault on the left of the American lines."[7]

If there was confusion among Gibbs's column there was bewilderment among General Keane's troops. A thick mist covered the ground when the sun came up. This was exactly what Pakenham needed. If he could not attack under cover of darkness, a fog would serve just as well. Then, slowly, as the light of the new day spread across the field separating the two armies, the mist thinned and rolled away, but objects were visible only two or three hundred yards distant.

Suddenly a rocket rose with a screech. But Keane's men were puzzled. Where did the rocket come from? The American side or British? As the rocket ascended it whizzed backward and forward in such a zigzag way, reported Captain Cooke, that his troops stared upward to see if it would descend upon them. So the men stood there, looking upward, like the apostles after Christ's ascension, and not advancing as the plan directed. Small wonder. Incredible as it may seem, they did not know that the rocket was the signal to begin the attack! Never, said Cooke, in all his years of military service, had he seen such a strange configuration of men standing in a circle, looking upward, and not knowing what they were expected to do or where the anticipated firing would begin.[8]

"All was silent." No one moved. It lasted about two minutes and then "the most vehement firing from the British artillery" on the right shattered the silence, answered immediately by the American artillery. Suddenly cannonballs came tearing through the ground, crisscrossing each other "and bounding along like so many cricket-balls through the air." Then, said Gleig, the Americans "opened upon us from right to left, a fire of musketry, grape, round-shot, and canister, than which I have certainly never witnessed any more murderous."[9]

The final great action in the Battle of New Orleans, which had been anticipated for over a month, had finally begun.

The general attack seemed to start well for the British. On the left side of the line, Colonel Rennie's troops crept forward to catch the outposts along the river before they could run for cover. Supposedly this was a diversion for Gibbs's main attack. Surprised by the sudden burst of the rocket and now with soldiers charging toward them, the American outposts could think of nothing but heading for the isolated redoubt. The British caught up with them, but it was so difficult to distinguish one soldier from the other because of the fog that Captain Humphrey withheld his fire. He feared killing his own men.

The outposts reached the redoubt and piled into it, their pursuers right after them. They fought hand-to-hand. Outnumbered, the Americans had no choice but to abandon the redoubt and cross the plank to find safety behind Jackson's lines. Once his men reached him, Humphrey then opened up on the redoubt and was joined by Patterson's marine battery three-quarters of a mile across the river. Rennie, two other officers, and three men from the column managed to reach the rampart near the edge of the Mississippi. Rennie, already hit in the calf by grape, climbed the parapet and shouted to his men, "Hurra, boys! the day is ours." As he spoke these words a volley from the New Orleans Rifles under Captain Beale struck him and his fellow officers and pitched them lifeless into the ditch. The rest of Rennie's column turned and ran, some along the levee, some along the road, and others below the road—all showered with cannonballs, musket fire, and grapeshot from Humphrey's and Patterson's battalions. Those who thought they could find protection by running along the riverbank under the protection of the levee found themselves blasted with volleys of grapeshot from the marine battery. Soon scores of dead and wounded lay strewn along the bank.

The three slain officers were dragged from the ditch and taken behind the lines. Almost immediately a contest broke out among the New Orleans company as to who would claim the honor of having dispatched the British colonel. A man named Withers, a merchant in town and recognized by all as the best shot in the group, settled the argument with the simple statement "If he isn't hit above the eyebrows, it wasn't my shot."

The others rolled Rennie's body over, and sure enough the fatal shot had caught the officer just over the eyebrows. Withers was therefore granted the recognition of having killed the colonel but also given the responsibility of returning Rennie's watch, purse, and other valuables to the officer's widow, who was among the wives stationed in the fleet off Lake Borgne. The other two officers had been riddled with rifle balls.[10]

Then, out of the mist, came a company of West Indian soldiers carrying ladders on their shoulders, but they were so confused by the noise that they dropped the ladders and fell flat on their faces. The sight of these "poor creatures," said Cooke, astonished us, knowing that such a responsibility "requires the very elite of an army," and "the most desperate efforts to lug [the ladders] along over broken ground, ditches, and other obstacles."[11]

This melancholy start to the British attack on the left was quickly repeated at the other end of the line. With the firing of the rocket, Gibbs's column began to move. But the 44th was nowhere to be seen. They were straggling in the rear, one officer reported, and they had the fascines and ladders needed to cross the ditch and mount the parapet. Mullens's disobedience and the confusion it caused among the attacking troops moved Gibbs to swear revenge. "Let me live till to-morrow and I'll hang him to the highest tree in that swamp."[12] Mullens, the son of a nobleman, had obtained his commission and promotions by influence, not ability. He was hardly the man to lead the charge of the storming Irishmen.

Gibbs's column soon reached the American outposts. The frontiersmen, fully alert to the probability of the attack that morning, began firing their muskets. They gave ground, slowly at first, but as the British continued to advance they turned and ran as fast as they could. They hurled themselves across the ditch and scrambled over the parapet to warn their comrades that the main attack had begun.

Lieutenant Spotts of Battery No. 6 was perhaps the first man in the American lines to catch sight of the advancing enemy. The fog continued to lift, and the light of the rising sun soon illuminated the entire plain. And there they were: the massed might of the British empire, all decked out in their splendid scarlet uniforms and shining accouterments.

It was a gorgeous and frightening sight. Thousands of men lined up in precise formations across two-thirds of the plain from the river to the woods, flags and standards fluttering in the slight breeze, rockets blazing as they whooshed into the sky, drums beating in unison, bugles blaring their call to advance, and men in the rear holding heavy fascines and unwieldy ladders. It was an extraordinary military spectacle, the kind that only His Majesty's army could provide. The sight alone had been said to overawe an enemy and send them rushing head-long in retreat.

Not this time. The Americans came to life on finally seeing them. Cheers erupted from Carroll's troops, followed by cheers from the Kentuckians standing behind them. But these were not the huzzas of approval; they were the cheers of men who welcomed the opportunity to prove once and for all that they were freemen whose liberty could be successfully defended against this implacable and ancient foe.

The British cheered too. They were the cheers of men who thought they could finally escape from their entrapment and smash through the American line, reach New Orleans and share the "Beauty and Booty" that awaited them. They were the cheers of the doomed.

When Gibbs ordered his column to advance, the troops swung into immediate action, heading directly towards Batteries No. 6, 7, and 8. The column was outside the reach of Patterson's marine battery but headed straight toward the part of Jackson's line that had the largest concentration of men and rifles.

As these troops drew closer, the three American artillery batteries opened up on them. The brass pieces, "the noisiest kind of varment," recorded one Kentuckian, "began blaring away as hard as they could, while the heavy iron cannon . . . joined in the chorus and made the ground shake under our feet." The guns punched large gaping holes in the ranks of the advancing troops that penetrated from front to rear. The holes were quickly filled by obedient and disciplined redcoats as the mud rampart rebuked them again and again—right into their faces. Men and body parts were hurled in every direction. It was the beginning of a slaughter.

Still the column advanced under a barrage that mowed down whole sections. A thirty-two-pounder "filled up to the very muzzle with musket balls" slammed into the head of the column at point-blank range "and served to sweep the center of the attacking force into eternity." It was later computed that two hundred casualties resulted from this single blast.[13]

It was only minutes before the British troops came within range of the small arms, the Tennessee rifles, the Kentucky muskets, and four lines of sharpshooters, lined up one behind the other. Before giving the order to open fire, General Carroll waited patiently for the enemy to reach the precise position he had previously designated in his mind as the spot where, when they fired, his men could inflict the most damage. It seemed to take an eternity.

Finally the British came to within two hundred yards.

Carroll screamed, "Fire! Fire!"

The entire line erupted as rifles, muskets, and small arms emptied into the ranks of the onrushing redcoats. The embankment was one long "line of spurting fire." The initial roar of defiance that echoed over the plain was answered by the British batteries, which showered rockets over the entire scene and kept it up throughout the battle. The marine battery also joined the ruckus, and the scene became one awful sight of exploding shells and bodies. It developed into a constant rolling fire of tremendous noise that resembled the "rattling peals of thunder." It seemed as if the earth was cracking or the heavens had been rent asunder, said Captain Cooke. "It was the most awful and the grandest mixture of sounds to be conceived." Adding to the din, the New Orleans band started playing "Yankee Doodle," and it continued playing every martial air in its repertory throughout the entire engagement.

"Stand to your guns," Jackson shouted as he continually glanced up and down the line, "don't waste our ammunition—see that every shot tells." He stood in a prominent position slightly to the right of Plauché's battalion so he could command a view of the entire line. But within minutes he could barely see from one battery to the next. "The morning had dawned to be sure," wrote an American, "but the smoke was so thick that every thing seemed to be covered up in it."[14]

Gibbs's column continued its forward momentum, but the 21st, which led the charge, was broken. British officers of the corps that followed managed to keep control of their troops by obliquing them to the left to avoid the fire of Battery No. 7, which hit them again and again and decimated whole files of men.

"Give it to them, my boys," Jackson cried. "Let us finish the business today."[15]

"Fire! Fire!" Carroll called out again, as the American ranks rotated, line after line. The first line discharged their death-dealing missiles and then stepped back to reload. Meanwhile the second line advanced, emptied their guns at the British, and then made way for the third line. After performing their duty, the third line retreated as the fourth line took their place. The fire of the Tennessee and Kentucky marksmen was therefore continuous, with no interruption or interval. "Our men," remembered one Kentuckian, "did not seem to apprehend any danger, but would load and fire as fast as they could, talking, swearing, and joking all the time."

What made it worse for the British was the fact that they could not see their enemy, "for the Americans, without so much as lifting their faces above the rampart, swung their firelocks by one arm over the wall, and discharged them directly upon [our] heads." We "were mowed down by the hundreds," moaned Gleig. Several times the column halted, only to re-form and start forward again.[16]

The front and flanks of the British line melted away under this unrelenting fire. The horror of the scene was orchestrated by the rolling thunder pounding out from the American rampart, by the pitiful screams and cries of wounded and dying men, by the incessant whoosh of the rockets, the roar of the cannons, the blast of chain shot and grape, and the bark of musketry. The carnage was simply frightful.

The Tennessee and Kentucky riflemen never seemed to miss a target, so skilled were they. With each shot a redcoat collapsed to the ground, many of them falling on their comrades. Soon the bodies seemed to be stacked, one on top of the other.

Major Harry Smith, one of Pakenham's aides, said he never in his life witnessed a more destructive fire poured upon a single line of men.[17]

One of the Kentucky officers, on seeing the redcoats lying on the ground, jumped on top of the parapet and called to his men in his Irish brogue, "Shoot low, boys! shoot low! rake them—rake them! They're coming on their all fours."[18]

Once the advancing troops caught sight of the ditch they realized they had no means of crossing it and scaling the rampart.

"Where are the 44th?" the men cried out. Where are the fascines and ladders?

General Gibbs turned around and saw the 44th coming toward him. "Here comes the 44th," he assured his men. "Here comes the 44th."

A large detachment of the 44th, some of whom still had their fascines and ladders, rushed forward, led by Pakenham himself. The general had called for Mullens to advance, but Mullens had disappeared, so Pakenham placed himself at the head of the 44th and led them toward the rampart. He tried to inspire these troops by reminding them of their ancient victories, especially in Egypt, and calling them countrymen.

Suddenly Pakenham's bridle arm was struck by a bullet; another killed his horse and dropped it to the ground. He quickly scrambled to his feet and mounted the Creole pony of his aide Captain Duncan McDougall.

Gibbs's column pressed on in the face of that murderous fire, their path strewed with the dead and wounded. Many of the officers were struck down, and with their number diminished, the column began to break into small detachments. Some of the men continued toward the ditch, throwing off their knapsacks as they went, but most of them turned and ran from the "flashing and roaring hell" in front of them.[19] It was too much. The horror that surrounded them could no longer be endured.

Pakenham tried to restore order. "For shame," he shouted; "recollect that you are British soldiers. *This* is the road you ought to take!" as he pointed toward the deathtrap in front of them.

He rode on and soon encountered Gibbs, who was screaming at his men to re-form and advance. But the troops continued their headlong flight.

"I am sorry to have to report to you," Gibbs cried out to Pakenham, "that the troops will not obey me. They will not follow me."

"Forty-third," Lieutenant Colonel Stovin shouted, "for God's sake, save the day!" What he obviously meant was the reserve under General Lambert's command.

At this point General Keane finally made his move. He had held his

Highlanders, the 93rd Regiment, in reserve until he saw where they were most needed. Now he pushed forward to support Gibbs's attack. He made a successful feint on the right side of Jackson's line and then ordered the nine hundred Highlanders, with a front of one hundred men, to oblique to the right and head into the fire. "Never," said Gleig, "was any step taken more imprudently, or with less judgment." Bagpipes began playing "Monymusk," the regimental charge, and the tartan-trousered Highlanders, their bayonets glittering in the sun, moved at a quick-step pace, Colonel Dale leading the way. At the sight of this solid phalanx of support running toward them, Gibbs's troops halted their flight. They removed their heavy knapsacks, re-formed, and prepared for a second charge at the rampart.[20]

But the Americans watched and waited. Then as the 93rd approached, the dirty shirts roared another order to halt. Rifle, grape, round, buckshot, and musketry raked the entire line, the front, and both flanks. Colonel Dale took a grapeshot that passed clean through his body and fell lifeless to the ground.

But the Highlanders kept coming, although their pace had slowed considerably. They finally reached a point about one hundred yards from the rampart, where, for some quite understandable reason, they halted. As they stood there motionless, Carroll's men rained down on them a torrent of fiery hell and slew nearly six hundred of them. As they awakened to the horror they faced, the Highlanders finally broke and fled. "Before they reached our small arms, our grape and canister mowed down whole columns," said General Coffee, "but that was nothing to the carnage of our Rifles and muskets."[21]

The British West Indian corps of blacks also advanced and made their way into the woods in a diversionary action, but Coffee's men and the Choctaws dispersed them with rifle fire in less than ten minutes and sent them scurrying to the rear.

The open plain from the river to the wood had become a killing field. Whole regiments had been shattered, broken, and dispersed. Order in the ranks vanished. Men were running in all directions so that it was impossible to know whether they were British or Americans. Captain Cooke was so astonished by the panic among the fleeing troops, something he had never seen before, that he halted a retreating soldier and asked, "Have we or the Americans attacked?"

"We attacked, Sir," came the despairing reply.

Lieutenant Duncan Campbell of the 43rd was running around in circles, staggering first in one direction, then another. Finally he fell to the ground but tried to raise himself. When help arrived it was obvious he was blind from a grapeshot that had torn open his forehead. As he was lifted and carried to the rear, Campbell still clenched the hilt of his sword, the blade having been broken off close to the hilt by grapeshot. He lived for a few days in a state of delirium.[22]

As General Pakenham looked around him he suddenly realized what was happening to his army. Utter and humiliating defeat stared him in the face.

"Order up the reserve," he shouted to his aide Major Tylden, meaning, of course, General Lambert's army, stationed a mile away.

Pakenham turned and saw the Highlanders. His right arm was useless, since it had taken a bullet, so he removed his hat with his left hand and waved it at them in salute.

"Hurrah! brave Highlanders!" he cried out.

No sooner had the words left his mouth than a terrible crash of grapeshot struck the group surrounding the commander. One shot pierced Pakenham's thigh, killed his horse, and pitched both to the ground. As he rolled from the horse, his aide Captain MacDougal rushed forward and caught him in his arms. As MacDougal and several other men attempted to raise the general, another shot struck Pakenham in the groin and immediately paralyzed him.

The unconscious and dying commander was moved to the rear and placed in the shade of an old oak tree out of reach of the American guns. A surgeon was summoned, and he declared the wound mortal. A few moments later, Lieutenant General Sir Edward Michael Pakenham died.[23]

General Gibbs suffered an even more painful death. Shortly after Pakenham fell, Gibbs tried to rally what was left of the column. He had gotten to within twenty yards of the rampart when he received a mortal wound and was carried to the rear, writhing in agony. He lingered for the remainder of the day and night, and finally found release the following day when he expired.

Keane too was badly wounded in the neck and thigh and removed from the field. Now not a single field officer remained to command and rally the broken column. The destruction of the high command, said General Lambert in his report to Lord Bathurst, "caused a wavering in the column which in such a situation became irreparable."[24]

Without their leader and completely demoralized, Gibbs's men ran from the killing field and hid themselves in wet ditches and behind trees and bushes near the swamps. Officers struck them with the flat of their swords, or pricked them from behind with the points of their weapons, all the while cursing them for their cowardice. But nothing could induce them to turn around and face the destruction behind them.

"Did you ever see such scene?" declared Lieutenant Colonel Smith, one of Pakenham's aides, to Captain Cooke. "There is nothing left but the seventh and forty-third!"

That damned rocket, cried Cooke. It had been fired before we were ready, before the troops had gotten into position. It had only served to alert every American gun behind the parapet that we were attacking.[25]

Still, a few courageous souls did not flee and did not lose heart. About two hundred men reached the ditch, including Lieutenant Gleig. They tried to scale the parapet, but without ladders they could not reach the top. They scrambled up the wall as best they could and got just so far before sliding down into the soft mud. Gleig himself finally reached the summit and was prepared to "spring among the enemy" when a bullet struck him in the head and he fell back into the ditch. Several of his men rescued him and later carried him to safety when the firing stopped.[26]

Major Wilkinson and Lieutenant Lavack, followed by about twenty men, also reached the ditch, jumped across it, and mounted the rampart, one man standing on the shoulders of another to reach the top. As

Wilkinson pulled himself above the breastwork he was riddled with Tennessee and Kentucky grape and rifle fire. But the Americans were amazed at Wilkinson's bravery, and so they gently moved his body from the parapet and carried it behind the lines.

Major Smiley, a kind-hearted Kentuckian, tried to minister to the dying man.

"Bear up, my dear fellow," he said, "you are too brave a man to die."

Wilkinson looked at Smiley and in whispered tones replied, "I thank you from my heart. It is all over for me. You can render me a favor; it is to communicate to my commander that I fell on your parapet, and died like a soldier and a true Englishman."

Wilkinson died two hours later.[27]

Lavack of the 21st Fusiliers enjoyed a happier fate. He mounted the breastwork unharmed, although two bullets tore through his hat. He immediately demanded the swords of the first two American officers he saw. They laughed at him. Surrender their swords? One of them said, "Oh, no; you are alone, and, therefore ought to consider yourself our prisoner."

Lavack looked around and to his amazement saw none but "dirty shirts." The men in his command had thrown themselves into the ditch, where they cowered under the protection of the embankment. At least it provided shelter from the withering American gunfire.[28]

General Lambert, meanwhile, was informed of Pakenham's death and the severe wounding of Gibbs and Keane. He then began to move forward with the reserve, but he moved slowly and cautiously. Pakenham had tried to summon him just before he took the fatal shot to the groin. He had told his aide Major Tylden to order up the reserve. Tylden gave the order, but as the bugler was about to sound the advance he was struck in the arm with a bullet and the bugle fell from his hand. So the order was never given and the reserve only served to cover the retreat of what was left of the two other brigades.

As the firing lessened and the smoke and mist began to dissipate, the shocking and unbelievable sight of a battlefield strewn with dead and wounded bodies was revealed. Of the three thousand who constituted the attacking British force, fewer than a thousand escaped death or injury. Captain Cooke noted, "They fell like the very blades of grass beneath the scythe of the mower."[29] His Majesty's army lay in shreds.

Still, one lone bugle boy of fourteen or fifteen had managed to climb a tree within 200 yards of the American line. He straddled a limb and throughout the battle kept blowing the charge with all the breath within him. While cannonballs and grapeshot whistled around him, tearing off branches of the tree and shaking the ground, the boy continued to blow the charge. Even when the remnants of the army retreated he did not stop. In fact, he blew with undiminished strength and determination.

He was finally captured by an American soldier and brought into the camp. To his amazement he was embraced and praised for his gallantry. He had stayed at his post to the bitter end, something few other British soldiers could claim.

Several other Americans rushed onto the field to take captives. One Tennessean came upon a slightly wounded British officer and demanded his surrender. The officer looked at his dirty, unkempt, wild-eyed captor with contempt. Surrender to such a person? Never. He disregarded the call and kept walking toward his own lines.

"Halt, Mr. Red Coat," the dirty shirt cried out, as he drew a bead on the officer. "One more step and I'll drill a hole through your leather."

The officer froze in his tracks, turned around, and with a look of profound resignation said, "What a disgrace for a British officer to have to surrender to a chimney-sweep!"[30]

The day's disaster was indisputably the most humiliating experience in the lives of virtually every member of the entire British force. Even so, most British officers and men had demonstrated incredible bravery in facing what one officer described as one of the most impossible enterprises ever conceived.

But who could believe it? Who could believe that this band of frontiersmen, privateers, men of color, local citizens, state militiamen, and army regulars had annihilated the most modern and most powerful army in the world? Captain Cooke said that it was "more like a dream, or some scene of enchantment, than reality."

Indeed! Three generals, seven colonels, seventy-five officers, and nearly two thousand men had fallen.[31]

How had it happened? What had gone wrong? One important fact in the catastrophe was the belief within the high command that the Americans would not fight—not a well-disciplined fighting machine like the one they faced—and that the people of Louisiana would throw off their allegiance to the United States and side with the English. Much of the invasion plans were based on these erroneous assumptions. Tactically, the army's attack on January 8 was sluggish against Jackson's lines. Small wonder when it is remembered what load the soldiers carried. In addition to their knapsacks, which usually weighed about thirty pounds, they carried muskets that were too heavy by at least a third. Also, many of them handled fascines from nine to ten inches in diameter and four feet long, made of ripe sugarcane and extremely heavy; or they hauled ladders ten to twelve feet long. The British army always had a reputation for moving slowly and doggedly, a tactic more suited to a pitched battle than an assault. They should have charged at full speed with fixed bayonets.

Then, too, there were the weather and ground conditions and the cantankerous Mississippi; also the lack of proper transports to navigate the lakes and bayous; finally the poorly synchronized segments of the assault. Pakenham was much too impetuous, much too arrogant about what he could accomplish with an army that should never have attacked when it did.

But what should not be forgotten in explaining why and how the battle turned out the way it did was the excellence of the so-called ragtag army of Americans. First of all, the rank and file were excellent marksmen. In addition, many of the officers and the Tennesseans had served with Jackson during the Creek War and were devoted to his leadership. And the regulars were officered by excellent and experienced men, led by a commander who even the British conceded was "first class both in attack and defence." Furthermore, a large number of Louisianians, including the battalion of free blacks, had served in the armies of France or in the Caribbean and had experienced military life and discipline. Perhaps most important of all were the privateers, who provided Jackson with supplies and ammunition and virtually the entire corps of gunners. And they performed miracles. The Americans owed their victory to their own skill and heroism, not simply the mistakes or bad luck of the British.[32]

The battle on the east bank of the Mississippi had now ended, and from start to finish it had lasted no longer than twenty-five minutes. But desultory shooting continued for five hours. As long as a British soldier showed any sign of renewing the charge, shots would ring out to put a stop to it.

As the broken columns retreated from the field, Major Hinds, whose Mississippi Dragoons were drawn up in the rear, approached Jackson and asked permission to pursue the fleeing troops and cut them to shreds. It certainly was tempting. It might also be a means of cutting them off from their ships. But the cautious Jackson hesitated. He summoned an informal council of his senior officers and asked their opinion. They unanimously opposed the idea.

"What do you want more?" asked Livingston. "Your object is gained. The city is saved. The British have retired. For the pleasure of a blow or two, will you risk against those fearless troops your handful of men, composed of the best and worthiest citizens, and rob so many families of their heads!"[33]

The temptation to pursue was indeed great, but Jackson instinctively knew that it had hazard written all over it. He still faced a dangerous and powerful army. To attempt an engagement in the open field could lead to disaster. Besides, the British troops were itching for "a renewal of the combat" in the keen anticipation of regaining their lost honor and brightening their tarnished laurels.[34] Wisely, Jackson refused to risk everything he had won and jeopardize the safety of his army. He later explained, "My reason for refusing was that it might become necessary to sustain him [Hinds], and thus a contest in the open field be brought on: the lives of my men were of value to their country, and much too dear to their families to be hazarded where necessity did not require it; but, above all, from the numerous dead and wounded stretched out on the field before me, I felt a confidence that the safety of the city was most probably attained, and hence that nothing calculated to reverse the good fortune we had met should be attempted."[35]

Interestingly, most of the carnage was inflicted by the extreme left and right of Jackson's lines. Plauché's, Daquin's, and Lacoste's battalions and the 44th Infantry in the middle hardly fired a shot, except where individual sharpshooters turned about forty-five degrees to score hits on the enemy. But the commanders of these groups tried to keep their men from firing so that they would be ready in an instant to repel a frontal attack if it came. The men at times grew impatient, so desperate were they to share in the active defense of their city. The fact that for the most part they obeyed their commanders, perhaps understanding the reason behind it, indicates not only their determination to do whatever would best protect the line, even if it meant sacrificing their chance to smite the enemy, but the degree of control that was exercised by their officers.

Finally an order went down the American line to cease fire. At that point, Jackson left his station near Plauché's battalion, and accompanied by his staff, began to congratulate his men and thank them for their heroism and skill. He walked from battery to battery, addressing all the commanders and their men, both those at the individual batteries and those strung along the line between the batteries. And as he walked the band played "Hail Columbia," while the men cheered their chief with loud bursts of "Huzza, huzza."

As the smoke cleared from the field, the American sharpshooters, regulars, militiamen, Indians, pirates, blacks, and others peered over the parapet and for the first time saw the apocalyptic scene of death and suffering. Bodies were piled on top of one another, indeed, whole platoons mowed down together as if by a single discharge. For two hundred yards in front of Carroll's position the bodies were so numerous that the area was literally covered by the dead and dying. It was like a sea of red, remembered one Kentucky militiaman, not because of the blood but because of the number of red coats lying side by side. One could walk on the bodies of the dead without touching the ground. There were also forty lifeless bodies in the ditch in front of the parapet and at least a hundred more who were wounded. What made it worse was the cries, the groans, and the shrieks of the wounded, the convulsive jerking of limbs, sometimes from underneath other dead soldiers, and the writhing and twitching of bodies in the final throes of an agonizing death. And there were body parts everywhere: arms, legs, heads, torsos. Tatum said it was "truly distressing." The horror of it all. "Arms, legs & thighs had been shattered, in great abundance, by our Grape & ball, as well as by our riffles & musquets." "Some had their heads shot off, some their legs, some their arms. Some were laughing, some crying, some groaning, and some screaming. There was every variety of sight and sound." Vincent Nolte, the New Orleans merchant, called it "the field of slaughter."[36]

From every quarter of the plain came awful cries for help. Boys not yet out of their teens, delirious in their agony, begged for release from their torment. Some Americans ventured onto the field to bring succor and render whatever assistance they could to the wounded. They brought water and lifted a number of British troops across the American lines to receive whatever medical aid was available. Not that it amounted to much.

Jackson himself stood transfixed when he surveyed the battle-field. For a long time he just stared at what seemed like a charnel house. "I never had so grand and awful an idea of the resurrection as on that day," he later confessed. "After the smoke of the battle had cleared off somewhat, I saw in the distance more than five hundred Britons emerging from the heaps of their dead comrades, all over the plain, rising up, and still more distinctly visible as the field became clearer, coming forward and surrendering as prisoners of war to our soldiers. They had fallen at our first fire upon them, without having received so much as a scratch, and lay prostrate, as if dead, until the close of the action."[37]

With the conclusion of the firing, scavengers roamed among the dead retrieving what looked valuable, such as swords, bayonets, knives, telescopes, money, guns, and ammunition, or anything that could serve as a souvenir. In some instances the bodies were stripped of their uniforms "to be hawked about the streets of New Orleans in triumph, or the caps placed on the heads of Americans, and the tufts and feathers of officers and soldiers stuck into their hats as trophies of the day." At least a thousand stand of arms were collected by these enterprising scoundrels, some of which had to be surrendered when it was discovered they belonged to Pakenham or one of the other generals.[38]

Prisoners were also rounded up and together with the wounded were placed in carts or lined up in groups to be hurried off to the city. Because the hospitals were filled with American patients a call went out to the citizens to assist in this operation of mercy. Almost immediately, 140 mattresses and a large number of pillows, lint, and linen to bind wounds were collected from all quarters. Food and drink were also provided, and "several women of colour offered their services" as nurses. The British later admitted that the Americans had shown great kindness and dutiful attention to their wounded. "To their credit," wrote Captain Cooke, "when once within their lines, [our injured soldiers] were treated with the greatest humanity, put into good houses, and their wants supplied with unsparing hand."[39]

Some of the prisoners seemed delighted with their capture, especially the Irish. They revealed under questioning that when they left their own country they had had absolutely no idea where they were going, and no one would tell them. Furthermore, they said they had never wanted to fight the Americans.

"Why, then," asked one of their guards, "did you march up so boldly to our lines, in face of such fire?"

"And 'faith were we not obliged," came the answer, "with officers behind, sticking and stabbing us with their swords."[40]

Throughout the battle the aged men and women in New Orleans, in their own particular way, assisted the heroic efforts of their countrymen on the firing line by tending the wounded and offering up prayers and supplications to the Almighty to spare the city the horror of capture. Madame Devance Bienvenu, a wealthy widow living in Atakapas, who had sent her four sons to the battlefield, wrote Governor Claiborne and expressed her regret that she did not have any more sons to offer her country. However, if her own services could be thought useful in caring for the wounded, she would hasten at once to New Orleans, despite her advanced age and the great distance of her residence. What is more, she would pray daily for the success of American arms and the safety of her boys.

Many other New Orleanians prayed as well. The cathedral was opened each day, and "devout Creoles and quadroons" crowded inside to pray and beg for deliverance. Ursuline nuns in their convent began the day by examining the calendar of saints, and to their surprise and delight they discovered that January 8 was the feast day of St. Victoria! What an auspicious sign! They prostrated themselves and implored the saint to intercede on their behalf and save the city.[41]

There can be no doubt that on the east bank their prayers had been answered. The victory was total. But on the west bank it was a completely different story. As Jackson went up and down his line from one end to the other, congratulating his men and heaping words of praise on their courage and skill, across the river a disaster of nearly equal magnitude was in the making. Jackson had no sooner completed his round of congratulations than he suddenly realized that Patterson's and Morgan's guns had been silent for some time.

Strange. Then came the flash of gunfire and the roar that trailed behind it. Jackson and Adair mounted the levee and turned a glass on the opposite shore. In a moment they saw Thornton's men advancing to attack and watched as Morgan's men returned the fire. Relieved and encouraged by the vigor of Morgan's response, Jackson turned to his men and asked them to send up a shout of victory to salute the troops on the other bank. "Take off your hats," he cried, "and give them three cheers!"[42]

The entire line on the east side crowded along the river to watch the ensuing battle. They expected that their own victory over the British columns would be repeated by their comrades across the river. They soon learned otherwise.

Thornton and his men had landed early in the morning about four miles below Morgan's position. Had the American troops been present onshore when they arrived, they might well have blocked Thornton's efforts to disembark. The boats were crowded. They could easily have been riddled with grapeshot. But it did not happen.

By the time the British finally came ashore and formed their column, the flashing and booming of cannons on the east bank announced that Pakenham had commenced his attack and that they were far behind schedule. Thornton therefore ordered his column to move at double-quick time as he headed north. In the river three small gunboats commanded by Captain Roberts with a carronade on each of their bows and manned by one hundred sailors covered his flank and kept abreast of the charging column.

To prevent a landing, Morgan had sent an advanced contingent of 120 men of the 6th Louisiana Militia under the command of Major Jean Arnaud three miles below his position. These men were badly armed. Most of them carried only fowling pieces and musket cartridges that were much too large for their guns. They erected a small breastwork during the night, and when they completed it they went to sleep leaving a single sentry on guard.[43]

Shortly after dawn a shower of grapeshot erupted from the carronades of the gunboats and roused the sleeping Americans and sent them fleeing for their lives. Thornton barely missed capturing them. A short distance farther north these retreating troops met Colonel John Davis's detachment of Kentuckians, whom Jackson had sent to reinforce Morgan's lines. These Kentuckians had arrived about the time Thornton landed. Although exhausted, hungry, poorly armed, and in no mood to do anything but sleep, they were ordered to move down the river and join Arnaud's men in attacking the enemy. Once the two forces joined they tried to make a stand in an open field. But they were no match for the better-armed and better-disciplined British. Their flank was quickly turned, sending the Louisianians dashing into a swamp, where they wandered for hours, unable to reach their lines. The Kentuckians fired a few rounds and then scurried back to Morgan's position in great confusion.

Morgan's line consisted of a ditch and a breastwork formed from the dirt that had been dug out of it. But the breastwork afforded little protection. It only reached waist level and exposed the men to enemy fire unless they lay flat on the ground.[44]

Thornton halted his advance about seven hundred yards from Morgan's position. He reconnoitered and prepared for a general assault. He immediately saw that the American line was weakest to his left, where the retreating Kentuckians had been posted. He also noticed that behind the Kentuckians was a totally undefended swampy wood. This, then, would be the point of his attack. He directed Captain James Money of the Royal Navy with his one hundred sailors to feint toward his right nearest the river, where the American line was strongest. At the same time, two divisions of the 85th Regiment under Lieutenant Colonel Richard Gubbins were ordered to assault the Kentuckians on his left. Marines were kept in the rear as reserve.

Morgan's line was too long to be properly defended without more troops than he presently commanded. In all he had about six hundred soldiers, most of them physically exhausted and one-third of them poorly armed. On this line were mounted three cannon: a twelve-pounder and two six-pounders.

A shrill bugle sounded the charge. A shower of rockets screamed aloft and exploded in the sky. The British sailors and troops rushed forward as Morgan's men opened up on their attackers. The American line closest to the river hit the sailors with crushing effect and brought them to a halt. Another round of well-directed grapeshot from the twelve-pounder and the two sixes sent the enemy recoiling from the murderous fire. One volley followed another as sailors crumpled to the ground, including their commander, Captain Money.[45]

But Gubbins's 85th struck the Kentuckians with full force. They were divided into two columns, one charging the center of the Kentucky position and the other attacking the flank. What took place was exactly what Thornton had predicted and planned. The extreme right of the Kentucky line was turned at the same time as the center gave way. The Americans quickly realized they were being enveloped by the two columns and exposed to fire from the front and rear. They fired three rounds and then abandoned their position and fled in wild panic.[46]

Morgan rode to his right and shouted to Colonel Davis to halt his men, but the colonel replied that it was impossible.

"Sir," Morgan barked, "I have not seen you try."

Then he raced after the fleeing Kentuckians and demanded that they turn and face the enemy.

"Halt, halt! men, and resume your position."

It had no effect.

A Kentucky adjutant continued running after them, hoping to humiliate them into doing their duty. "Shame, shame! Boys," he cried. "Stand by your general."

They continued running to the rear with Morgan galloping after them, trying desperately to rally them.[47]

With the right side of the American line now uncovered, the British vaulted over the ditch, mounted the rampart, and poured inside Morgan's position. At the other end, where the British sailors had been repulsed, Colonel Thornton rushed to their aid with a division from the 85th Regiment. Despite a severe wound he succeeded in adding strength to the attack in that area. Meanwhile the carronades on the gunboats bombarded the batteries alongside the river.

The American batteries, having discharged their last cartridges, now faced the danger of capture, so the gunners spiked their guns (that is they drove spikes into the vents of these cannons, which rendered them useless), pitched them into the Mississippi, and abandoned their post under heavy fire from the enemy.[48]

Some three hundred yards behind Morgan's line, Patterson's marine battery had been trained on the east bank since daybreak to order to provide Jackson with additional and necessary support to enfilade the enemy columns as they attacked. But when he saw that Morgan's lines had been pierced and the men were running madly from their pursuers, Patterson wheeled his guns around so as to aim at Thornton's onrushing troops. But the more he saw the Kentuckians fleeing in wild disorder the more incensed and outraged he became, so that he ordered a young midshipman to fire his cannon right into the faces of those "d——d cowards."

The midshipman lighted his match and was about to touch it to the gun when Patterson countermanded the order. Once he calmed down and recovered his wits, he came alive to his situation and realized his position was no longer tenable. He directed that his guns be spiked and together with the remaining powder thrown into the Mississippi. He turned his back on the enemy and walked away.

Thirty of his men walked ahead of him as Patterson invoked curses against the British and the Kentuckians. He was followed by the Louisiana militia, who retired in fairly good order. Together they reached the *Louisiana*, which had been moored about three hundred yards behind the marine battery. They succeeded in moving the ship into the river and away from enemy fire.

Jackson observed what was happening on the west bank, and he too cursed the fleeing Kentuckians. They had marred his victory, and he never ceased accusing them of cowardice. He wrote to Secretary Monroe the following day and complained that "the Kentucky reinforcement in whom so much reliance had been placed, ingloriously fled—drawing after them, by their example, the remainder of the force; & thus, yielding to the enemy that most fortunate position."[49]

As Jackson watched his troops retreat he dispatched General Humbert, who had volunteered his services, to cross over with four hundred men to support Morgan in "Carrying the enemy if necessary at the point of the Bayonet. . . . I rely upon your determination with the aid I have sent you to accomplish it." He also sent Jean Laffite as well, because the pirate had expert knowledge of the canals and bayous of the area and could help devise the strategy to block the advance of the enemy.[50]

Meanwhile Thornton had moved up and occupied Patterson's position. It was now 10:00 A.M., and Thornton sent a message to Pakenham announcing his victory. He boasted that one of Morgan's guns captured in the engagement had the inscription "Taken at the surrender of Yorktown, 1781."

The British soldiers on the east side of the river first heard about the American defeat about an hour after they had begun their attack on Jackson lines. "Pop, pop, pop," came the report from across the Mississippi, "followed by a volley of musketry, interspersed with a few hasty rounds of artillery." Then it stopped, and the troops instantly knew that Thornton and his men had gained a victory and would soon turn the American guns on Jackson's line and enfilade it from left to right exactly the way the *Louisiana* had raked the British position.

"Bravo!" shouted the redcoats. "The batteries are taken, and the Americans are done for." Here was "another opening to the streets of New Orleans, and dame Fortune soared aloft in favour of the English general." But then all of a sudden "dame Fortune" fell to earth.

"We waited and waited," moaned Captain Cooke, "still exposed to a cannonade from the front. . . . But no such agreeable sounds greeted our ears." The Americans had spiked their guns before they were captured.[51]

Still, Thornton and his men might have slogged their way northward, but Lambert, who had ordered a stop to the senseless killing on his side of the river, sent over his artillery chief, Colonel Sir Alexander Dickson, to ascertain the number of men it would take to hold the captured batteries now that Morgan had been reinforced by the four hundred men under Humbert. Dickson estimated that it would take at least two thousand soldiers.

And that ended that. A messenger was immediately dispatched to Thornton with an order to retire from his position, recross the river, and return to the main body of the army. In intense pain because of the severe wound he had received, Thornton was forced to transfer command of his troops to Gubbins. He and his command set fire to several sawmills, destroyed the guns, ammunition, and stores they had captured, and regretfully reboarded their boats and sailed back across the river.

The Americans threatened to attack the retiring column by sending out sixty or a hundred men to reconnoiter, but the British made a show of advancing and the "dirty shirts" fled. Once Thornton's men returned, the entire army knew that the battle, and with it New Orleans, had been lost. "Then, and not till then, all further hopes of victory were blasted."

Cooke was livid. "Was this not enough, I say, to make His Majesty's officers hold hard the breath of suppressed indignation at being reined in when so much blood had been spilled, and when the words of their dying comrades still called on them to advance?"[52]

When the redcoats entered their boats and headed across the river, the Americans returned to their lines on the west bank, and Patterson restored his battery at an even more advantageous position than he had occupied before the battle. On January 10, Jackson informed Morgan that he wanted him "to set fire to and destroy every house, and remove the fences, in front of your position which may in the Smallest degree interfere with its defence. . . . Your post must be defended—the safety of the Country and my army in a great measure depends on it."[53]

One reason for Thornton's success, despite his inferior force, had to do with the speed with which he moved once he crossed the river. His men were also better armed and disciplined, and the American defense was totally inadequate. Had Thornton rather than Keane commanded the army upon its arrival in Louisiana, the outcome of the Battle of New Orleans might well have ended with the capture of the city.

When Thornton and his troops arrived back in the British camp they were struck dumb by what they saw and encountered. Only twenty hours earlier, all had been "life and animation. . . . Now gloom and discontent everywhere prevailed." Rage, grief, disappointment, and sorrow were etched on the faces of their comrades. The loss of honor, the thought of laurels tarnished, the sense of failure filled the minds of the survivors. Virtually every one of these men had suffered the personal loss of a friend. Still, they did not despair. They cursed those—especially the 44th Regiment—who had caused their defeat, and expected to exact a fearful vengeance in the near future against their American foes.

They exacted one revenge against the American deserter who had provided the information that had led Gibbs's column into the very jaws of fiery destruction. They labeled him a spy sent by Jackson to mislead Pakenham, and despite the unfortunate man's vehement denials they hanged him.[54]

Meanwhile Jackson kept his men on alert for any untoward movement by the enemy on his side of the Mississippi. Lookouts posted ahead of the lines kept a close watch on any activity that might appear threatening. About noon, several of them spotted the approach of a party from the British camp. It included an officer in full uniform, a trumpeter, and a soldier carrying a white flag. They advanced to within three hundred yards of the American lines and stopped. The trumpeter then let out a loud blast and the soldier waved his flag. Instantly the parapet came alive with soldiers wanting to see what was happening. Jackson ordered his aide Major Butler and two other officers to meet the British delegation and learn what they wanted.

The Americans climbed the parapet, crossed the ditch, and advanced toward the three emissaries. The British officer very courteously handed Butler a note for Jackson. It was accepted, and the two parties separated and returned to their respective lines.

Jackson was still at the Macarty house when he received the note. In it Lambert said that he had observed the "humane attention" shown to the wounded close to the Americans rampart, for which he was grateful. He then asked for the names of these men and added, "It would be a satisfaction, as numbers are now laying there dead, and perhaps more wounded, to allow an unarmed party to bury the former, or bring such away whose cases are dangerous." The note was signed "Lambert, Major-General."[55]

Jackson had no idea who this Lambert was or the extent of his authority. It may have been Lambert's intention to conceal the deaths of Pakenham and Gibbs. And it took several notes and several days before Lambert admitted the loss of these generals and the fact that he was now the ranking officer of the British army. But Jackson had to prod him. By that time he no doubt knew the British high command had been wiped out, but he decided to confirm it. On January 11 he told Lambert that for the correspondence to continue it was necessary that the "Commanders in Chief of the two armies" identify themselves and state their authority. "I have the honor to Command the American forces in this quarter," he wrote.

Lambert promptly replied, "I have the Honor to . . . inform you that I am Commr. of the Forces on the left Bank of the Mississippi."[56]

Responding to Lambert's initial request for a day's truce so that the dead could be buried and the wounded attended to, Jackson established a line three hundred yards in advance of the rampart and informed Lambert that the wounded within that line would be taken to his hospital; those dead would "be intered by my troops." The dead on the field beyond the line "you can inter." This precaution was taken by Jackson, said Major Reid, so "that the enemy might not have an opportunity to inspect, or know any thing of his position." As for prisoners, Old Hickory reminded Lambert that for weeks Patterson had been trying without success to learn from Admiral Cochrane the fate of the men taken in the battle of the gunboats on December 14. Then, very pointedly, he added that when he had the report of these prisoners and wounded men, as well as those taken on the night of December 23, then, and only then, would Lambert receive the information he requested about the wounded prisoners.

Jackson also proposed that hostilities on the east bank cease until the next day at noon, during which time the wounded could be gathered and the dead interred. He further stipulated that hostilities would not cease on the west bank but that no further reinforcements were to be sent by either army until noon of the following day. He of course had already sent over reinforcements to retake the position Morgan had lost. Lambert agreed, but felt that more time would be necessary to complete the operation of tending the wounded and burying the dead and therefore proposed a cut-off time of 2:00 P.M. Jackson had no objection.[57]

And so the grisly business began of collecting the dead and giving them a decent burial. Squads of American and British soldiers came forward from both camps, and it was immediately clear that nearly a thousand bodies lay on the ground, "all of them arrayed in British uniforms. Not a single American was among them; all were English." The sight proved shocking and humiliating to His Majesty's officers. One of them hung his head in sorrow and anger. He related how an American officer, with a look of "savage exaltation," supervised the operation of collecting the dead while smoking a cigar. To each British officer who approached him he bragged that the American losses amounted to only eight killed and one wounded.

The bodies of several of the slain British officers, including Pakenham, Gibbs, Dale, and Rennie, were reportedly disemboweled and the cadavers encased in casks of rum to be shipped back to England. Most of the regular troops were buried in simple ceremonies in the rear of Bienvenu's plantation. Jackson himself stated that on January 9, "upwards of 300 of the dead were picked up by my troops, and delivered over to the enemy for burial. We took about 500 prisoners; the greater part of whom were dangerously and many of them *mortally* wounded."[58]

At Laronde's mansion every room was crowded with the wounded. "The scene presented . . . was one I shall never forget," reported one British captain. He watched many amputations, heard the piteous cries of his countrymen, and saw "a *basket nearly full of legs* severed from these fine fellows, most of which were still covered with their hose."[59]

Lieutenant Gleig awoke from his unconscious state to find himself lying on a mattress in a small room surrounded by a half-dozen other wounded officers. He had been unconscious for thirty-six hours. A doctor attended him and removed a bandage from his head. "I regained my strength slowly and painfully," he later wrote, "and did so, only to witness the agonies of those who surrounded me."[60]

And the numbers of the dead and wounded told an unbelievable story. The day after the battle, Jackson informed Secretary Monroe that he estimated fewer than 1,500 British "killed wounded & prisoners." Four days later he revised the figure to more than 2,600, of which 400 were killed, 1,400 wounded, and 500 taken prisoner. But the British themselves reported 2,037 casualties, of which 291 were killed, 1,262 wounded, and 484 taken prisoner. Two out of the four British generals had been killed, including the commander in chief, and a third severely wounded. Of particular sadness was the loss of 50 percent of the men from one of the best units in the army, the magnificent 93rd Regiment of Highlanders.

As for the American losses, Jackson reported to Monroe "only seven killed & six wounded" for the battle itself but admitted that "afterwards a skirmishing was kept up in which a few more of our men was lost." For the entire four days of fighting on both the east and west banks the total came to 333, of which 55 were killed, 185 wounded, and 93 missing. Jackson had to admit that on the face of it "such a disproportion in loss, when we consider the number and the kind of troops engaged must, I know, excite astonishment, and may not, every where, be fully credited; Yet I am perfectly satisfied that the amount is not exaggerated on the one part, nor underrated on the other." In fact, admitted Captain Cooke, it was "a circumstance unparalleled in modern history."[61]

Put in better perspective it should be remembered that the British landed almost fifteen thousand soldiers and sailors below New Orleans and sustained more than two thousand casualties. They should never have attempted to fight in the place and at the time that they did. But British arrogance and pride drove them forward. And more than two-thirds of the *attacking* force suffered the consequence.

The "morning of the 8th of January," Jackson wrote, ". . . will be ever remembered by the British nation, and always hailed by every true american."[62]

Chapter 8

❧

The Final Assault

Not that the danger of a renewal of the battle ended on January 8. The British just sat and waited while Lambert tried to figure his next move. Among his senior officers there was a sense that the advantage gained on the west bank by Thornton should be followed up. The idea was feasible, and flanking Jackson's line had enormous military merit, but it meant dividing the army—always a risky enterprise, as Morgan learned—and ferrying a large contingent of soldiers across the river. By experience Lambert knew that the Mississippi could play tricks with any organized plan of operation. And who could guess what Jackson would do in the interim?

Admiral Cochrane, Admiral Edward Codrington, the fleet captain, Colonel John Burgoyne (the illegitimate son of General John Burgoyne, who surrendered at Saratoga in 1777 during the American Revolution), and others felt that abandoning the west bank had been a grave mistake. They also felt that if the fleet could sail unopposed up the Mississippi it could bombard New Orleans with a hundred or more cannon and guns of various sizes and land troops behind Jackson's lines. The only real obstacle to the plan was Fort St. Philip at Plaquemine, a heavily armed fortification some eighty miles south of the city and thirty miles north of the mouth of the river. A rude, irregular structure, it stood at the bend of the Mississippi and had a broad sweep of the river above and below it. The fort was surrounded by a swampy morass and was additionally protected by a deep water-filled ditch. Furthermore, Bayou Mardi Gras, a stream forty-five yards wide, flanked its eastern side. It was therefore virtually unapproachable and impregnable to a land attack.

Jackson had inspected the fort when he first arrived in the city and, recognizing its importance in his plans for defense, had ordered its reinforcement. Several detachments of troops were added to the garrison, and a number of slaves were sent down to help in erecting gun emplacements and generally strengthening the entire structure. Major Walter H. Overton of the rifle corps commanded the fort, and he built small magazines in different parts of the garrison so that if a bomb hit one of these magazines "he could resort to another." He also disguised these structures and protected them with a covering of timber, scantling, and soil. In addition he removed from the fort all combustible materials, such as wooden barracks, and erected bomb shelters to protect his men from flying shrapnel.

The garrison itself consisted of two companies of United States artillery numbering 117 men under Captains Charles Wollstonecraft, Thomas Murray, and Michael Walsh; two companies of the 7th Infantry of 163 men under Captains Narcissus Brontin and James S. Waide; 54 men of the Louisiana volunteers commanded by Captain Francois Lagan; 30 free men of color under Ferdinand Listeau; and 40 sailors from Gunboat # 65—for a total of 406 soldiers and sailors. Within the fort, thirty-four pieces of ordnance were mounted: twenty-nine twenty-four-pounders, one six-pounder, one 13-inch mortar, one 8.5-inch howitzer, and, in the covered area, two thirty-two-pounders, placed level with the river.[1]

Once the British had captured or destroyed Fort St. Philip, the only remaining obstacle in their way would be the rather weak American fortification at the English Turn, which was particularly vulnerable to a land assault. Quite easily the British could brush aside any opposition they encountered at the Turn and sail right on to New Orleans.

The decision was therefore made to attempt this nautical feat. Cochrane had long boasted of what his ships and men could accomplish, and now he had the chance to prove it. He probably decided to make this attempt several days prior to the major battle of January 8. In any event he dispatched two "bomb-ships," the *Herald* and *Sophia*, along with a brig, a sloop of war, and a tender, to take out Fort St. Philip. However small this fleet, if it managed to get past Fort St. Philip and the English Turn it undoubtedly would decimate Jackson's lines.

The British had already blockaded the entrance of the Mississippi, and once Cochrane gave his order the five ships ascended the river and headed for the Plaquemine Turn. Early on January 8 an American "look-out boat" caught sight of this fleet and reported to it Overton. But nothing happened, and the fleet kept its distance and stayed out of the range of the American guns. Then on January 9 at 10:15 A.M. the five ships hove into view and anchored two and a quarter miles below the fort. They waited. At 11:30 A.M. and at 12:30 P.M. two barges approached to within a mile and a half of the fort, apparently intent on sounding the depth of the water. At that moment Overton ordered Lieutenant Cunningham of the navy, who commanded the sailors of the gunboat and now manned the two thirty-two-pounders inside the fort, to open fire. This was what Overton called his "water battery."

As the two cannons roared their defiance, the barges withdrew, having completed their assignment. The Americans tensed for the expected attack. The furnace for hot shot was lighted, and the troops took their assigned positions in three separate areas. The right battery of the fort was commanded by Captain Walsh. Captain Wollstonecraft commanded the center bastion with its mortar and howitzer, and Captain Murray had charge of the battery on the left. Unfortunately the ammunition for the mortar proved to be faulty, so messages were immediately dispatched to Jackson to send the proper fuses. The Louisiana troops assisted the artillerists in the center and on the left side. The infantry under Captain Broutin was stationed to support the artillery if needed. Meanwhile they melted lead for making canister and grapeshot and helped prepare the ammunition charges. Gunboat # 65 took a position in the bayou so as to flank the rear of the fort.

Hours passed. It started raining again. In fact, it had rained on and off since the start of the invasion and would continue to rain for days.

Finally, at 3:30 P.M., the British fleet moved to a position behind a bend in the river at a distance of 3,960 yards from the fort and anchored. Then the two "bomb-ships" opened up on the fort with "four sea-mortars, two of thirteen inches, [and] two of ten." To Overton's "great mortification," the ships were outside the range of the American guns, inasmuch as the mortar was inoperable. Nevertheless, Overton hoisted the United States flag, and below it, as a gesture of defiance, he nailed the Union Jack.

The first British shell fell short, and the next one burst above the interior of the fort, showering its shrapnel below but causing no serious damage. The following bombshells struck the soft dirt within the compound and buried themselves so deep that they only shook the ground. No one was hurt. Some bombs failed to explode, but the bombardment continued hour after hour, a missile bursting every two minutes. And this went on and on into the evening hours.[2]

Once it got dark, the British reconnoitered in small boats, and since the wind was blowing up the river the conversations of the sailors could be distinctly heard in the fort. That is how close they came. These sailors fired several rounds of grape and round shot over and into the fort, but the defender paid them little heed. They kept their eyes peeled for any movement by the five ships, recognizing that the action by the small boats was intended as a diversion to turn their attention away from the fleet. When these boats found the Americans impervious to their ploy, they retired.

The following day the bombardment was resumed with the same intensity as the previous day, except that the firing ceased for about two hours at noon and at sunset. Obviously the British needed a sufficient period of time to enjoy a proper lunch and dinner. It would be unseemly for the British navy to allow a bombardment to interfere with regular meals. Occasionally the Americans would respond with a salvo or two, but the shots fell short, and so Overton ordered a halt. On the third day a lucky shot struck the flagstaff, and it took a fair amount of work to restore the American ensign to the mast. This feat was accomplished by a sailor who had the courage to stand high on the crossbars and reattach the flag. He was a living target who might well have been killed. Enemy fire was very brisk and well directed at him, and several shells burst over his head. Miraculously, he escaped injury. It was important to Overton and his men that the Stars and Stripes remain visible to all, "flying in all its glory."

That evening the British made a concerted effort to target the contractor's store in what they assumed from information provided by their spies was the main magazine in the fort. Here again was an instance of the enemy acting on information that was no longer true. The situation had changed when Overton decided to redistribute his ammunition in different parts of the garrison. It proved to be a very wise move. British accuracy that evening was extraordinary. Two bombs tore through the target and burst within it, killing one man and wounding another.

Once more Overton decided to open up on the bomb-ships. Although he knew he could not inflict any real damage on them, he wanted to give them a demonstration of American firepower and accuracy should they decide to come closer. He also felt that it would "animate" his men. They chafed at doing nothing. They needed a means of venting their anger and frustration; they needed the sense that they were active participants in the defense of their country.[3]

For the next three days the bombardment continued as before with the usual intermissions for lunch and dinner. By this time the British realized their shelling was ineffective, and they decided to rearrange their fuses so that the bombs would burst in midair over the interior of the fort so that the shrapnel could inflict more personnel damage. And their luck improved. On the evening of the 14th, one man was killed on the right battery, another lost a leg, and a third suffered a slight wound. Several gun carriages were also badly damaged. The thirty-two-pounder in the covert was struck five times and rendered inoperable for over an hour.

With the British change of tactics, Overton ordered the building of safer covers between the guns facing the river to protect the men at the batteries from flying shell fragments. He also wanted to protect them from the rain, which had continued day after dreary day. By this time the center of the fort was one enormous pool of water, the ground surrounding it a veritable quagmire. To the amazement of all, no one was hurt while they labored, despite a great deal of coming and going of work parties collecting materials for the covers. The various magazines were also provided greater protection by heaping more dirt on top of them.

Finally several boats arrived from New Orleans with additional ammunition, including fuses for the thirteen-inch mortar. By the evening of the 15th the work was completed and the fort was better prepared not only to torment the enemy, which its defenders were itching to do, but to rout any attempted naval assault.

The rain stopped on the 16th, and with good weather the garrison continued strengthening the fort and bringing in additional supplies from the north. Spirits ran high. The men now sensed that they had repulsed the invasion and that the British knew they had been thwarted and defeated.

On the morning of January 17 the bombardment slackened off a bit, and in the evening the Americans, having readied their heavy mortar with the much-needed fuses, returned the fire and actually hit one of the bomb-ships. "We distinctly heard the shock, and for near five minutes the fire from one of the vessels was discontinued." The bombardment continued sporadically throughout the night of the 17th, but that was the end of it. Just before daybreak on the 18th the British left their anchorage, turned around, and sailed down the Mississippi toward the Gulf.

The Americans roared. The fort stood proudly in defiance of its attackers. It had not been damaged in any significant manner, although

Overton admitted that "the enemy left scarcely ten feet of this garrison untouched." The mighty British navy had failed to sail past it or dislodge its defenders and capture their city. The Americans had endured near-constant bombardment from January 9 to the morning of the 18th. During that period the British had thrown up more than "one thousand shells and carcases, expending upwards of seventy tons of shells and more than twenty thousand pounds of powder, besides small shells [from howitzers], and round shot and grape from their [small] boats." The American casualties consisted of two dead and seven wounded. They had lived nine days without adequate cover, suffered exposure and constant rain. "They cannot be denied praise for the unremitted exertions they made to receive the enemy," wrote Latour, "the fatigues they underwent during the bombardment, which was almost incessant, and the patience they exercised thus exposed." Their sense of accomplishment was profound, however. They knew they had prevented the enemy from getting past their keep and inflicting incalculable damage on Jackson's army. They had helped save New Orleans.[4]

The bombardment of Fort St. Philip could be distinctly heard by Jackson at Chalmette, and he knew that danger still faced him, despite Lambert's withdrawal back to his camp. If the British could get past the fort they could easily subdue any opposition at the English Turn and subject him to great jeopardy. So, once the temporary cession of fire to gather the dead and wounded had expired, Jackson began a regular cannonading of the British position. If nothing else it would harass the enemy and maybe even encourage Lambert and his army to depart. Indeed, deserters reported to the Americans that the constant fire of the artillery deprived the troops of sleep and that they were irritable, fault-finding, and outraged that they had been subjected to needless butchery. Moreover, they expected an attack by the Americans and had doubled their outposts. So Jackson kept up the cannonading day after day. Anytime a group of British soldiers came together within range they were immediately greeted with gunfire. At night the Tennesseans resumed their marauding parties to shoot pickets—all of which continued to erode the spirit of the defeated army. Lambert tried to restore confidence in his troops by holding daily parades. But it was hopeless.

Then the rains came, day after unrelenting day, usually with thunder and lightning. The situation was no longer tolerable, and Lambert began to plan a general withdrawal of his troops, particularly after the attempted assault against Fort St. Philip had failed. "We passed *ten days* after the repulse in as uncomfortable a manner as could fall to the lot of most *militaires* to endure," wrote Captain Cooke. Some days the redcoats ate nothing, and when they did have food it was served in such small portions "as only to tantalize our voracious appetites." They found a grove of orange trees, picked the fruit, and put them in a pot half filled with sugar and mixed with a little water. The result was candied orange peels "which in some degree satisfied the cravings of hunger."

To intensify their agony the redcoats were rudely awakened one morning before daybreak by water pouring into their makeshift huts. The Mississippi had suddenly overflowed its banks "and nothing but a sheet of water could be seen." It was as though the mighty river wished to flush the unwelcome intruders back into the sea whence they had come. Not until sunset did the waters finally recede.[5]

It was time to depart and try again somewhere else. And Lambert knew it. He needed to move his army out of the swamps and muck of Louisiana. But he did it carefully and cautiously and as expeditiously as possible.

Always alert to the actions of his foe, Jackson instantly suspected the enemy was about to do something. As early as January 15 and 16, according to Major Tatum, Jackson had evidence, confirmed by deserters, that the British were planning to retire. He told Governor Claiborne that "the Enemy is, from his Manovers is about to make a movement—And all hands must be at their posts." He also ordered Chef Menteur reinforced and requested that the governor accompany these troops.[6]

The movement came on January 17. Lambert proposed that "a cartel of prisoners" be drawn up in preparation for an exchange. To do this Jackson appointed Livingston to meet with Lambert's representative, Major Harry Smith, between the lines of the outposts and draw up "Provisional Articles for an Exchange of Prisoners." Under the terms of this agreement, as finally worked out, Cochrane would return the American prisoners presently on board ships of the British fleet. Upon the release of these Americans, English prisoners of equal rank and number would be received by designated ships appointed by the admiral. In addition, all American prisoners held in the British camp would be exchanged for an equal number of English prisoners. Finally, "Officers of Equal Rank shall be exchanged for Equal Rank & wounded for wounded as far as circumstances will permit."[7]

The following day, Lambert began his general withdrawal. During the ten-day period from January 9, the day after the disastrous defeat on the east bank, until January 18, Lambert had been making preparations for the retreat. It was necessary to plan ahead, because he faced a problem that could be treacherous. There were not enough boats to transport more than half the army down the bayou at one time, and to divide the army invited possible attack by the entire American force, which could result in the total annihilation of his command. And even if the attack was repulsed, "it would be impossible to take to our boats in their presence," said Lieutenant Gleig, "and thus at least one division, if not both, must be sacrificed." Consequently, during the ten days they waited for the outcome at Fort St. Philip, Lambert directed that the road along which the army had formed on landing (after sailing up the bayou) be continued to the rim of Lake Borgne. It meant traversing "the very center of a morass which human foot had never before trodden."[8]

Still Lambert decided that the task had to be completed before he dared move his army. He immediately assigned large working parties under the guidance of engineers to lengthen the road, keeping as close to the bayou as possible. But it was another herculean undertaking. Long stretches provided no firm footing on which to build a path nor enough trees to supply construction material. So they bound together large amounts of reeds and laid them across the quagmire. They also collected large branches from trees in the woods to construct bridges over broad ditches.

It took nine days "of incessant and most arduous labor" to prepare this road, and on the tenth day, January 18, Lambert began to move his wounded to the fleet. The abandoned guns were spiked and broken. At 9:00 P.M., in the stillness of the night, the main body of the army began to withdraw, leaving pickets to follow as a rear guard. And a "most profound silence" accompanied the movement. Even necessary orders were whispered.

Fortunately the weather cooperated. A heavy fog shrouded their departure, and not until 8:00 A.M. the next day, after the fog had lifted, did Jackson discover that the British were gone. If there had been another heavy rain during the withdrawal, said Cooke, "we must all have perished in the slough." At first the troops had no difficulty as they took the high road next to the river, but once they began to head east through the marsh their problems mounted. The first corps managed to get through easily enough, but as one squad followed another the reeds were driven into the mud and water welled up and finally obliterated the road. With each step the soldiers sank ankle then knee deep into the swamp, and sometimes even deeper than that. The blackness of the night only worsened their situation. Gleig came upon a man who was sinking into the morass and raced forward to help him. The unfortunate soldier cried out for help, but as Gleig advanced he too became enveloped in muck as high as his chest. The soldier disappeared completely while Gleig sank to his armpits. He could feel nothing solid beneath his feet. He too called out for assistance, and fortunately a leather canteen strap was thrown to him and he grabbed hold of it and was dragged to safety. But the poor soldier had been swallowed by the swamp.[9]

Meanwhile the Americans had begun a systematic campaign to encourage the British soldiers to desert, particularly the sentinels. Printed notices held out promises of land and money. Unfortunately, reported Lieutenant Gleig, "in the course of a week, many men quitted their colours, and fled to the enemy."[10]

For the entire night the army kept up its grueling march, finally reaching Fishermen's Village near the lake. A large number of slaves had followed, hoping that they too could embark with the army. They were assembled, said Cooke, "to dance for our amusement, accompanied by a sort of rude *pipe* and *tabor.*" The gyrations of these unfortunates and their "violent contortions of countenance" no doubt provided the "amusement" the troops craved. But Lambert later insisted in a letter to Jackson that "every pain has been taken to persuade them to remain peaceably at home." However, it was reported that the British had carted off two hundred slaves, and one plantation owner claimed that he alone had lost forty-three slaves to the English wolves.[11]

As dawn broke on January 19 the troops peered around and "as far as the eye could reach a perfect ocean of weeds everywhere presented itself." The order came to halt the march, and, said Gleig, "I never rejoiced more sincerely at any order than at this." He threw himself to the ground, pulled off his mud-soaked clothes, and fell sound asleep. After several hours he awoke cold and stiff. He huddled near a fire of reeds, which like straw blazed up quickly but soon died out, and ate his last morsel of salt pork.[12]

The troops bivouacked along the rim of the lake, a line of outposts was drawn, and orders went out for the men to make themselves comfortable, which only brought howls of derision. They had no shelter and few provisions. In fact, they were starving. For two days men made do with "crumbs of biscuit and a small allowance of rum." A flotilla of boats in the lake already loaded with the black corps and the 44th had a distance of sixty miles to travel to discharge these troops before it could return with provisions. And who knew how long that would take, considering the treachery of the wind and sea?

While waiting, Gleig decided to go hunting for wild ducks, which abounded in the bog. A crack shot, he bagged three as a large flock flew over him. But they fell into the water about twenty yards away. It was biting cold, and the edge of water was coated with ice. His dog, more tired than Gleig, refused to fetch them. So he tried again at a different spot and shot down two more ducks. But once again they fell into the lake. "This was too much for a hungry man to endure," he said. So he stripped off his clothes, broke the ice, plunged into the frigid water, snatched his prey, and returned to shore with the two birds. He reckoned himself one of the lucky ones as he devoured his kill.[13]

Here the troops passed "some wretched days," starving, on constant guard against the danger of the swamp and the snakes and alligators that inhabited it. Captain Cooke related how he spent the whole night in a state of "apprehension that an alligator might push a broad snout through the reeds and gobble me up."[14]

As soon as the loading ships returned, the embarkation began according to plan. First went the wounded, next the baggage and stores with the civil officers, commissaries, purveyors, and other administrative officials, and then the light artillery. Of the heavy artillery only ten remained, and they were so heavy and cumbersome that Lambert decided to abandon them. The last to go was the infantry.

Regiment after regiment embarked and headed for the fleet, but because of the wind and rough seas it took several days to transport all the troops back on board. When the wounded first arrived at the anchorage they were met by anxious wives who on learning that their husbands had died broke down in grief. Their tears and moans added to the universal misery aboard the ships. Here they had accompanied their husbands over a distance of thousands of miles to grace the fashionable circles of New Orleans, and now they faced a long journey home alone. Lady Mullens was deeply grieved when she heard the accusations hurled at her husband. She locked herself in her room and refused to see anyone. Later she insisted that her husband had been falsely accused and would be exonerated. Instead he was court-martialed and cashiered for cowardice.[15]

During this evacuation a group of Louisianians decided that a few well-armed boats could harass the enemy on Lake Borgne and teach them another lesson in the superiority of American arms. On January 19, thirty-four men, including officers, led by Dr. Robert Morrell and Thomas Shields, proceeded to Bayou St. John in four boats, one of which carried a twelve-pound carronade. The next day they were

joined by two other boats and nineteen men from Fort Petites Coquilles, and together they continued past Chef Menteur to a campsite
about three miles from Lake Borgne. It was 2:00 P.M. They watched
the enemy's ships moving back and forth from the shore to the fleet. At
9:00 P.M. they got underway, and within half an hour they had entered
the lake. Rowing with muffled oars, they headed toward the Rigolets
and at 11:00 P.M. discovered an unarmed barge at anchor. Six men and
an officer pulled up to her, boarded her at the bow, midships, and stern,
and captured thirty-eight men of the 14th Dragoons, thirteen sailors, a
lieutenant, and a master's mate. They delivered the prisoners to the
camp and at 1:00 A.M. went out on another sortie. They searched the
entire night and found nothing. At 7:00 A.M. on January 22 they tried
again. They steered toward the Rigolets and bagged a transport boat.
An hour and a half later they captured a schooner of 110 tons, and still
later three more boats. Because of the sandbar at the Rigolets the
schooner could not be brought in, and so Shields set it on fire. The
British tried in vain to board the burning ship and then landed three
boats filled with soldiers on their way to the fleet to attack the Americans on shore.

Dr. Morrell and twenty men marched to meet then. Concealed in
the high grass, they managed to drive the enemy back to their boats.
The British soldiers "embarked in great confusion."[16]

Because of these marauding Americans the troops being evacuated
were put aboard several ships to form little squadrons and kept close
together. Armed launches accompanied each squadron. But adverse
winds slowed the operation and it took many days to complete it. Finally the 85th embarked, or what was left of it, followed by the 7th.
Not until January 27 did the entire army rejoin the fleet. From the day
following their defeat on the battlefield the British needed two and a
half weeks to withdraw completely from the Louisiana coast.

Captain Cooke left the "morass" on the morning of January 25 in a
ship's barge that carried fifty other men and was rowed by twelve
sailors. He was astounded that the tars "could have continued such exertions for so many successive hours." They too had endured a terrible
ordeal, just like the troops. It was deeply discouraging for all of them

to leave having failed in their mission. But they rejoiced that they were finally departing this "wretched" land.[17]

As Lieutenant Gleig boarded his ship to be taken to the anchorage he kept remembering the honors and rewards they had expected to achieve and the horrors they had actually encountered. "We, who only seven weeks ago had set out in the surest confidence of glory, and, I may add, of emolument, were brought back dispirited and dejected. Our ranks were wofully thinned, our chiefs slain, our clothing tattered and filthy, and even our discipline in some degree injured." Gloom permeated the fleet, punctuated "by the voice of lamentation over fallen friends; and the interior of each ship presented a scene well calculated to prove the short-sightedness of human hope and human prudence."[18]

On reaching the anchorage, Gleig found that a large contingent of troops had just arrived from England, consisting of the 40th Foot of about a thousand men. But the war-weary veterans of the struggle for New Orleans felt that even with three times the number they could never hope to capture the city.

Even after the disastrous battle performance, the evacuation was managed so well that Lambert was later knighted for his achievement. Another council of war was held and Admiral Cochrane convinced the general that they should revert to their original plan and attack Mobile. It was their only hope for ultimate success. Once Mobile was taken, he argued, an overland assault on New Orleans would be possible and would assuredly bring them victory.

So the ill-fated expedition sailed away. The American picket guard reported that at 11:30 A.M. on January 27, 1815, they lost sight of the last sail of the British navy. "Louisiana may again say, " Jackson wrote to Governor Blount, "her soil is not trodden by the sacrilegious footsteps of a hostile Briton."[19]

But the Britons had not entirely given up their invasion plans. Not yet. Twenty-four hours later they dropped anchor opposite Dauphin Island outside Mobile Bay. The first thing they did was disembark and steal the cows and hogs of "a Mr. Cooney, of Irish extraction, who had been banished to that island for some misdemeanor committed in the

American navy." For the next week they shot every four-footed animal they could find on the island. Having starved on "salt provisions" for months they could hardly restrain themselves. However, the meat was so "rank" and tasted so much like the "rushes" that the cattle had fed on that it was impossible to "stomach the flesh until well salted down."[20]

Finally, after several delays involved in digging formal siege works and seeking Indian assistance for an attack on the Georgia frontier, they launched a land and sea operation against Fort Bowyer outside Mobile on February 8, and it was surrendered to them three days later by the American commander, Colonel William Lawrence. The 375-man garrison and a large supply of guns and ammunition thus fell into British hands. The redcoats suffered thirty-one casualties in the assault, including thirteen killed.[21]

Mobile would surely have fallen if news had not arrived that a treaty of peace had been signed in Ghent, Belgium, on Christmas Eve, 1814, and that the war was over. The Wellington heroes never had another chance to win vindication for their disastrous defeat at the hands of the dirty shirts at the Battle of New Orleans. And it mattered a great deal to the Americans that they had defeated the veterans of the Duke of Wellington's Peninsula War. Even General Jackson trumpeted the claim. "I have defeated this Boasted army of Lord Wellington," he bragged.[22]

On March 15, 1815, the army of Lord Wellington set sail for England.

Chapter 9

"Who Would Not Be an American?"

As General Andrew Jackson peered through his telescope from the top floor of the Macarty mansion on the day following the "Agreement for the Exchange of Prisoners," he could see no discernible difference in the British camp. Flags were flying and sentinels posted as before. What were the British up to? What were they doing? Were they "playing possum"?

Jackson turned to General Humbert and asked for his evaluation. Humbert took the glass and stared at the open field.

"They are gone," he finally said as he lowered the glass.

"How do you know?"

Look at that crow flying near to one of the British sentinels, Humbert directed. Notice anything strange? The fact that the crow would fly so near the so-called sentinel showed that it was no sentinel at all but a "dummy," a "stuffed paddy," and a badly made one at that. So bad, in fact, that it could not even serve as a decent scarecrow.[1]

Then, just as Jackson was about to order a reconnoitering party to move forward and occupy the enemy camp, a flag of truce was seen approaching the American position. It was carried by a British medical officer left behind to tend the wounded. He declared that he had a letter from Lambert to Jackson announcing that his army was departing and that he had left behind eight badly wounded men who could not be moved and who he hoped General Jackson would help obtain needed medical assistance. A few days later these wounded were ferried by steamboat to New Orleans, attended by three surgeons who had also been left behind by Lambert.

There was once again an appeal by several American officers to pursue and engage the retreating British army, but the general refused. He fully expected the enemy to attack again, and until he knew where that might take place he had no intention of abandoning his position or reducing his force. However, he did order a detachment of Hinds's dragoons to sting the enemy as they pulled back. The dragoons fought a brief skirmish at the mouth of Bayou Bienvenu with the British rear guard on January 25, but this operation failed to achieve any tangible results, owing to Lambert's skillful management of the withdrawal. Still, this brief skirmish had significance in that it marked the last land fighting of the war below New Orleans.

Major Lacoste and a detachment of Louisianians were also sent to scour the woods and pick up stragglers and any slaves who might have attempted to escape with the British. At least four stragglers were found, but when Lacoste realized that he and his men were very close to a large contingent of British soldiers as they headed for the lake he very wisely withdrew.

With his aides in tow, Jackson rode into the enemy's camp and inspected what had been left behind. He found fourteen broken guns and a great deal of private and public property. Three thousand cannonballs were picked up in the field, and the Kentucky troops piled them behind the Rodriguez rampart. Jackson visited the hospital and assured the patients that everything possible would be done to provide for their care and comfort. Now convinced that the British would head for Mobile in another attempt to capture New Orleans, Jackson decided to return to the city and there await the enemy's next action.

By now Old Hickory and his troops understood the significance of their overwhelming victory. They had achieved something no other nation could match: the thorough and complete thrashing of a British army. What an unparalleled triumph for supposedly undisciplined militiamen, not one-fourth of whom had any idea what war was about or had ever seen a military camp.[2] Their extraordinary victory called for a day of rejoicing and thanksgiving. So on January 19, Jackson sent a message to the Abbé Guillaume Dubourg, the apostolic administrator of the diocese of Louisiana and the Floridas, and asked him to conduct a public service in the cathedral "in token at once of the great assistance we have recd. from the *ruler of all Events* and of our humble sense of it."[3]

The general also decided to add as much pomp and ceremony as possible to the army's return to the city so that the citizens could express their gratitude to the heroes who had saved them and their city.

Before marching his army back to New Orleans, he stationed the 7th Regiment at the parapet while a like number of Kentucky and Louisiana militia were posted at Villeré's plantation. He also ordered the building of a strong fortification at the junction of Bayou Mazant and Bayou Bienvenu. But a determined detachment of British troops at the junction, prior to their departure, prevented any such undertaking. Then Jackson set about the creation of a permanent roll of honor in which every corps that had served in the siege, every commanding officer, and every man who had distinguished himself were listed together with glowing words of praise for their heroic deeds. And those who fell in action were also recorded. In all some seventy names decorated this honor roll.[4]

Jackson also prepared an address to his troops in which he recounted the main events of the campaign, excoriating the enemy for their arrogance and extolling those who had fought for freedom and their homeland. "The enemy has retreated," he began, "and your general has now leisure to proclaim to the world what he has noticed with admiration and pride—your undaunted courage, your patriotism, and patience, under hardships and fatigues." He alluded to their many sectional, ethnic, and racial differences and how they had come together for the sake of their country. "Natives of different states, acting together, for the first time, in this camp, differing in habits and in language . . . and from the seeds of discord itself have reaped the fruits of

an honourable union." All of which has inspired you "with a just confidence in yourselves." The nation has been saved, "unanimity established," the city spared the horrors of pillage, "confidence restored,
your country saved from conquest. . . . These, my brave friends, are
the consequences of the efforts you have made, and the success with
which they have been crowned by Heaven."[5]

The address was read at the head of each corps that had assembled
for the last time behind their mud rampart. When the reading ended,
the ranks wheeled into marching order and began their triumphal return to New Orleans. It was January 21, and Jackson's first visit since
December 23.

And it was quite a spectacle. The aged, the infirm, mothers, daughters, wives, and children crowded into the streets to welcome their
deliverers. "Every countenance," said Latour, "was expressive of
gratitude—joy sparkled in every feature, on beholding fathers, brothers, husbands, sons, who had so recently saved the lives, fortunes, and
honour of their families, by repelling an enemy come to conquer and
subjugate the country."[6]

The Abbé Dubourg had wanted Jackson to fix the day for the
thanksgiving service, but when the general failed to respond to his request the abbé set the date for January 23. Again, it was a splendid
pageant, "which displayed the talent of the French in devising em-
blematic shows." A temporary triumphal arch was erected in the middle of the great square, opposite the main entrance to the cathedral.
Uniformed companies of Plauché's battalion lined both sides of the
square between the river and the cathedral. The balconies and windows of the city hall and all the adjacent buildings were crowded with
spectators. The entire square and the streets leading to the square were
thronged with people.

The arch was supported by six columns, and on each side stood a
young girl. The one on the left represented Liberty, the one on the
right Justice. Under the arch were two children, each on a pedestal and
each holding a crown of laurel. From the arch in the middle of the
square to the church, young women were stationed at regular intervals
representing all the states and territories that made up the United

States in 1815. They were dressed in white and wore transparent veils with silver stars on their foreheads. Each young lady carried a flag in her right hand inscribed with the name of the state she represented. In her left hand she carried a basket of flowers trimmed with blue ribbons. A shield behind each of them, with the name of a state or territory inscribed on it, was suspended on a lance that had been driven into the ground. Garlands of evergreens and flowers linked the shields together and stretched from the arch to the cathedral.[7]

Finally General Jackson himself arrived at the entrance of the square, accompanied by the officers of his staff. He was asked to walk the distance to the church, and as he passed under the arch the two children lowered the crowns of laurel to his head. The eight-year-old daughter of Dr. David Kerr, who represented the state of Louisiana, stepped forward and read an address of congratulations from the people of her state. Mrs. Ellery of New Orleans then sang a ballad to the tune of "Yankee Doodle," all of which so moved the general that he stopped and spoke to the young ladies, thanked them for their wonderful tribute, and asked for a copy of the ballad, which he subsequently sent to his nieces. As he continued toward the cathedral the young girls strewed flowers in his path and recited an ode.

> *Hail to the chief! who tried at war's alarms,*
> *To save our threaten'd land from hostile arms;*
> *Preserv'd, protected by his gallant care,*
> *By his the grateful tribute of each fair:*
> *With joyful triumph swell the choral lay—*
> *Strew, strew with flow'rs the hero's welcome way.*
> *Jackson, all hail! our country's pride and boast,*
> *Whose mind's a council, and whose arm's an host;*
> *Who, firm and valiant, 'midst the storm of war,*
> *Boasts unstain'd praise—laurels without a tear:*
> *Welcome, blest chief! accept our grateful lays,*
> *Unbidden homage, and spontaneous praise;*
> *Remembrance, long, shall keep alive thy fame,*
> *And future infants learn to lisp thy name.*[8]

Resplendently garbed in his ecclesiastic robes, the Abbé Dubourg greeted the general at the porch of the cathedral and welcomed him in a long-winded speech that lavishly praised him for his exploits and gave thanks to the Almighty for having sent the country and the city of New Orleans such a sublime savior. "In proving yourself the worthy instrument of Heaven's merciful designs," he said, "the first impulse of your religious heart was to acknowledge the *signal interposition of providence*—your first step, a solemn display of *your humble sense of his favours*. . . . Immortal thanks be to his Supreme Majesty for sending us such an instrument of his bountiful designs." He then handed Jackson a laurel wreath that he had blessed as a "prize of victory, the symbol of immortality."[9]

Over the years the general had become quite adept at speaking before large crowds. He had frequently addressed his army before and after major engagements, and he therefore responded to the abbé in a speech that was both graceful and brief. *"Reverend sir,"* he began, "I receive with gratitude and pleasure the symbolic crown which piety has prepared. I receive it in the name of the brave men who have so effectually seconded my exertions for the preservation of their country—they will deserve the laurels which their country will bestow." He concluded, "For myself, to have been instrumental in the deliverance of such a country is the greatest blessing that heaven could confer."

With the conclusion of these ceremonies the group entered the cathedral. Jackson was escorted to a seat prepared for him close to the altar. The Te Deum was chanted "with impressive solemnity," and at its conclusion an honor guard accompanied the general to his quarters. In the evening with the curfew lifted the city was brilliantly illuminated and New Orleans, in its own distinctive and extravagant way, gave itself over to pleasure and feasting.[10]

As the city celebrated, its citizens suddenly realized that out of their commonality of purpose a disparate ethnic population of French, Spanish, Portuguese, Germans, Italians, Anglos, Indians, and blacks of various social classes had been brought together and welded into a force that had brought about the nation's first military victory of any significance. The past ethnic and social distinctions that had kept them divided and rendered state unity all but impossible had been blurred. Moreover, they had united with outsiders in a common cause: Creoles and Tennesseans, Cajuns and Kentuckians, blacks and whites, slaves and freemen. For the first time they came to realize they were Americans, no matter their ethnic background, social class, or residence. And as Americans they had achieved an extraordinary feat. All of a sudden the city was unified.

The identical transformation occurred around the nation. In Washington the climate had been one of despair and apprehension. The nation had gone to war and suffered one military disaster after another. The country had been invaded, its coastline blockaded, its capital burned by an enemy who held the country in supreme contempt. Worse, the government had ignominiously fled the capital to escape the British invaders.

Gloom shrouded Washington. And the unrelenting doleful news included the gossip that representatives from the convention meeting in Hartford, Connecticut, were on their way to Washington bearing constitutional amendments as the price of their continued allegiance to the Union. Furthermore, it was learned that an enormous invasion force of British soldiers had departed the West Indies and were headed for the Gulf Coast with the intention of capturing New Orleans. Once the invasion succeeded the British would certainly march up the Mississippi Valley, cut off the west, and link up with forces moving south from Canada. Additional armies would likely sail into the Chesapeake, take Philadelphia, and march on to New York. The nation would be shredded.[11]

And many feared that New Orleans could be easily captured. After all, it was "not a regular fortification, requiring a large army, and a powerful battering train, for its reduction." Once it was taken, the British, as Lieutenant Gleig admitted, would have "kept the entire southern trade of the United States in check; and furnished means of commerce to our merchants, of incalculable value."[12] In addition, the city would have been sacked. Wellington himself readily admitted that as far as the officers and troops involved in the invasion of New Orleans were concerned, "plunder was its object."[13] Nor was plunder its only object, according to several American officers. While it was true, wrote Jackson's aide John Reid, that Pakenham "promised the wealth of the city [to his troops], as a recompense for their gallantry and desperation," it should also "be remembered" that "with brutal licentiousness, they were to revel in lawless indulgence, and triumph, uncontrolled, over female innocence. Scenes like these, our nation, dishonoured and insulted, had already witnessed" at Hampton. The British might deny this charge, Reid added, "but its authenticity is too well established to admit of doubt."[14]

Not until mid-January did Washington hear that the British were before New Orleans and that a night battle had occurred on December 23. Then nothing. Silence. Day after day. It was nerve-racking. After a particularly bad snowstorm one packet of mail did get through with the discouraging news of the gunboat battle on Lake Borgne and how American arms had been defeated. Enemy forces had scored a major victory, and "they are now masters of the lake."[15] Ultimate defeat seemed inevitable. "We are a lost country," cried several opposition newspapers. "A wicked administration has ruined us." On January 26 the *National Intelligencer*, a Washington journal, reported a rumor from Baltimore to the effect that the British had been driven from New Orleans. But the paper doubted the veracity of the rumor. After all, it said, the British were not likely to be driven from their objective so easily. The enemy was too powerful for that.

Several more weary days and nights of suspense passed, and still no word. A good many people believed that when the news arrived of the outcome in New Orleans it would be a tale of utter and complete disaster. Congressman Charles J. Ingersoll of Pennsylvania reported that he had conferred with a naval officer and together they had examined a number of maps of New Orleans and how it could be defended against a siege. The officer finally concluded that the defense of the city was impossible.[16]

Then, on February 4, the stupendous word flashed across the capital: Victory! What was more, a victory that was almost impossible to believe. Thousands of British troops killed, wounded, and captured while Americans suffered only a handful of casualties. It seemed too wonderful, too spectacular, to be true. "History," James Monroe told Jackson, "records no example, of so glorious a victory, obtained, with so little bloodshed, on the part of the victorious."[17]

Washington exploded with cries of delight. People thronged the streets, shouting and singing and praising Providence for the nation's deliverance. They thronged about the President's residence, surged to the homes of the secretaries, and filled the air with shouts of "huzza." The mayor recommended the illumination of the city. That evening the town blazed with light. Newspapers spread the joyful information and used their largest type to do it. "ALMOST INCREDIBLE VICTORY!!!" The "Enemy . . . beaten and repulsed by Jackson and his brave associates with great slaughter. The Glorious News . . . has spread around a general joy, commensurate with the brilliance of this event, and the magnitude of our Victory."

Newspapers were quick to quote from Shakespeare's *Henry VI*:

> *"Advance our waving colors on the walls,*
> *Rescued is Orleans from the English wolves."*

And they quoted the newly written "Star Spangled Banner":

> *"The star spangled banner in triumph shall wave,*
> *O'er the land of the free and the home of the brave."*

The news of the victory shot up to Baltimore, and the reaction was the same as in Washington. "Glory be to God that the barbarians have been defeated," proclaimed *Niles' Weekly Register*. "Glory to Jackson . . . Glory to the militia. . . . Sons of freedom . . . benefactors of your country . . . all hail!"[18]

The extraordinary news spread rapidly around the country, "kindling everywhere the maddest enthusiasm." In Philadelphia, parades were spontaneously organized and transparencies devised to depict what might be a likely picture of the New Orleans battle. One transparency showed Jackson on horseback in pursuit of the enemy. A motto on it proclaimed: "This day shall ne'er go by, from this day to the ending of the world, but He, in it, shall be remembered."[19] A broadside printed in New York predicted that "Gen. JACKSON will be immortilized—the bravery of the Kentuckians, the Tennesseans &c. will be handed down to the latest posterity."[20]

In fact, Americans in the first half of the nineteenth century did believe that January 8 would be remembered like July 4—both dates representing the nation's first and second declaration of independence from Great Britain. Indeed, some called the War of 1812 the Second War for Independence.[21] Generally speaking, widespread observance of January 8 as a day of national celebration continued for the next fifty years, with parades and toasts in most major cities. But, as with so many other traditions of the antebellum period, the Civil War and its aftermath more or less extinguished the commemoration of this event.

For nine glorious days in 1815 the nation celebrated its newfound claim to military power and achievement. Then in mid-February dispatches arrived from Europe announcing that the commissioners in Ghent had signed a treaty of peace with their British counterparts and that the War of 1812 had ended. There had been rumors of a peace treaty as early as January 21, but they were only rumors. Not until Saturday, February 11, when the British sloop-of-war *Favorite* arrived in New York with an official copy of the treaty that had been ratified by the Prince Regent, was it certain that the war had finally ended. Late in the afternoon of February 14, this news reached Washington and was taken immediately to the President, who was meeting with his cabinet. This electrifying announcement seemed so unexpected and so joyful that men ran through the streets screaming, "Peace! Peace! Peace!" The same cry echoed from town to town. Parades were organized and men and women marched through the streets carrying lighted torches and lamps and weeping with pride and happiness that this frightful war had at last been concluded.[22]

And concluded magnificently! Concluded with a display of arms that any nation on earth would be proud to claim. Never mind that the battle occurred after the peace treaty had been signed;[23] never mind that the treaty failed to address many of the issues that had produced the war. The nation had escaped with its independence intact and had achieved its first truly triumphant military victory. "Who is not proud to feel himself an American," cried Charles J. Ingersoll on the floor of the House of Representatives, "—our wrongs revenged—our rights recognized." With pride and a deep sense of relief, the Senate of the United States unanimously (35–0) ratified the Treaty of Ghent on February 16, 1815. Now the war was officially over.[24]

The rumor that a peace treaty had been signed in Ghent reached New Orleans on February 10. Edward Livingston had been sent on a mission to the British fleet involving the exchange of prisoners and the return of slaves, and while he was there the sloop *Brazen* brought word that peace had been declared. Still it was not official. No matter. Livingston hurried back to New Orleans "with the glad tidings, which was received with universal joy."[25] But Jackson would not yield his dictatorial powers nor end martial law until official confirmation of the ratification of the treaty arrived, and that news did not reach New Orleans until March 13. Only then did Old Hickory revoke martial law. Only then did he order a cessation of hostilities against Great Britain, proclaim a general pardon for all military offenses, and finally dismiss the militia and volunteers of Tennessee, Kentucky, Mississippi, and Louisiana. "Go, then, my brave companions," he told them, ". . . full of honor, and crowned with laurels which will never fade. . . . Farewell, fellow soldiers. The expression of your General's thanks is feeble, but the gratitude of a country of freemen is yours—yours the applause of an admiring world."[26]

A few days after the announcement of peace, Jackson's wife, Rachel, and their adopted son, Andrew, Jr., arrived in New Orleans, much to the general's delight. Rachel had grown into an extremely stout, dark-complexioned, forty-seven-year-old woman whose religious views bordered on fanaticism. In no time at all she came to regard the city as a veritable "Babylon-on-the-Mississippi," given over to every sin in the Decalogue. At one grand ball which she was obliged to attend with her husband, complete with transparencies, flowers, colored lamps, a sumptuous dinner, and dancing, Rachel could scarcely believe the brilliance of the setting. After dinner, Jackson and his lady led the way to the ballroom and there treated the guests to "a most delicious *pas de deux,*" country-style. "To see these two figures, the General, a long, haggard man, with limbs like a skeleton, and Madame la Generale, a short, fat dumpling, bobbing opposite each other like half-drunken Indians, to the wild melody of *'Possum up de Gum Tree,'* and endeavoring to make a spring into the air, was very remarkable, and far more edifying a spectacle than any European ballet could possibly have furnished."[27]

It was a grand finale to a spectacular victory. A few days later, on April 6, 1815, Jackson, Rachel, and their son left New Orleans and returned to their home in Tennessee.

The Battle of New Orleans was one of the great turning points in American history. The country had gone to war with England in a desperate effort to prove that its independence won in the Revolution was no fluke, no accident, no grant by a reluctant mother country to her rebellious colonies. Over the past several decades, foreign powers had treated the United States at times with outragious contempt, the British in particular, starting with the Jay Treaty and continuing with the seizure of American ships and the impressment of American sailors. As Gleig said several times, "We have long been habituated to despise the Americans, as an enemy unworthy of serious regard."[28] Even France, the nation's former ally, had acted with such disregard for American rights that a so-called Quasi-War broke out between the two countries in 1797–98 and only the determination of President John Adams prevented it from escalating into something more serious.

But everything changed with New Orleans. In that one glorious moment the nation had demonstrated that it had the strength, will, and ability to defend its freedom and prove to the world that it was here to stay, that its sovereignty and rights were to be respected by all. An British expeditionary force of the finest professional soldiers, fitted out by "an immense treasury," had been "entirely destroyed" by a small army of citizen-soldiers commanded by a man whose military career had "commenced but two years before." And the slaughter they inflicted on the invading army was "on their side never surpassed at any other battle."[29] To the modern world it is virtually impossible to convey what this victory meant to contemporary Americans. Never again—ever—did they feel compelled to prove to themselves or anyone else the worth of their unique experiment in liberty and constitutional government.

The men and women of New Orleans really believed they had fought for their liberty—certainly Jackson said so repeatedly—and having defeated their former monarch could now say with confidence that they were not subjects of a foreign power but Americans.

The fantastic triumph on the Plains of Chalmette was a defining moment in the national character. After New Orleans the country changed dramatically. Just as the battle had brought men and women of different ethnic and social classes together in the crescent city, so too the battle united men and women from all sections and states around the country. A powerful surge of nationalism resulted from the successful conclusion of this war. Citizens of all eighteen states in the Union in 1815 had discovered at last their true identity. They were no longer Englishmen or colonists. They were Americans.

At the time of the loss of the gunboats in Lake Borgne when the British first invaded Louisiana, Jackson said that the sailors aboard those gunboats acted "nobly . . . and sustained the american Character."[30] To him the *American* character had become real.

It was also real to the administration in Washington. "It is known," wrote Secretary of War James Monroe, "that the enemy promises to themselves, from the waste of our country and distress of our people, a base submission to their will. Little do they understand, the true character of this virtuous and free nation. They deceive themselves by those visionary calculations, in our revolution, and the result of this contest will prove that the American people are not less faithful to their principles, than the British Government is, to its vindictive & barbarous policy."[31]

As this new nationalistic impulse resonated throughout the country it brought enormous changes. For one thing, Americans no longer looked or sounded or acted like their forebears. Certainly Andrew Jackson in trousers hardly looked like George Washington, Thomas Jefferson, James Madison, or Benjamin Franklin in their silk stockings and powdered wigs. And like so many of his countrymen, he spoke differently as well. Old Hickory did not talk or sound like an Englishman; the rhythm and accents of his speech were different. Nothing about him was European.

With his victory at New Orleans, General Jackson became a hero such as the people of America had never enjoyed before. "Columbus had sailed," wrote an early biographer; "Raleigh and the Puritans had planted; Franklin had lived; Washington fought; Jefferson written; . . . the population of the country had been quadrupled and its resources increased ten fold; and the result of all was that the people of the United States had arrived at the capacity of honoring Andrew Jackson before all other living men."[32] And in honoring him the American people needed and wanted to reward him. Nothing was too good for him. Nothing was too good for "The Hero of New Orleans."

Following this victory, Jackson went on to seize Florida from the Spanish in 1818, having been directed by President Monroe to pursue marauding Seminole Indians who raided Georgia settlements and then retired to the safety of their villages inside the Florida border. As a result of the seizure the Spanish government was persuaded to sell Florida to the United States in a treaty that also settled the western boundary of the Louisiana Purchase. Jackson subsequently served as the territorial governor of Florida, and in October 1823 he was elected to the Senate of the United States from Tennessee. Clearly, he was being groomed as a presidential candidate.

And the continuing changes around the country helped that grooming process. One of those changes included a steady development toward democratic government. Within a decade of the Battle of New Orleans the constitutions of many states were amended to provide universal white male suffrage. The nation was moving from a republican to a more democratic form of government, and what subsequently developed was something that historians would later call Jacksonian Democracy.

In 1828 the democracy lifted Andrew Jackson to the highest office in the land. The American people chose to elect as their President an uneducated westerner whose credentials for this high office could not begin to match those of any of his predecessors. Yet the people felt it was an appropriate reward for the man who had helped them prove the superiority of their free republic over all the other forms of government. Americans were never reluctant to put their victorious military heroes in the White House, even those who were singularly unqualified to hold the office. As one woman in Salisbury, North Carolina, exclaimed on hearing of Jackson's nomination, "What! Jackson up for the President? *Jackson? Andrew* Jackson? The Jackson that used to live in Salisbury? . . . Well if Andrew Jackson can be President, anybody can!"[33]

Indeed.

The great Battle of New Orleans produced a President and an enduring belief in the military ability of free people to protect and preserve their society and their way of life. "The last six months is the proudest period in the history of the republic," declared *Niles' Weekly Register*. "We . . . *demonstrated* to mankind a capacity to acquire a skill in arms to conquer 'the conquerors of the conquerors of all' as Wellington's *invincibles* were *modestly* stiled. . . . *Who would not be an American? Long Live the republic! . . . Last asylum of oppressed humanity! Peace is signed in the arms of Victory!*"[34]

Peace in the arms of Victory. What better way for the American nation to start building a new society? After the War of 1812 the country began to develop a truly national domestic economy. It produced a market revolution. It slowly moved from a purely agricultural to an industrial society. Within fifty years it spanned a continent and fashioned roads, bridges, highways, canals, and railroads to bind the country together. Religious fervor spawned by the Second Great Awakening swept across the nation and triggered a host of reform movements, such as abolitionism, temperance, women's rights, world peace, and many others, reforms that reshaped American society and life. "The demon of reform," said Ralph Waldo Emerson, had been loosed in the land in a powerful surge among citizens of all the states to improve social conditions developing from an increasingly industrial and materialistic age.

From this moment on, Americans also believed wholeheartedly in the superiority of American institutions such as representative government, and that they had created a society which rewarded talent and individual initiative instead of class and blood lines. They also believed that this kind of society would ultimately spread around the globe and that its institutions would lift people out of their humiliating subjugation to kings and emperors and czars. Such a conceit was possible because the united efforts of a free people, when challenged on the battlefield, had pulverized the pretensions of an ambitious, class-dominated, and arrogant empire. "[W]e have unqueened the self-stiled Queen of the Ocean," trumpeted the *Boston Yankee*, and "we have beaten at every opportunity, *Wellington's Veterans!*"[35]

Americans had matured into something distinct, even unique, in the Western world, and visitors came to inspect "this new man" and publish what they observed. Some of their works, like Alexis de Tocqueville's *Democracy in America*, have become classics in recognizing and identifying many of the essential elements of American life and government.

Virtually all the characteristics that can be ascribed to Americans today evolved at this time. Prior to the nineteenth century, Americans were fundamentally colonists with a European culture. Even when they won their independence their society, dress, and manner remained essentially English. But following the War of 1812 they reinvented themselves, and what emerged had a distinctly New World cast, and their society, except perhaps for New Orleans, which retained some of its European flavor, evolved into the America we know today. And clearly the Battle of New Orleans played an important role in that evolution. It was one of the great defining moments in the history of the republic.

Notes

CHAPTER 1: THE WAR IN THE SOUTH

1. Remark of Castlereagh in Paris, mid-December 1814, in Alexander Walker, *Jackson and New Orleans* (New York, 1956), p. 58.
2. John Lewis Thomson, *Historical Sketches of the Late War Between the United States and Great Britain Blended with Anecdotes* (Philadelphia, 1816), p. 344.
3. The most recent book and a most excellent study of this war is Donald R. Hickey, *The War of 1812: A Forgotten Conflict* (Urbana and Chicago, 1989).
4. Sources do not agree as to the actual number of men, women, and children killed. One figure runs as high as 517. Frank Lawrence Owsley, Jr., *Struggle for the Gulf Borderlands: The Creek War and the Battle of New Orleans, 1812–1815* (Gainesville, 1981), pp. 30, 33, 34, 36–39; Michael Green, *The Politics of Indian Removal* (Lincoln, Neb., 1982), pp. 40–42; John Claiborne, *Mississippi as a Province . . .* (Jackson, Miss., 1880), p. 324; H. S. Halbert and T. H. Hall, *The Creek War of 1813 and 1814* (Chicago, 1895), p. 156; Albert J. Pickett, *History of Alabama . . .* (Charleston, 1851), II, 275; James Holland, *Andrew Jackson and the Creek War Victory at the Horseshoe* (University, Ala. 1968), p. 10.
5. Blount to Jackson, September 14, 1813, in John Brannon, *Official Letters of the Military and Naval Officers of the United States . . .* (Washington, 1823), p. 215; Blount to Jackson, September 25, 1813, Jackson Papers, Library of Congress.

6. Jackson to Rachel Jackson, November 4, 1813, Jackson Papers, Library of Congress; Davy Crockett, *Life of Davy Crockett* (New York, 1854), p. 75.

7. John Reid and John H. Eaton, *The Life of Jackson* (Philadelphia, 1817), p. 149; Jackson to Blount, March 31, 1814, in John S. Bassett, ed., *Correspondence of Andrew Jackson* (Washington, 1926–33), I, 490; Jackson to John Armstrong, April 2, 1814, National Archives.

8. Jackson to Pinckney, March 28, Jackson to Blount, March 31, 1814, in Jackson, *Correspondence*, 488–91. Jackson always warned his men against being intimidated by the horrifying din set up by the Indians.

9. Jackson to Blount, March 31, Jackson to Pinckney, March 28, 1814, in ibid., I, 491, 489; Jackson to Blount, April 1, 1814, Jackson Papers, Library of Congress; Reid to Elizabeth Reid, April 1, 1814, Reid to Nathan Reid, April 5, 1814, Reid Papers, Library of Congress; Coffee to Jackson, April 1, 1814, Jackson Papers, Library of Congress.

10. Jackson to Blount, March 31, Jackson to Rachel Jackson, April 1, 1814, in Jackson, *Correspondence*, I, 491–92, 493.

11. Green, *Politics of Indian Removal*, p. 42.

12. Jackson to Rachel, August 10, 1814, in Jackson, *The Papers of Andrew Jackson* (Knoxville, 1980–), III, 114.

13. Jackson to Rachel, August 5, 1814, Jackson Papers, Huntington Library.

14. Jackson to González Manrique, August 24, 1814, Jackson Papers, Library of Congress.

15. John K. Mahon, "British Command Decisions Relative to the Battle of New Orleans," *Louisiana History* VI (Winter 1965), 58.

16. Ibid., pp. 59, 63; Robin Reilly, *British at the Gates* (New York, 1976), pp. 163–64; Owsley, *Struggle for the Gulf*, p. 96.

17. Cochrane probably developed his plan from suggestions first offered by Governor Charles Cameron of Nassau and Admiral Sir John Borlase Warren.

18. A. Larriere Latour, *Historical Memoir of the War in West Florida and Louisiana . . .* (Philadelphia, 1816), Appendix II, vi.

19. Jackson to Armstrong, June 27, 1814, in Jackson, *Papers*, III, 83.

20. Armstrong to Jackson, July 18, 1814, in ibid., 90.

21. Latour, *Historical Memoir*, Appendix II, vi.

22. Jackson to Rachel, August 10, 1814, in Jackson, *Papers*, III, 114.

23. Latour, *Historical Memoir*, p. 31; Mahon, "British Command Decisions," p. 62.

24. Lawrence to Jackson, September 15, 1814, in Brannon, *Official Letters*, pp. 424–25; Reid and Eaton, *Jackson*, pp. 214–15; Thomson, *Historical Sketches*, pp. 345–46; James Parton, *Life of Andrew Jackson* (New York, 1861), I, 608.

25. Jackson to Monroe, October 26, 1814, in Jackson, *Correspondence*, II, 82–83.

26. Jackson to Monroe, October 26, 1814, in ibid.
27. Jackson to González Manrique, November 6, 1814, Cuba leg. 1795, Archivo General de Indias, Seville, Spain.
28. Jackson to Blount, November 14, 1814, in Brannan, *Official Letters*, p. 452; Jackson to Rachel, November 15, 1814, Miscellaneous Jackson Papers, Harvard University Library; Thomson, *Historical Sketches*, p. 346; Latour, *Historical Memoir*, p. 49.
29. Jackson to Monroe, November 14, 1814, in Jackson, *Correspondence*, II, 99.
30. Ibid.
31. Robert V. Remini, *Andrew Jackson and the Course of American Empire* (New York, 1977), I, 243.
32. Cochrane to Major General John Lambert, February 3, 1815, quoted in Owsley, *Struggle for the Gulf*, p. 118; Jackson to Rachel, November 15, 1814, in Jackson, *Papers*, II, 187.
33. Jackson to González Manrique, November 9, González Manrique to Jackson, November 9, 1814, Cuba leg. 1795, Archivo General de Indias.
34. Earlier Monroe in a letter dated September 27 informed Jackson of an invasion against Louisiana "thro' the mobile . . . [which would allow them] to take possession of the lower parts of that State, and of all the Country along the mobile." Jackson acknowledged receiving this letter on October 26. Monroe to Jackson, September 27, Jackson to Monroe, October 26, 1814, in Jackson, *Papers*, II, 149, 173.
35. Monroe to Jackson, October 21, 1814, in ibid., 170–71.

CHAPTER 2: NEW ORLEANS

1. Vincent Nolte, *Memoirs of Vincent Nolte* (New York, 1854), p. 189; Charles Gayarré, *History of Louisiana* (New York, 1866), IV, 218.
2. Jane de Grummond, *The Baratarians and the Battle of New Orleans* (Baton Rouge, 1961), p. 11; Wilburt S. Brown, *Amphibious Campaign for West Florida and Louisiana, 1814–1815* (University, Ala., 1969), p. 36.
3. On the lives of the Laffite brothers see, in addition to de Grummond, Stanley Clisby Arthur, *Jean Laffite, Gentleman Rover* (New Orleans, 1952); and Lyle Saxon, *Lafitte the Pirate* (New York and London, 1930). It will be noticed that the brothers' family name is spelled differently by these two authors.
4. de Grummond, *Baratarians*, pp. 4, 8–9.
5. John S. Bassett, ed., "Major Howell Tatum's Journal," *Smith College Studies in History* VII (October 1921–April 1922), 111.
6. Brooks, *Siege of New Orleans*, p. 16.
7. Ibid., p. 14; Liliane Crété, *Daily Life in Louisiana, 1815–1830* (Baton Rouge and London, 1978), pp. 36, 39, 61.

8. Reilly, *British at the Gates*, p. 171.
9. Crété, *Daily Life*, pp. 97, 71–72; Bernard Marigny, "Reflections on the Campaign of General Andrew Jackson," in *Louisiana Historical Quarterly* VI (1923), 63, 66; Rachel Jackson to Mrs. Eliza Kingsley, April 27, 1821, Parton, *Jackson*, II, 595–96.
10. Nolte, *Memoirs*, p. 215; Bernard Marigny, "Reflections on the Campaign," VI, 63; Robert V. Remini, "Andrew Jackson's Account of the Battle of New Orleans," *Tennessee Historical Quarterly* XXVI (Spring 1967), 37. On Claiborne see Wiley W. Jenkins, *William C. C. Claiborne, Governor of the Creoles* (Austin, Tex., 1951) and Joseph T. Hatfield, *The Public Career of William C. C. Claiborne* (Ann Arbor: University Microfilms, 1972).
11. On Livingston, see William B. Hatcher, *Edward Livingston: Jeffersonian Republican and Jacksonian Democrat* (University, La., 1940); and Louise Livingston Hunt, *Memoir of Mrs. Edward Livingston with Letters Hitherto Unpublished* (New York, 1896).
12. Gayarré, *History of Louisiana*, IV, 302; de Grummond, *Baratarians*, p. 21.
13. Proclamation, August 12, 1814, Nicholls to Laffite, August 31, 1814, in Latour, *Historical Memoir*, Appendix III, ix, viii.
14. Laffite to Blanque, September 4, 1814, Laffite to Claiborne, in ibid., Appendix I, xii, xiv.
15. Quoted in de Grummond, *Baratarians*, p. 43.
16. Ibid., pp. 43–44.
17. Ibid., pp. 46–48. Claiborne told Jackson that among the Baratarians were "some St. Domingo negro's of the most desperate characters and probably no worse than most of their white associates." Claiborne to Jackson, September 20, 1814, in Jackson, *Correspondence*, II, 56.
18. Brown, *Amphibious Campaign*, pp. 9–10.
19. Claiborne to Jackson, August 12, 1814, in Jackson, *Papers*, III, 115–16; Crété, *Daily Life in Louisiana*, pp. 77–78; Jackson to Claiborne, August 22, September 21, 1814, in Jackson, *Correspondence*, II, 27, 56–57.
20. Jackson's Proclamation to the People of Louisiana and the free colored of Louisiana, September 21, 1814, ibid., 57–59. Unfortunately, Jackson's letter and proclamations did not reach Claiborne until October 15, having been misdirected to Natchez. The proclamation to the people of Louisiana was published on October 17; the one to the free blacks was delayed until October 24. See Claiborne to Jackson, October 17, 1814, in Jackson, *Correspondence*, II, 76.
21. Jackson to Claiborne, September 30, 1814, in ibid., 63.
22. Committee of Public Safety to Jackson, September 18, 1814, in ibid., 51, 52; Nolte, *Memoirs*, p. 205.
23. Mahon, "British Command Decisions," p. 63.
24. Thomson, *Historical Sketches*, p. 347; Walker, *Jackson and New*

Orleans, pp. 89–92; George R. Gleig, *Campaigns of the British Army at Washington and New Orleans* (London, 1827), p. 248.

25. Jackson to Carroll, October 31, Carroll to Jackson, November 26, 1814, in Jackson, *Papers*, III, 175, 197.

26. Louise Livingston Hunt, *Memoir*, pp. 53–54; Marigny, "Reflections on the Campaign," VI, 63.

27. Nolte, *Memoirs*, pp. 202–3.

28. Crété, *Daily Life in Louisiana*, p. 97.

29. Walker, *Jackson and New Orleans*, p. 14; Parton, *Jackson*, II, 29.

30. Division Orders, March 7, 1812, Jackson Papers, Library of Congress.

31. Nolte, *Memoirs*, p. 205; Marigny, "Reflections on the Campaign," VI, 64.

32. Jackson to Claiborne, December 10, 1814, in Jackson, *Papers*, III, 202.

33. Jackson to W. Allen, December 23, 1814, Jackson Papers, Library of Congress.

34. Walker, *Jackson and New Orleans*, p. 73.

35. Nolte, *Memoirs*, p. 207.

36. Marigny, "Reflections on the Campaign," VI, 65–66.

CHAPTER 3: THE INVASION BEGINS

1. Walker, *Jackson and New Orleans*, p. 94.

2. Thomson, *Historical Sketches*, p. 347.

3. Reilly, *British at the Gates*, p. 215.

4. Latour, *Historical Memoir*, pp. 60–61, Jones to Patterson, March 12, 1815, Appendix XIX, xxxiv–xxxv; Brooks, *Siege of New Orleans*, pp. 92–96; Horsman, *War of 1812*, pp. 238–39; Owsley, *Struggle for the Gulf*, p. 139.

5. Gleig, *Campaigns of the British Army*, p. 261.

6. Jackson to Coffee, December 16, 1814, Jackson Papers, Library of Congress; Parton, *Jackson*, II, 56.

7. Carroll to Jackson, December 14, 1814, in Jackson, *Papers*, III, 203; Jackson to Coffee, December 16, 1814, Jackson Papers, Library of Congress.

8. Bassett, ed., "Tatum's Journal," p. 104.

9. Jackson to Citizens and Soldiers, December 15, 1814, in Jackson, *Papers*, III, 204.

10. Latour, *Historical Memoir*, pp. 67–68.

11. Order to the Citizens of New Orleans, December 16, 1814, in Jackson, *Papers*, III, 206–7.

12. Bassett, ed., "Tatum's Journal," p. 105.

13. Parton, *Jackson*, II, 62.

14. Jackson's Address to the Troops in New Orleans, December 18, 1814, in Jackson, *Correspondence*, II, 118–19.

15. Latour, *Historical Memoir*, p. 72; Parton, *Jackson*, II, 67.

16. Jackson to Holmes, December 25, 1814, in Jackson, *Correspondence*, II, 124.

17. George R. Gleig, *A Subaltern in America* (Philadelphia, 1833), pp. 196–97. Gleig's *Campaigns of the British Army*, which was issued in several editions, was later republished under the title *A Subaltern in America* but without the author's name and with significant additions and changes to the original. Both books will be cited here.

18. Diary of a British Officer, in Jackson, *Correspondence*, II, 109; Gleig, *Campaigns of the British Army*, p. 265; Gleig, *Subaltern in America*, p. 201.

19. Walker, *Jackson and New Orleans*, pp. 113–14.

20. Parton, *Jackson*, II, 53; Walker, *Jackson and New Orleans*, p. 114. However, Major Tatum reported in his journal that boats were seen passing Chef Menteur in the direction of Bayou Bienvenu on December 22. Bassett, ed., "Tatum's Journal," p. 106.

21. Walker, *Jackson and New Orleans*, p. 119.

22. Gleig, *Campaigns of the British Army*, pp. 267–68; Gleig, *Subaltern in America*, p. 206.

23. Gleig, *Subaltern in America*, pp. 207–10.

24. John Henry Cooke, *A Narrative of Events in the South of France and of the Attack on New Orleans in 1814 and 1815* (London, 1835), p. 163; Gleig, *Campaigns of the British Army*, p. 267; Jackson to Villeré, December 19, 1814, in Jackson, *Papers*, III, 210.

25. Latour, *Historical Memoir*, pp. 78, 82–86.

26. Ibid., pp. 86–87; Walker, *Jackson and New Orleans*, pp. 124–26; Gleig, *Campaigns of the British Army*, p. 278.

27. Latour, *Historical Memoir*, pp. 86–87; Gleig, *Campaigns of the British Army*, p. 278; Walker, *Jackson and New Orleans*, pp. 126–27; Gayarre, *History of Louisiana*, IV, 420–21.

28. Latour, *Historical Memoir*, p. 88.

29. Gleig, *Campaigns of the British Army*, p. 280.

30. *Niles' Weekly Register*, January 14, 1815.

31. Ibid., p. 283; Walker, *Jackson and New Orleans*, pp. 150–51.

32. Nolte, *Memoirs*, p. 209–10; Reid to Elizabeth Reid, December 20, 1814, Reid Papers, Library of Congress.

33. Latour, *Historical Memoir*, pp. 89–92.

34. Walker, *Jackson and New Orleans*, pp. 154, 160; Latour, *Historical Memoir*, p. 105.

35. Gleig, *Campaigns of the British Army*, pp. 284–85; Cooke, *Narrative of Events*, p. 190.

36. Gleig, *Subaltern in America*, p. 221; Gleig, *Campaigns of the British Army*, p. 286. Cooke says the voice exclaimed, *"Now, d—n their eyes, give it 'em." Narrative of Events*, p. 191.

CHAPTER 4: THE NIGHT ATTACK

1. Parton, *Jackson*, II, 86.
2. Ibid., 88.
3. Gleig, *Subaltern in America*, p. 222.
4. Gleig, *Campaigns of the British Army*, p. 286; Walker, *Jackson and New Orleans*, pp. 171–72.
5. Nolte, *Memoirs*, p. 211.
6. Gleig, *Subaltern in America*, p. 224.
7. Walker, *Jackson and New Orleans*, p. 173.
8. Bassett, ed., "Tatum's Journal," p. 109.
9. Latour, *Historical Memoir*, p. 98; Gleig, *Campaigns of the British Army*, p. 289; Cooke, *Narrative of Events*, p. 194.
10. Cooke, *Narrative of Events*, p. 175.
11. Parton, *Jackson*, II, 94.
12. Reid and Eaton, *Jackson*, pp. 297–98.
13. Latour, *Historical Memoir*, p. 100.
14. Morgan to Jackson, December 25, Jackson to Morgan, December 26, 1814, Jackson Papers, Library of Congress.
15. Latour, *Historical Memoir*, pp. 102–3; Report of Killed, Wounded and Missing . . . December 23 and 24, 1814 . . . , Jackson Papers, Library of Congress.
16. Gleig, *Subaltern in America*, pp. 226–27.
17. Latour, *Historical Memoir*, p. 107.
18. Gleig, *Campaigns of the British Army*, pp. 307–8.
19. Gleig, *Subaltern in America*, pp. 232–33.
20. Gleig, *Campaigns of the British Army*, pp. 290, 299–303.
21. Jackson to David Holmes, December 25, 1814, in Jackson, *Papers*, III, 219.
22. Robert V. Remini, ed., "Andrew Jackson's Account of the Battle of New Orleans," *Tennessee Historical Quarterly* XXVI (Spring 1967), 26–31.
23. Reid and Eaton, *Jackson*, p. 332.
24. Bassett, ed., "Tatum's Journal," pp. 112, 119.
25. Livingston to Nicholas Girod, December 29, 1814, in Jackson, *Papers*, III, 225.
26. Reid and Eaton, *Jackson*, p. 324.
27. de Grummond, *Baratarians*, p. 97; Remini, *Jackson and the Course of American Empire*, p. 272; Bassett, ed., "Tatum's Journal," p. 119.
28. Gleig, *Campaigns of the British Army*, p. 306.
29. Walker, *Jackson and New Orleans*, p. 211.
30. Cooke, *Narrative of Events*, p. 200.
31. Morgan to Jackson, December 25, Jackson to Morgan, December 26, 1814, Jackson Papers, Library of Congress; Morgan to Jackson, December 26, 1814, in Jackson, *Papers*, III, 222.

32. Gleig, *Campaigns of the British Army*, p. 308; Walker, *Jackson and New Orleans*, p. 205.
33. Cooke, *Narrative of Events*, p. 178.
34. De Grummond, *Baratarians*, p. 98 and note 7.
35. Gleig, *Campaigns of British Army*, pp. 383–84.
36. Cooke, *Narrative of Events*, p. 178.
37. Parton, *Jackson*, II, 126–27.
38. Ibid., 84
39. Cooke, *Narrative of Events*, p. 203.
40. Gleig, *Campaigns*, p. 303; Cooke, *Narrative of Events*, p. 203
41. Cooke, *Narrative of Events*, p. 203; Walker, *Jackson and New Orleans*, pp. 212–13.
42. Walker, *Jackson and New Orleans*, p. 214; Gleig, *Campaigns of the British Army*, p. 310.
43. Cooke, *Narrative of Attack on New Orleans*, pp. 201–2.
44. Brown, *Amphibious Campaign*, p. 112; de Grummond, *Baratarians*, pp. 97–103.
45. Gleig, *Campaigns of the British Army*, p. 311.
46. Ibid., pp. 313–14.
47. Ibid., pp. 314–16.
48. Nolte, *Memoirs*, pp. 215–16
49. Unfortunately Jackson's order was not carried out with respect to the buildings on the Bienvenu plantation.
50. Parton, *Jackson*, II, 116–17.
51. Walker, *Jackson and New Orleans*, p. 227.
52. De Grummond, *Baratarians*, p. 104.
53. Latour, *Historical Memoir*, pp. 120–21.
54. Fairfax Downey, *Sound of Guns* (New York, 1955), pp. 68ff; de Grummond, *Baratarians*, p. 106 and note 25.
55. Gleig, *Campaigns of the British Army*, p. 318.
56. Thomson, *Historical Sketches*, p. 349
57. Gleig, *Subaltern in America*, pp. 235–36.
58. Latour, *Historical Memoir*, p. 123; Bassett, ed., "Tatum's Journal," p. 118.
59. Cooke, *Narrative of Events*, p. 165; Gleig, *Subaltern in America*, pp. 205–6.
60. Nolte, *Memoirs*, p. 214; Reid and Eaton, *Jackson*, pp. 320–21; Parton, *Jackson*, II, 143.

CHAPTER 5: THE ARTILLERY DUEL

1. Walker, *Jackson and New Orleans*, pp. 239–40.
2. Gleig, *Campaigns of the British Army*, pp. 323–24.

3. Latour, *Historical Memoir*, pp. 147–48.
4. *Niles' Weekly Register*, February 4, 1815.
5. Parton, *Jackson*, II, 150.
6. Latour, *Historical Memoir*, pp. 126–27.
7. Parton, *Jackson*, II, 151.
8. Walker, *Jackson and New Orleans*, p. 243.
9. Ibid., p. 244.
10. Ibid, pp. 246–47; Gleig, *Subaltern in America*, p. 244.
11. Gleig, *Campaigns of the British Army*, pp. 323–24; Gleig, *Subaltern in America*, pp. 246–47.
12. Gleig, *Subaltern in America*, p. 249.
13. Walker, *Jackson and New Orleans*, pp. 252–53.
14. Ibid., p. 255.
15. Lawrence Owsley, *Struggle for the Gulf*, p. 150, doubts that a parade took place and says there is not a good source for the story. But Gleig, *Campaigns of the British Army*, is an excellent source, and the scene is described on pp. 325–26. Walker, *Jackson and New Orleans*, pp. 254–55, and Parton, *Jackson*, II, pp. 156–57, also describe the review. However, it is not mentioned by Latour or Nolte.
16. Walker, *Jackson and New Orleans*, p. 255.
17. Gleig, *Campaigns of the British Army*, p. 326.
18. Reid and Eaton, *Jackson*, p. 326.
19. Walker, *Jackson and New Orleans*, pp. 256–57.
20. Gleig, *Campaigns of the British Army*, p. 326.
21. Nolte, *Memoirs*, p. 218.
22. Walker, *Jackson and New Orleans*, p. 265.
23. Ibid., pp. 264–65.
24. John Reid to Elizabeth Reid, February 10, 1815, Reid Papers, Library of Congress.
25. Bassett, ed., "Tatum's Journal," p. 121.
26. Walker, *Jackson and New Orleans*, pp. 267–270.
27. Jackson to Monroe, January 2, 1815, Jackson Papers, Library of Congress.
28. Gleig, *Subaltern in America*, p. 250.
29. Diary of a British Officer, in Jackson, *Correspondence*, II, 110.
30. Ibid.
31. Gleig, *Campaigns of the British Army*, pp. 326–27; Cooke, *Narrative of Events*, p. 212; Latour, *Historical Memoir*, Appendix XXIX, lix. Tatum estimated that the British lost between 140 and 200 men killed, wounded, and taken prisoner. Bassett, ed., "Tatum's Journal," p. 122.
32. Nolte, *Memoir*, p. 218.
33. Gleig, *Subaltern in America*, p. 251.
34. Jackson to Monroe, January 3, 1814, in Jackson, *Correspondence*, II, 130; see also his letter to Monroe of January 2, 1815, in ibid.
35. de Grummond, *Baratarians*, p. 121.

36. Latour, *Historical Memoir*, p. 143.
37. Reid and Eaton, *Jackson*, p. 333.
38. Gleig, *Subaltern in America*, pp. 249–50; Cooke, *Narrative of Events*, pp. 214–15; Parton, *Jackson*, II, 163.
39. Henry Adams, *History of the United States During the Administrations of Thomas Jefferson and James Madison* (New York, 1890), VIII, 365.
40. Nolte, *Memoir*, p. 219.

CHAPTER 6: FINAL PREPARATIONS

1. Latour, *Historical Memoir*, pp. 139–40; Walker, *Jackson and New Orleans*, p. 284.
2. Walker, *Jackson and New Orleans*, pp. 287, 295–96.
3. Latour, *Historical Memoir*, pp. 141–42; Parton, *Jackson*, II, 168–69.
4. Ibid., 172–72.
5. Latour, *Historical Memoir*, p. 150; Nolte, *Memoirs*, p. 211.
6. Latour, *Historical Memoir*, p. 150.
7. Owsley, *Struggle for the Gulf*, p. 158.
8. Parton, *Jackson*, II, 178.
9. Gleig, *Campaigns of the British Army*, pp. 328–29.
10. Walker, *Jackson and New Orleans*, p. 299.
11. Gleig, *Campaigns of the British Army*, p. 329.
12. Cooke, *Narrative of Events*, p. 217.
13. Ibid., p. 169.
14. Ibid., pp. 219–20.
15. Parton, *Jackson*, II, 191.
16. Saxon, *Lafitte the Pirate*, p. 181.
17. Parton, *Jackson*, II, 176.
18. Owsley, *Struggle for the Gulf*, p. 158.
19. Latour, *Historical Memoir*, p. 153.

CHAPTER 7: THE EIGHTH OF JANUARY

1. Parton, *Jackson*, II, 186–88.
2. Ibid., p. 188.
3. Brooks, *Siege of New Orleans*, p. 229.
4. Ibid., pp. 227–29.
5. Parton, *Jackson*, II, 192.
6. Ibid., 191–92.
7. Cooke, *Narrative of Events*, pp. 250–51.
8. Ibid., p. 229.

9. Ibid., p. 231; Gleig, *Subaltern in America*, p. 260.
10. Walker, *Jackson and New Orleans*, pp. 335–37; Parton, *Jackson*, II, 200–1.
11. Cooke, *Narrative of Events*, pp. 231–32.
12. Walker, *Jackson and New Orleans*, p. 326.
13. "A Contemporary Account of the Battle of New Orleans by a Soldier in the Ranks," in *Louisiana Historical Quarterly* IX (January 1926), 11; Gleig, *Subaltern in America*, pp. 261–262.
14. Latour, *Historical Memoir*, pp. 154–55; Cooke, *Narrative of Events*, p. 234; Parton, *Jackson*, II, 194–95; Walker, *Jackson and New Orleans*, pp. 326–27; "A Contemporary Account of the Battle of New Orleans," IX, 11.
15. Ibid., p. 327.
16. "A Contemporary Account of the Battle of New Orleans," in *Louisiana Historical Quarterly* IX (January 1926), 11; Gleig, *Campaigns of the British Army*, pp. 334–35.
17. Sir Harry Smith, *The Autobiography of Lieutenant General Sir Harry Smith* (London, 1902), I, 236; see also Claiborne to Monroe, January 9, 1815, in Dunbar Rowland, ed., *Official Letter Books of W.C.C. Claiborne* (Jackson, 1917), VI, 332.
18. "A Contemporary Account of the Battle of New Orleans by a Soldier in the Ranks," *Louisiana Historical Quarterly* IX (January 1926), 11.
19. Parton, *Jackson*, II, 196–97.
20. Gleig, *Subaltern in America*, pp. 262–63.
21. Coffee to John Donelson, January 25, 1815, in *American Historical Magazine* VI (April 1901), 186.
22. Cooke, *Narrative of Events*, pp. 235–36.
23. Lambert to Lord Bathurst, January 10, 1815, in Latour, *Historical Memoir*, Appendix LXVI, cli.
24. Ibid.
25. Cooke, *Narrative of Events*, p. 236.
26. Gleig, *Subaltern in America*, pp. 263–64.
27. Walker, *Jackson and New Orleans*, pp. 331–32.
28. Cooke, *Narrative of Events*, pp. 255–56.
29. Ibid.
30. Walker, *Jackson and New Orleans*, p. 344.
31. Cooke, *Narrative of Events*, p. 239.
32. Owsley, *Struggle for the Gulf*, pp. 162–63.
33. Nolte, *Memoirs*, p. 224; Parton, *Jackson*, II, 235.
34. Gleig, *Campaigns of the British Army*, p. 343.
35. Reid and Eaton, *Jackson*, p. 344; Parton, *Jackson*, II, 207.
36. Tatum, "Journal," p. 125; "A Contemporary Account of the Battle of New Orleans," IX, 11; Nolte, *Memoirs*, p. 222.
37. Parton, *Jackson*, II, 208–9.

38. Cooke, *Narrative of Events*, p. 263.
39. Latour, *Historical Memoir*, p. 177; Cooke, *Narrative of Events*, pp. 263–64.
40. Walker, *Jackson and New Orleans*, pp. 344–45.
41. Latour, *Historical Memoir*, p. 229; Speech of Senator Edward Livingston in Congress, quoted in Parton, *Jackson*, II, 228.
42. Jackson to Adair, July 1817 in *Kentucky Reporter*, quoted in Parton, *Jackson*, II, 212.
43. Reid and Eaton, *Jackson*, p. 345
44. Ibid., pp. 344–347.
45. Thornton was very complimentary about the initial effort of the Americans to defend their line. "At first," he wrote Pakenham, "the Enemy, confident in his own security, shewed a good countenance, and kept up a heavy fire." Thornton to Pakenham, January 8, 1815, quoted in Jackson, *Papers*, III, 238, note 3.
46. Reid and Eaton, *Jackson*, pp. 346–48.
47. Walker, *Jackson and New Orleans*, p. 353; Remini, ed., "Andrew Jackson's Account of the Battle of New Orleans," 35.
48. Louis Foelckel to Jackson, January 8, 1815, in Jackson, *Papers*, III, 237.
49. Jackson to Monroe, January 9, 1815, in ibid., 240.
50. Jackson to Morgan, January 8, 1815, in ibid., 238.
51. Cooke, *Narrative of Events*, p. 259.
52. Ibid., pp. 264–65.
53. Jackson to Morgan, January 10, 1815, in Jackson, *Papers*, III, 241.
54. Gleig, *Campaigns of the British Army*, pp. 382–84; Parton, *Jackson*, II, 221–22; Reid and Eaton, *Jackson*, p. 358.
55. Lambert to Jackson, January 8, 1815, in Jackson, *Correspondence*, II, 133.
56. Jackson to Lambert, January 11, Lambert to Jackson, January 11, 1815, in Jackson, *Papers*, III, 243.
57. Lambert to Jackson, January 8, 9, Jackson to Lambert, January 8, 9, 1815, in Jackson, *Correspondence*, II, 134, 138; Reid and Eaton, *Jackson*, pp. 354–55.
58. Gleig, *Campaigns of the British Army*, pp. 341–42; Jackson to General James Winchester, January 10, 1815, in Jackson, *Papers*, III, 242.
59. Captain Hill quoted in Parton, *Jackson*, II, 234.
60. Gleig, *Subaltern in America*, p. 264.
61. Jackson to Monroe, January 9, 13, 1815, in Jackson, *Correspondence*, II, 137, 143; Latour, *Historical Memoir*, Appendix XXIX, lx; Reid and Eaton, *Jackson*, p. 350; Cooke, *Narrative of Events*, p. 257.
62. Jackson to Robert Hays, February 9, 1815, Jackson Papers, Library of Congress.

CHAPTER 8: THE FINAL ASSAULT

1. Walker, *Jackson and New Orleans*, pp. 370–71; Jerome A. Greene, *The Defense of New Orleans, 1718–1900* (Denver, Colo., 1982), pp. 91–92; Reid and Eaton, *Jackson*, p. 361.

2. Overton to Jackson, January 19, 1815, in Latour, *Historical Memoir*, Appendix XXXIV, lxix–lxx, 191–92; Walker, *Jackson and New Orleans*, pp. 372–73; Greene, *Defense of New Orleans*, p. 93.

3. Latour, *Historical Memoir*, p. 195.

4. Overton to Jackson, January 19, 1815, in Latour, *Historical Memoir*, Appendix XXXIV, lxix–lxx, 191–92, 195–96; Thomson, *Historical Sketches*, p. 351.

5. Cooke, *Narrative of Events*, pp. 269–70.

6. Bassett, ed., "Tatum's Journal," p. 134; Jackson to Claiborne, January 16, 17, 1815, in Jackson, *Papers*, III, 246–47 and note 2.

7. Agreement for Exchange of Prisoners, January 17, 1815, in Jackson, *Papers*, III, 247; Cochrane to Jackson, February 12, 1815, in Jackson, *Correspondence*, II, 163.

8. Gleig, *Campaigns of the British Army*, p. 345.

9. Cooke, *Narrative of Events*, pp. 271–72; Gleig, *Campaigns of the British Army*, pp. 351–52.

10. Gleig, *Campaigns of the British Army*, p. 349.

11. Cooke, *Narrative of Events*, p. 275; Lambert to Jackson, January 20, 1815, in Jackson, *Papers*, III, 253; de Grummond, *Baratarians*, p. 147; Latour, *Historical Memoir*, Appendix LXVIII, clxxxi.

12. Gleig, *Campaigns of the British Army*, pp. 352–53.

13. Ibid., pp. 354–55.

14. Cooke, *Narrative of Events*, p. 274.

15. Brooks, *Siege of New Orleans*, pp. 257–58. Mullens was convicted of neglecting and disobeying orders, which produced the disorder and disaster that ensued. But he was found not guilty to the charge of "scandalous and infamous misbehavior." "General Court Martial . . . for. the Trial of Brevet Lieutenant Colonel Hon. Thomas Mullin [*sic*]," reprinted in *Louisiana Historical Quarterly* IX (January 1926), 109.

16. Latour, *Historical Memoir*, pp. 180–83; Gleig, *Campaigns of the British Army*, p. 358.

17. Cooke, *Narrative of Events*, p. 276.

18. Gleig, *Campaigns of the British Army*, p. 357.

19. Jackson to Willie Blount, January 27, 1815, in Parton, *Jackson*, II, 270.

20. Cooke, *Narrative of Events*, p. 277.

21. Owsley, *Struggle for the Gulf*, p. 171.

22. Jackson to James Winchester, January 19, 1815, in Jackson, *Papers*, III, 252.

CHAPTER 9: "WHO WOULD NOT BE AN AMERICAN?"

1. Walker, *Jackson and New Orleans*, p. 382; Parton, *Jackson*, II, 267.
2. Latour, *Historical Memoir*, pp. 184–85, 201.
3. Jackson to Dubourg, January 19, 1815, in Jackson, *Correspondence*, II, 150.
4. Reid and Eaton, *Jackson*, p. 366.
5. Latour, *Historical Memoir*, Appendix LXIX, clxxxiii–clxxxv.
6. Ibid., p. 197.
7. Ibid., p. 199. John Reid, one of Jackson's aides, said the children carried roses and garlands. Reid to Elizabeth Reid, February 10, 1815, Reid Papers, Library of Congress.
8. Latour, *Historical Memoir*, pp. 198–200; Reid to Elizabeth Reid, February 10, 1815, Reid Papers, Library of Congress; Parton, *Jackson*, II, 273; Jackson to Robert Hays, February 9, 1815, Jackson Papers, Library of Congress; Reid and Eaton, *Jackson*, p. 369.
9. Address of Abbé Dubourg to Jackson, January 23, 1815, in Brannan, *Official Letters*, pp. 467ff.
10. Jackson's response to Dubourg, January 23, 1815, in Latour, *Historical Memoir*, Appendix XXXV, lxxiii.
11. Parton, *Jackson*, II, 244.
12. Gleig, *Campaigns of the British Army*, pp. 383–84.
13. Wellington to Longford, May 22, 1815, *Louisiana Historical Quarterly* IX (January 1926), 8.
14. Reid and Eaton, *Jackson*, p. 352.
15. *National Intelligencer*, January 9, 1815.
16. Parton, *Jackson*, II, 244–46.
17. Monroe to Jackson, February 5, 1815, in Jackson, *Papers*, III, 271.
18. *National Intelligencer*, February 7, 1815; *Niles' Weekly Register*, February 11, 14, 18, 1815; Parton, *Jackson*, II, 247.
19. John Binns, *Autobiography*, quoted in Parton, *Jackson*, II, 248.
20. Broadside, Rare Book Division, Library of Congress.
21. In 1989 the little town of Ghent in Belgium celebrated the 175th anniversary of the signing of the treaty that ended the war between Great Britain and the United States. The town is proud of the part it played in bringing an end to such a needless and foolish war. I was invited to participate in that celebration because at the time I was writing a biography of Henry Clay, one of the five U.S. commissioners who wrote the treaty. In the course of the festivities I was asked by one official what Americans did each year to commemorate such an important event in our history. I was astonished by the question, and a little embarrassed. Nothing, I sheepishly replied. Absolutely nothing. The official could scarcely believe it.
22. *Niles' Weekly Register*, February 11, 18, 1815.
23. As a matter of fact, although the treaty had been signed it had not been

ratified by either country, and it is certain that had the British won the Battle of New Orleans the treaty would have been repudiated or drastically altered to take such a victory into account.

24. *Annals of Congress*, 13th Congress, 3rd session, p. 1161.
25. Latour, *Historical Memoir*, p. 216.
26. Ibid., Appendix LI, ciii, cv; Jackson, *Correspondence*, II, 195–96.
27. Rachel to Robert Hays, March 5, 1815, Jackson Papers, Library of Congress; Rachel to Mrs. Eliza Kingsley, April 27, 1821, quoted in Parton, *Jackson*, II, 595; Nolte, *Memoirs*, pp. 238–39.
28. Gleig, *Campaigns of the British Army*, p. 384.
29. Thomson, *Historical Sketches*, p. 351.
30. Jackson to William Carroll, December 16, 1814, in Jackson, *Correspondence*, II, 116.
31. Monroe to General Joseph Bloomfield, September 4, 1814, Marion S. Carson Collection, Library of Congress.
32. Parton, *Jackson*, III, 684–85.
33. Ibid., I, 109.
34. February 18, March 4, 1815.
35. *Boston Yankee*, March 3, 1815, quoted in Hickey, *The War of 1812*, p. 309.

Bibliography

Although the Battle of New Orleans and the War of 1812 that produced it are dim recollections for most Americans today, historians have been much more attentive to their significance and have provided a rich collection of studies that explore in depth the military, diplomatic, political, and economic aspects of the struggle. The availability of a wide assortment of primary sources is one reason for their notice, but with respect to the great battle that took place outside New Orleans I suspect that the drama, the vivid personalities involved, and the crucial meaning of the event to Americans in the early nineteenth century have attracted their interest and involvement.

For myself a fifty-year connection with the life and times of Andrew Jackson has made a profound impression on me about what he and his army accomplished by their stupendous victory on January 8, 1815. Fortunately there are both British and American sources by the participants of the struggle, and in writing this book I have relied heavily on a number of memoirs, correspondence, and official papers written at the time or shortly thereafter.

Of primary importance are the letters written by and to General Jackson during the invasion, as well as related government documents, which can be found in Volumes II and III of *The Papers of Andrew Jackson*, edited by Harold Moser et al. (Knoxville, 1980–). However, Volume II of the *Correspondence of Andrew Jackson*, edited by John Spencer Bassett (Washington, D.C., 1926–35), contains additional letters that shed valuable light on the siege. See also Robert V. Remini, ed., "Andrew Jackson's Account of the Battle of New Orleans," *Tennessee Historical Quarterly* XXVI (Spring 1967). An important early biography of Jackson that stresses his military career is John Reid and John H. Eaton, *The Life of Andrew Jackson, Major General, in the Service of the United States, Comprising a History of the War in the South, from the Commencement of the Creek Campaign to the Termination of Hostilities Before New Orleans* (Philadelphia, 1817). Even more important in fleshing out the details of the struggle is a work by one of Jackson's chief engineers, Major A. Lacarrière Latour. His *Historical Memoir of the War in West Florida and Louisiana in 1814–1815* (Philadelphia, 1816) was written at the time and included valuable maps as well. Less important was the journal kept by Jackson's other engineer, Howell Tatum, "Major Howell Tatum's Journal," in John Spencer Bassett, ed., *Smith College Studies in History* VII (1921–22). A view of events by a participant and New Orleans businessman can be found in Vincent Nolte, *Fifty Years in Both Hemispheres* (New York, 1854), while Bernard de Marigny, *Réflections sur la Campagne du Général André Jackson en Loouisiana 1814 et 1815* (New York, 1848), provides a Creole perspective. The latter work has been edited and translated by Grace King and can be found in *Louisiana Historical Quarterly* VI (January 1923).

Although they were not present during the battle, both Alexander Walker, author of *Jackson and New Orleans* (New York, 1856), and James Parton, author of *Life of Andrew Jackson* (New York, 1861), knew and spoke to a number of individuals who were. I have found Parton particularly reliable in what he reports, and although Walker tends to embroider what he was told, nonetheless he is an important source for dramatic and colorful material that is essential for the proper telling of what took place during the long siege. See also Dunbar Rowland, ed., *Official Letter Books of W. C. C. Clairborne, 1810–1816* (Jackson, Miss., 1907); Jean Laffite, *The Journal of Jean Laffite* (New York, 1958); *American State Papers, Indian Affairs* (Washington, 1832); John Brannan, ed., *Official Letters of the Military and Naval Officers of United States During the War with Great Britain in the Years 1812, 13, 14, 15* (Washington, 1823); "A Contemporary Account of the Battle of New Orleans by a Soldier in the Ranks" and "A Massachusetts Volunteer in the Battle of New Orleans," both in *Louisiana Historical Quarterly* IX (January 1926); H. S. Halbert and T. H. Ball, *The Creek War of 1813 and 1814* (University, Ala., 1969); and Louise Livingston Hunt, *Memoir of Mrs. Edward Livingston, with Letters Hitherto Unpublished* (New York, 1886).

On the British side I have relied heavily on George R. Gleig, *The Campaigns of the British Army at Washington and New Orleans Under Generals Ross, Pakenham and Lambert, in the Years 1814–1815* (London, 1827), and that author's anonymously published and revised *A Subaltern in America; Comprising His Narrative of the Campaigns of the British Army, at Baltimore, Washington, During the Late War* (Philadelphia, 1833). I also made extensive use of Captain John Henry Cooke, *A Narrative of Events in the South of France and of the Attack on New Orleans in 1814 and 1815* (London, 1835). Additional points of view from the invader's side can be found in Benson Earle Hill, *Recollections of an Artillery Officer* (London, 1836); Thomas Pakenham, ed., *Pakenham Letters 1800–1815* (London, 1914); G. C. Moore, ed., *The Autobiography of Lieutenant-General Sir Harry Smith* (London, 1901); John Buchan, *The History of the Royal Scots Fusiliers: 1678–1918* (London, 1925); Hugh Rankin, ed., *The Battle of New Orleans: A British View* (New Orleans, 1961); and John Spencer Cooper, *Rough Notes of Seven Campaigns* (Carlisle, England, 1869).

Among secondary sources the most recent and best study of the war itself is Donald R. Hickey, *War of 1812: A Forgotten Conflict* (Urbana and Chicago, 1999). See also Harry L. Coles, *The War of 1812* (Chicago, 1965); Reginald Horsman, *The War of 1812* (New York, 1969); John K. Mahon, *The War of 1812* (Gainesville, Fla., 1972); and Bradford Perkins, *The Causes of the War of 1812* (New York, 1962). Of special significance is Roger H. Brown, *The Republic in Peril: 1812* (New York, 1964). A popular account that includes an appendix that explains such things as military terminology, ordnance, and tactics is James R. Jacobs and Glenn Tucker, *The War of 1812: A Compact History* (New York, 1969).

Jackson's war against the Creeks and subsequent defense of New Orleans are fully and expertly analyzed in Frank Owsley, Jr., *Struggle for the Gulf: The Creek War and the Battle of New Orleans, 1812–1815* (Gainesville, Fla., 1981). But there are a whole slew of books that deal directly with the battle itself, and among the best are Charles Brooks, *The Siege of New Orleans* (Seattle, 1961); Wilbur S. Brown, *The Amphibious Campaign for West Florida and Louisiana, 1814–1815* (University, Ala., 1969); Samuel Carter III, *Blaze of Glory: The Fight for New Orleans: 1814–1815* (New York, 1971); Charles Gayarré, *History of Louisiana* (New York,

1866); Powell A. Casey, *Louisiana in the War of 1812* (Baton Rouge, 1963); and D. B. Chidsey, *The Battle of New Orleans* (New York, 1961).

Among secondary works written by British writers the following studies are useful: Jane Bourchier, *Memoir of the Life of Admiral Sir Edward Codrington* (London, 1873); J. W. Forester, *A History of the British Army* (London, 1899–1930); Michael Lewis, *The History of the British Navy* (London, 1957); and Robin Reilly, *The British at the Gates: The New Orleans Campaign in the War of 1812* (New York, 1974).

For the Laffite brothers and the pirates see Jane Lucas de Grummond, *The Baratarians and the Battle of New Orleans* (Baton Rouge, 1961). A reprint of this work in 1963 also includes *Biographical Sketches of the Veterans of the Battalion of Orleans, 1814–1815* by Ronald R. Morazan (Baton Rouge, 1963). Older works include Lyle Saxon, *Lafitte the Pirate* (New York, 1930); Stanley C. Arthur, *Jean Laffite: Gentleman Rover* (New York, 1952); Gaspar Cusacks "Lafitte, the Louisiana Pirate and Patriot," *Louisiana Historical Quarterly* II (October 1919); Charles E. Gayarré, "Historical Sketch of Pierre and Jean Lafitte," *Magazine of American History* X (October–November 1883); and Edward A. Parsons, "Jean Lafitte in the War of 1812: A Narrative Based on the Original Documents," *Proceedings of the American Antiquarian Society* L (October 1940).

Except for those of Jackson, there are not many biographies of the leading characters in this momentous event. But the general himself has had his life narrated by each succeeding generation of historians who find him both fascinating and controversial. The earliest study, by John Reid and John H. Eaton, and that by James Parton a little over forty years later, both cited above, each include important data about the battle. Parton, the father of American biography, not only presents a critical study of Jackson's life but one that is exciting and a pleasure to read. Marquis James, *The Life of Andrew Jackson* (Indianapolis and New York, 1933, 1937), won the Pulitzer Prize for the excellence of its writing and breadth of its research. My own three-volume biography is the most recent work on the Hero of New Orleans, and the first volume, *Andrew Jackson and the Course of American Empire, 1767–1821* (New York, 1977), treats the battle at length.

One of the best ways of approaching and enjoying this forgotten war is through Benson J. Lossing, *The Pictorial Field-Book of the War of 1812* (New York, 1868). Lossing toured the battle sites and spoke to survivors of the conflict. He included in his book not only illustrations and maps but songs, poems, and other related material.

Index